Thinking without Words

PHILOSOPHY OF MIND SERIES

Series Editor
David J. Chalmers, University of Arizona

Self Expressions
Minds, Morals, and the Meaning of Life
Owen Flanagan

The Conscious Mind
In Search of a Fundamental Theory
David J. Chalmers

Deconstructing the Mind
Stephen P. Stich

The Human Animal
Personal Identity Without Psychology
Eric Olson

Minds and Bodies
Philosophers and Their Ideas
Colin McGinn

What's Within?
Nativism Reconsidered
Fiona Cowie

Purple Haze
The Puzzle of Consciousness
Joseph Levine

Consciousness and Cognition
A Unified Account
Michael Thau

Thinking
without
Words

José Luis Bermúdez

OXFORD
UNIVERSITY PRESS
2003

OXFORD
UNIVERSITY PRESS

Oxford   New York
Auckland   Bangkok   Buenos Aires   Cape Town   Chennai
Dar es Salaam   Delhi   Hong Kong   Istanbul   Karachi   Kolkata
Kuala Lumpur   Madrid   Melbourne   Mexico City   Mumbai   Nairobi
São Paulo   Shanghai   Taipei   Tokyo   Toronto

Copyright © 2003 by Oxford University Press, Inc.

Published by Oxford University Press, Inc.
198 Madison Avenue, New York, New York, 10016

www.oup.com

Oxford is a registered trademark of Oxford University Press

Library of Congress Cataloging-in-Publication Data
Bermúdez, José Luis.
Thinking without words / José Luis Bermúdez.
p. cm.—(Philosophy of mind series)
Includes bibliographical references and index.
ISBN-13 978-0-19-515969-1
ISBN 0-19-515969-1
1. Philosophy of mind. I. Title. II. Series.
BD418.3 .B47   2003
128'.3—dc21   2002029277

Printed in the United States of America
on acid-free paper

Acknowledgments

This book was begun during a two-year period of leave from teaching and administration that started in September 1998. The first year was spent at the Centre de Recherche en Epistémologie Appliquée (CREA) at the Ecole Polytechnique in Paris. I am extremely grateful to the Ecole Polytechnique for appointing me as Chargé de Recherche for the 1998-99 academic year. During this period I benefited from a European Research Fellowship jointly funded by the Royal Society of Edinburgh and the Caledonian Research Foundation. The second year was made possible by a semester's sabbatical from the University of Stirling and a matching period of leave under the Arts and Humanities Research Board's Research Leave scheme. I owe a considerable debt to my colleagues in the Philosophy Department at Stirling for allowing me to benefit from these opportunities.

A very preliminary version of the material in this book was presented in Paris in spring 1999 in a course of lectures entitled "La pensée sans le langage," offered as part of the DEA en Sciences Cognitives run by the Ecole Polytechnique, the Ecole des Hautes Etudes en Sciences Sociales, and the Université de Paris IV. My thoughts were sharpened by the questions of the students who attended the course. A slightly later version was delivered in Spanish under the title "El pensamiento sin el lenguaje" at the University of Barcelona in April 2000. I am very grateful to Manuel García Carpintero for extending the invitation and to Carolina Arrowsmith for helping me with translating the lectures into Spanish. In August 2000 I delivered the same set of lectures at the Universidad Nacional in Bogotá, Colombia. In Bogotá each lecture was followed by a commentary and a period of probing and fruitful discussion with students and faculty. A version of chapters 7 and 8 was presented on a second visit to the Universidad Nacional in November 2001. Thanks are due to Juan José Botero and his colleagues and students.

Material from the book has been presented at various colloquia and conferences. The minimalist conception of nonlinguistic thought discussed in chapter 3 was initially put forward in my contribution to a symposium entitled "Thought without Language," organized by John Campbell at the 1998 annual conference of the European Society for Philosophy and Psychology in Lisbon. Some of the ideas in chapters 4 and 5 were originally developed for a conference entitled "Animal Minds," at Oxford University, organized by Susan Hurley in April 1998. Later versions were delivered at CREA in June 1998 and at the Belief Ascription Conference in San Marino organized by Marina Sbisá in December 2000. Very early versions of the discussion of the language of thought hypothesis were delivered at the University of Aix-en-Provence in January 1999 and the University of Geneva in March 1999. The distinction between three levels of rationality that occupies most of chapter 6 was first worked out during a fortnight's stay at the Universidao Nacional Autonoma de Mexico (UNAM) Centro de Neurobiología in Querétaro, Mexico, in November 1998. My thanks to José Luis Díaz for his hospitality and encouragement. The basic idea of chapters 8 and 9, that intentional ascent requires the capacity for semantic ascent, was arrived at in Paris during various meetings of the Action, Perception, Intentionalité, Conscience (APIC) seminar—in response to the refusal of participants in the seminar to believe the arguments I offered in *The Paradox of Self-Consciousness* for the dependence of conceptual thought on language. François Recanati, Elisabeth Pacherie, Joelle Proust, Jerome Dokic, and Pierre Jacob were particularly helpful.

The first version of the manuscript was greatly improved by comments from four referees who have waived their right to anonymity. Donald Griffin, Colin Allen, David Braddon-Mitchell, and Chris Gauker made numerous probing criticisms and helpful suggestion. I have also greatly benefited from written comments from Peter Sullivan and Jonathan Lowe.

The final reworking of the manuscript was carried out at Simon Fraser University in Vancouver, where I was Visiting Professor for the 2002 spring semester. I am very grateful to the faculty and students who attended my Thinking Without Words course and helped me toward better formulations of many of my claims and arguments. My final revisions of the manuscript were greatly helped by extensive comments from David Chalmers, who has been an exemplary series editor.

Preface

Can creatures who do not have a language think? On the one hand, many types of nonlinguistic creatures behave in ways that seem to require treating the creatures in question as thinkers. The evidence is not simply anecdotal. Much of the most exciting and influential recent research in developmental psychology, cognitive archeology, and cognitive ethology explicitly assumes that the capacity for thought is not in any way tied to language possession. On the other hand, we do not really have any way of attributing thoughts to nonlinguistic creatures other than by crude analogy with the attribution of thoughts to language-using creatures. We have no theoretical framework for understanding the content and nature of nonlinguistic thought or the mechanisms of reasoning and reflection of which nonlinguistic creatures might be capable. And in the absence of such a theoretical framework, the practices of explanation within which the attribution of thoughts to nonlinguistic creatures seems so necessary remain without a secure foundation.

In this book I develop a framework for thinking about the thoughts of nonlinguistic creatures that acknowledges the differences between thinking without words and thinking with words while nonetheless enabling us to attribute to nonlinguistic creatures thoughts with many of the characteristic features of language-based thoughts. As will emerge, the thoughts of nonlinguistic creatures can have compositional structure—they have distinguishable components that can feature in further thoughts. They possess determinate contents, and it is often possible, despite the claims of many philosophers, to identify and spell out with reasonable accuracy the precise way that nonlinguistic creatures are thinking about their environment. Yet there are limits to the range of thoughts that nonlinguistic creatures can entertain because, as I argue in chapters 8 and 9, certain types of thinking (all those involving *intentional ascent*, or thinking about thoughts) require a linguistic vehicle.

Theoretical discussions of nonlinguistic thought tend either to deny that there can be any such thing or to speculate about the vehicles of nonlinguistic thought. Each of these general approaches is associated with a particular conception of the relation between thought and language. One very influential philosophical conception of the nature of thought, derived from the writings of Frege, is based on the principle that the study of thoughts can only proceed via the study of the sentences that express them. Theorists impressed by this conception of the nature of thought will find the notion of thought without language deeply problematic. Many of the problems that appear insuperable from the perspective of the classical philosophical approach seem less threatening if we shift paradigm and adopt the dominant understanding of the nature of thought within cognitive science, construing all thoughts (those of language-using creatures as well as those of nonlinguistic creatures) as relations to sentences in an internal language of thought. Yet, whatever the merits of the language of thought hypothesis as an account of the mechanics of cognition, it cannot provide a full account of nonlinguistic thinking. In particular, it does not provide us with an appropriate epistemology for the thoughts of nonlinguistic creatures.

In this book I develop a different approach to thought without language. Unlike the two approaches just outlined, the account I offer of thinking without words emphasizes the epistemological and explanatory dimensions of the problem. The best way of approaching the problem of thought without language, I suggest, is through providing an epistemological basis for the practice of attributing thoughts to nonlinguistic creatures and for the psychological explanations within which those attributions take place. Accordingly, the book contains considerable detailed discussion of empirical material from developmental psychology, cognitive psychology, and studies of animal behavior, both experimental and ethological. The theory that emerges is philosophical, in the sense that it is based on a particular philosophical conception of the nature of thought and thinking, but that philosophical view is developed and refined through detailed consideration of the practical implications of attributing thoughts to non-language-using creatures.

The basic problems that set the framework for this book are set out in chapter 1, where I outline the different types of question posed by the forms of psychological explanations of the behavior of nonlinguistic creatures given in various parts of the cognitive and behavioral sciences. Chapter 2 explores the differing responses to these questions given by the two approaches to the nature of thought outlined earlier, and shows how neither can provide a fully satisfying account of thinking without words. Chapter 3 considers a deflationary or minimalist construal of the nature of nonlinguistic thought that might be deployed to finesse the apparent need to attribute thoughts to creatures that are not language-users. The aim of the minimalist proposal is to show that thinking behavior in nonlinguistic creatures can be understood in nonpropositional and perceptual terms, rather than through the attribution of propositional attitudes such as beliefs and desires. In opposition to this I suggest that there are important types of nonlinguistic thought that cannot be accommodated in the manner proposed by the minimalist. The requirements of psychological explanation often demand that we attribute to nonlinguistic creatures thoughts that are structured, represent the world in a highly determinate way, and reflect the particular mode of presentation under which the creature apprehends its environment. Chapters 4 and 5 are devoted to showing how we might go about attributing such determinate and structured thoughts to nonlinguistic creatures. In chapter 4 I explain how a theorist might fix an ontology in a way that will allow the theorist to determine what objects a particular non-language-using creature is capable of thinking about—or, in other words, that will elucidate how the creature "carves up" its world into bounded individuals. Chapter 5 explores how a semantics can be provided for nonlinguistic thoughts in a way that both does justice to philosophical constraints on acceptable theories of content and provides the ethologist or developmental psychologist with a workable method of assigning contents to the beliefs and desires of nonlinguistic creatures.

A theory of nonlinguistic thought is incomplete without an account of nonlinguistic reasoning and the norms of rationality by which such reasoning is governed. In chapter 6 I show how an account of nonlinguistic rationality emerges when we pose the question: What could count as evidence that a nonlinguistic creature is behaving rationally? There are several different forms of evidence that can come into play here. At the most sophisticated level, a creature is behaving rationally when it is sensitive to the consequences of different courses of action, but there are types of rationality that do not involve such consequence-sensitivity. Different forms of rationality are appropriate to different types of explanation, and I draw a distinction between level 1 rationality and level 2 rationality that maps onto the distinction between explanations of the type proposed by the minimalist and explanations that make use of belief-desire psychology. Reasoning and rationality are, of course, correlative notions, and in chapter 7 I pursue the question of the forms of inference available at the nonlinguistic level. I offer an account of protoinference that respects the differences between linguistic and nonlinguistic thought (and in particular the impossibility of explaining nonlinguistic reasoning in formal terms), while at the same time offering analogues at the nonlinguistic level of some basic forms of inference.

In chapters 8 and 9 I address in more general terms the scope and limits of nonlinguistic thought. I argue that there are certain types of thinking for which a linguistic vehicle is essential—and by this I mean a public language rather than a private language of thought. Roughly speaking, a linguistic vehicle is required for all types of thinking that involve intentional ascent, or what is sometimes called metarepresentation. I argue in chapter 8 that intentional ascent requires semantic ascent, on the grounds that intentional ascent requires the ability "to hold a thought in mind" in a way that can only be done if the thought is linguistically vehicled. In chapter 9 this argument is developed and the limits of nonlinguistic thought plotted in the context of a range of different types of thought. These language-dependent cognitive abilities range from second-order reflection on one's own beliefs and desires and the capacity to attribute thoughts to others to the ability to entertain tensed thoughts and to deploy logical concepts. Many of these language-dependent cognitive abilities, however, have primitive analogues that do not involve intentional ascent and hence are available at the nonlinguistic level.

A final word. In previous work I have mapped the distinction between linguistic and nonlinguistic cognition onto a distinction between conceptual and nonconceptual content. In *The Paradox of Self-Consciousness* I proposed that genuine concept mastery involves an ability not simply to make judgments involving those concepts but also to justify those judgments and to reflect on the grounds for them. Since these are paradigmatically language-dependent activities, it follows that concept mastery requires the possession of a language. This line of thought still seems to me to be fundamentally correct, and the discussion of the differences between linguistic and nonlinguistic cognition in chapters 8 and 9 provides tools for developing it further. However, I have deliberately written this book in a manner that does not involve or require a particular interpretation of the distinction between conceptual and nonconceptual content. It seems to me that a clear view of the distinction between conceptual and nonconceptual content is more likely to emerge from a clear understanding of the differences between linguistic and nonlinguistic cognition than vice versa.

Contents

Note to the Reader

The problems with which this book is concerned are of broad interdisciplinary interest, and I have written the book with an interdisciplinary audience in mind. I hope that the general line of argument will be of interest to anyone with a theoretical, experimental, or practical interest in nonlinguistic creatures and how they represent and think about the world. The book does not presuppose a philosophical background, but there are certain sections that will perhaps be most directly of immediate concern to philosophers. Readers without a philosophical background could omit sections 2.1, 2.2, and 2.3 on an initial reading, moving straight from the end of chapter 1 to the final section of chapter 2. In chapter 3, section 3.2 could initially be omitted.

Thinking without Words

1

The Problem of Thinking without Words

The recent "cognitive turn" in the behavioral and cognitive sciences has drastically expanded the domain of the cognitive. High-level cognitive abilities are being identified and studied in an ever-increasing number of species and at ever-earlier stages of human development. The contemporary behavioral sciences have almost completely abandoned a longstanding tenet in the study of cognition, namely, that language and thought go hand in hand, and hence that the study of thought can only proceed via the study of language. Until recently, even those who held that thought could in principle exist without language had little idea how to study thought except through the language by which it is expressed. But current practice in the study of animal behavior, in the study of prelinguistic infants, and in the speculations of cognitive archaeologists about the evolutionary prehistory of *Homo sapiens,* has left these assumptions far behind.

Our understanding of the early stages of human development has undergone a sea change. Many developmental psychologists have come to speak of prelinguistic infants as little scientists, possessing, testing, and refining theories about the nature of the physical world (Gopnik and Meltzoff 1997). Complex experiments are regularly set up to identify the predictions that infants as young as 3 months make about the structure of physical objects and their dynamic and kinematic properties; about the trajectories that objects take through space-time; and about what will happen when objects interact (Baillargeon 1995, Spelke 1990). For example, when they are 3 months old infants are sensitive to the solidity of objects. They show surprise when one object appears in a place that it could only reach by passing through another object. It is tempting to conclude, and many developmental psychologists have concluded, that these infants have classified something as an object and have correlative expectations about how that thing will behave on the basis of that classification. There are important differences, of course, between how different developmental psychologists interpret these expectations and accompanying inferences. Some see them as involving the operation of a primitive theory (a naïve physics) and correlatively as involving something approaching inference. Others see them as primarily perceptual. All are agreed, however, in rejecting the traditional view of the prelinguistic infant as operating in a more or less unstructured perceptual universe with a small range of sensorimotor schemas enabling primitive types of behavior.

The study of animal behavior has been no less drastically transformed (Allen and Bekoff 1997, Dawkins 1986, Griffin 2001, Hauser 2000). The new discipline of cognitive ethology is essentially the study of the mental states of animals and of how those mental states manifest themselves in behavior. Unlike traditional approaches that have remained in the laboratory and attempted to account for animal performance on complicated but artificial tasks in terms of various forms of associationist learning, cognitive ethologists are prepared to study animals in the wild as they deal with the practical problems that arise in foraging, finding mates, constructing shelters, and raising their young. Cognitive ethologists, unlike the older generation of comparative psychologists, have little time for the project of trying to explain how an animal behaves in terms of nonrepresentational stimulus-response mechanisms or the fixed behavior patterns known as innate releasing mechanisms. They start from the assumption that animals have certain desires and certain beliefs about how the world is organized and act on the basis of those beliefs to try to ensure the satisfaction of their desires. Then they look at a species' natural behaviors, interpreting them as sophisticated strategies for pursuing the desires the members of that species seem to have. A good illustration of the degree of cognitive sophistication now attributed to animals are the various behaviors that have been analyzed as conscious attempts to manipulate conspecifics and members of other species. Deception behaviors have been identified at all levels of the phylogenetic ladder, from the much-studied examples in higher primates such as chimpanzees (Byrne 1995) to the broken-wing display of the plover (Ristau 1991), the false alarm calls of the great tit (Møller 1988), and the role of sentinel birds in mixed flocks (Munn 1986).

The study of human prehistory has taken on a new face. Cognitive archaeologists are finding evidence of thinking behaviors long before even the earliest plausible dates for the emergence of language (Corballis and Lea 1999, Mellars and Gibson 1996, Mithen 1990, 1996). Influential current accounts of the mind of prehistoric man identify evolutionary stages of high-level but manifestly nonlinguistic cognition. Stephen Mithen has argued, for example, that the early prehistory of the human mind was characterized by highly specialized cognitive modules, bodies of knowledge dedicated to specific aspects of the natural and social world (Mithen 1996). These "multiple intelligences" permitted complex intellectual skills and inferences. The social intelligence of the early human mind initially emerged from the constraints of social living, but then rapidly in its turn expanded the possibilities and parameters of communal existence. The natural history intelligence was tied up with what appear to have been the complex hunting and foraging strategies of the omnivorous early hominids. On Mithen's view the emergence of language proper did not make cognition possible. Rather, it permitted the integration of previously separated domain-specific modules. Merlin Donald has offered a rather different, but no less cognitivist, conception of the life of the prelinguistic hominids (Donald 1991). Prelinguistic hominids were capable of representing the world intentionally, of learning complex motor skills by imitation, and of constructing novel motor routines from a recursively structured motor vocabulary of basic movements. The integration of these individual skills into a social environment, with group mimetic acts, social coordination, and simple forms of teaching, facilitated the emergence of complex tool making, patterns of hunting that varied according to the season, primitive rituals, and a highly ramified social structure. For Donald, as indeed for Mithen and many other students of human prehistory, these sophisticated forms of instrumental and social cognition are a precondition for the emergence of language, not a consequence of that emergence.

These three areas of cognitive ethology, developmental psychology, and cognitive archaeology are becoming ever more closely integrated. It is usual to find cognitive archaeologists appealing to developmental work on infant grasp of naïve physics or naïve biology to support their claims about the domain-specific special intelligences of early man, just as they draw on the various studies of social cognition in nonhuman primates in developing theories about the social life of our earliest hominid ancestors. Research into animal cognition is now employing the dishabituation paradigm, which has proved so fruitful in the study of infant cognition (Hauser 1998, Munakata et al. 2001). Similarly, in developmental psychology arguments from evolution are playing an increasingly prominent role in the identification and explanation of the different levels of cognitive development, as indeed are arguments from the theory of animal learning (Gallistel et al. 1991). These interconnected bodies of knowledge and research share the common assumption that the domain of the cognitive far outstrips the domain of the linguistic.

This assumption that language is not necessary for thought will be the subject of this book. Relatively little work has been done on elucidating the types of thinking that are being attributed to different types of non-language-using creatures. The consequences of the basic assumption have been far more deeply explored than its theoretical background. This, of course, is how science proceeds. Niceties of conceptual framework are not at the fore when there is a major paradigm shift. But the new paradigms in ethology, developmental psychology, and the study of hominid prehistory are sufficiently well established for the more theoretical questions now to demand attention. In this book I will work toward providing a framework for understanding nonlinguistic thought, drawing on experimental work but trying to integrate it with the researches of philosophers on the nature of thought in a way that does justice to the more important insights that have emerged from very different approaches to the study of thought, language, and the relation between them. The remainder of this chapter is devoted to clarifying the precise challenges posed by the practice of explaining the behavior of nonlinguistic creatures in psychological terms.

1.1   Morgan's Canon and Psychological Explanations of Behavior

Experimental psychologists, particularly those concerned with comparative psychology (the psychological study of nonhuman animals) frequently appeal to a methodological principle originally proposed by Lloyd Morgan in 1894. The first formulation of Morgan's canon, as it is known, came in Morgan's book *An Introduction to Comparative Psychology*, where he writes that

> In no case may we interpret an action as the outcome of the exercise of a higher psychical faculty, if it can be interpreted as the outcome of the exercise of one which stands lower in the psychological scale. (Morgan 1894, 53)

Morgan himself did not provide a worked-out theory of what he terms the psychological scale, but it seems clear from his later formulations of the canon that he interpreted it in an evolutionary and developmental manner. In the revised edition of the *Introduction* he explicitly formulates the canon in evolutionary terms.

> In no case is an animal activity to be interpreted in terms of higher psychological processes, if it can be fairly interpreted in terms of processes which stand lower in the scale of psychological evolution and development. (Morgan 1903, 59)

Morgan's canon has frequently been taken to motivate an extreme distrust of attributing psychological states to nonhuman creatures, and is often cited as an objection to the whole enterprise of cognitive ethology. Clearly, given that it is explicitly formulated in evolutionary and developmental terms, it can hardly be applied without begging the question as a methodological principle for the study of prelinguistic infants and early hominids (since in both these cases the issue at stake is precisely when the "higher psychological processes" emerge in the course of psychological evolution and development). Nonetheless, Morgan's canon is frequently held to impose requirements on explanation that are incompatible with the attribution of thoughts to prelinguistic infants and early hominids. Consider, for example, the following exposition of Morgan's canon.

> In Morgan's case, the principle amounted to this. Where there is a pattern of animal behavior which must be explained, both as to form and to origin, and in the simplest, but at the same time most adequate way, the experimenter should appeal to factors observable in the situation in which the animal has been placed, in the behavior itself, and in the machinery by which the behavior is made possible. It is not incumbent on him to pass over these factors in order to appeal to a verbal construct, to a mind, or to any other kind of mental factor which lies outside of, behind, or within the behavior-situation. (Griffith 1943, 322)

The injunction here to seek an explanation in purely behavioral terms is just as applicable to developmental psychology and cognitive archeology as it is to ethology.

There are important questions about whether the appeals that have been made to Morgan's canon do justice to Morgan's own approach to comparative psychology. It is clear, for example, that Morgan was not simply advocating that one always seek the simplest explanation. Explaining a behavior in terms of beliefs and desires is frequently much simpler than explaining it as the result of a complex process of instrumental conditioning. But, at a minimum, Morgan was suggesting that we should not trust psychological explanations of behavior unless we are convinced that those explanations are indispensable—that is to say, unless we are convinced that the behavior in question cannot be explained in nonpsychological terms. This is not, I suspect, a methodological principle with which very many of the authors cited in the preceding section will disagree.

The roots of the cognitive explosion in the study of nonlinguistic creatures lie in an increasingly widespread sense that the existing tools for the nonpsychological study of behavior have produced patently inadequate pictures of infant and animal cognition and human evolution. Psychological explanations are appealed to because they seem required to make sense of the complex behaviors that can be both observed and experimentally demonstrated. And of course they are appealed to very selectively. Few advocates of extending psychological explanation to the realm of the nonlinguistic think that we should completely set aside our nonpsychological models of behavior. Few would deny, for example, that the cognitive ethologist should be ready to characterize many types of behavior in terms of *innate releasing mechanisms*—namely, fixed patterns of behavior that are more complex than reflexes, often involving a chained sequences of movements rather than a simple reaction, and that yet seem to be instinctive (Tinbergen 1951). Nor is it being proposed that the experimental study of animal behavior should completely abandon explanations formulated in terms of processes of conditioning, whether classical or instrumental.[1] It seems clear that much of infant behavior is best understood in terms of the sensorimotor schemas so carefully studied and documented by Piaget. And many cognitive archeologists have devoted considerable time to learning the techniques of stone-knapping and Neolithic tool construction with a view to investigating just how cognitively sophisticated they are.

Psychological explanations of nonlinguistic behavior are hard won—and, of course, only provisional. It may well be that a nonpsychological explanation will emerge for behavior that we currently think requires a psychological explanation. It is hard to see how any such possibility could be ruled out in principle. What seems highly unlikely, however, is that satisfactory explanations in wholly nonpsychological terms will be found for all the behaviors for which psychological explanations are canvassed. It is difficult to imagine that researchers into animal behavior, infant development, and human evolution will return to the methodological precepts of behaviorism. Even though they might, in any given situation and in complete conformity with Morgan's canon, always investigate whether a nonpsychological explanation might be forthcoming, it is (I think) inconceivable that psychological explanations will be banished from the study of nonhuman creatures. The shift to the cognitive has now cast too many roots and the independence of thought from language is now too deeply engrained for that to be possible.

If Morgan's canon is to be applied effectively, however, we require both a specification of the distinctive features of psychological explanation and some sort of understanding in operational terms of how behavior requiring such explanation is to be identified. The issues that this raises will recur throughout this book, but in the remainder of this section I will sketch out some of the principal respects in which psychological explanations are to be distinguished from nonpsychological or mechanistic explanations.[2]

The first distinguishing characteristic is that psychological explanations are teleological. That is to say, they explain an organism's behavior either in terms of the purposes and desires that the behavior is intended to satisfy or, more minimally, simply in terms of those that it does satisfy. On either construal, however, the behavior will come out as goal-directed in a way that mechanistically explicable behavior is not. It may be the case, for example, that a particular innate releasing mechanism brings about the satisfaction of a desire. Consider, for example, the pecking response in herring gull chicks (Tinbergen 1973). Newly hatched herring gulls are particularly sensitive to the sensory input correlated with the length, movement, and coloration of the adult herring gull's bill, and when they encounter such input they respond by pecking vigorously at whatever it is that presents the appropriate input (usually, of course, the adult's bill tip). The adult herring gull responds by feeding the chick. Yet the chick's pecking is not a goal-directed response, even though it can be described as bringing about the satisfaction of a desire. It is not a goal-directed behavior because it is an invariant response to the appropriate stimuli.

This brings us to the second characteristic of psychological explanations, namely, the fact that the behavior they seek to explain cannot be explained and predicted as a function of invariant responses to detected stimuli. Innate releasing mechanisms, such as the herring gull pecking response, have the following characteristics (Lea 1984).

- They are triggered by specific stimuli.
- They always take the same form.
- They occur in all members of the relevant species.
- Their occurrence is largely independent of the individual creature's history.
- Once launched they cannot be varied.
- They have only one function.

This means, of course, that if one can identify a member of a given species and has some understanding of the innate releasing mechanisms characteristic of members of that species at the appropriate stage of development, then one will be able straightforwardly to predict what the creature will do when it registers stimuli of the appropriate type. Registering the relevant stimulus causes the appropriate response, and this can be fully understood, explained, and predicted without any appeal to an intermediary between stimulus and response. Similar input-output links can be seen in the case of sensorimotor schemas and various types of conditioned behavior. Psychological explanations of behavior only become necessary when no such input-output links can be identified. The essence of a psychological explanation is that it explains behavior in terms of how the creature in question *represents* its environment, rather than simply in terms of the stimuli that it detects. Psychological explanations involve appealing to representational states that function as intermediaries between sensory input and behavioral output.

How does this work? How can the appeal to psychological states allow us to make sense of behaviors that cannot be understood as invariant responses to stimuli? When we appeal to representational states to explain behavior we rarely, if ever, appeal to single states operating in isolation. The issue here is one of *cognitive integration*. The behavior of organisms that are suitably flexible and plastic in their responses to the environment tends to be the result of complex interactions between internal states. Organisms respond flexibly and plastically to their environments in virtue of the fact that their representational states respond flexibly and plastically to each other, most obviously through the influence of stored representations on present representations. The possibility of learning and adaptation depends on past representations contributing to the determination of present responses, and hence interacting with them. Moreover, representing a particular feature of the environment does not have effects on behavior just when a creature is confronted by that very feature. It can also be effective when the creature is confronted by something that is relevantly similar to the represented feature, or when the feature is absent and there is nothing relevantly similar in the environment (as when a creature determines to leave its shelter because it cannot detect either a predator or anything predator-like in the vicinity).

The role of representations in explaining behavior is closely tied to the possibility of misrepresentation. Tropistic and classically conditioned behavior can be explained without reference to representational perceptual states because the response is invariant once the creature in question has registered the relevant stimuli. That is to say, the behavior can be explained by the way things are in the immediate environment, together with the assumption that the creature is appropriately sensitive to the relevant stimuli. The need to appeal to how things are taken to be comes in only when the law-governed correlation between stimulus and response breaks down. This can come about either when the response occurs in the absence of the stimulus, or when the stimulus occurs and is registered without the response following. In the first of these cases one might say that there is a representation of the stimulus and that this is what generates the response, and in the second case one might say that even though the stimulus is there it is not represented in a way that would bring about the appropriate response. Both of these are different types of misrepresentation, and the existence or possibility of misrepresentation is a useful index of the need to advert to psychological explanations.

Jerry Fodor has suggested how the possibility of misrepresentation might be explained by the lack of a lawlike correlation between stimulus and response (Fodor 1986, 14–16). Explaining why there should be an invariant connection between stimulus and response requires postulating the existence of *transducers* (devices that transfer sensory stimuli into physical output that is in a suitable form to interact with the motor system). We need transducers to explain how an organism can pick up stimuli at all, and when there is an invariant connection between stimulus and response we need to postulate the existence of transducers that are sensitive to specific properties—what are often known as *dedicated* transducers. The existence and operation of these dedicated transducers, hooked up in the appropriate ways to the motor system, is all that we need to explain the invariant behavior in question. Now, in the case of intentional behavior that does not involve a lawlike connection between stimulus and response, it is clear that we are not dealing with dedicated transducers. Creatures that are behaving intentionally are of course sensitive to particular properties of the stimulus, but these are not properties that can be detected by dedicated transducers. So how are they detected? In some sense their presence needs to be "inferred from" the presence of properties that can be picked up by transducers. The need for such a process of inference, however, brings with it the possibility of error. Hence the possibility of misrepresentation.

I will show later on in the book how these characteristics of psychological explanations and the behavior that they are proposed to explain can be applied in practice. For the moment I need simply note the following three characteristics of psychological explanations.

1. They serve to explain behavior in situations where the connections between sensory input and behavioral output cannot be plotted in a lawlike manner.
2. They rely on the cognitive integration of different psychological states.
3. They appeal to psychological states that admit of misrepresentation.

That such explanations are, as a matter of fact, applied to nonlinguistic creatures is beyond doubt. That they are applied to nonlinguistic creatures as a matter of necessity is highly plausible. As remarked earlier, there are no good reasons for thinking that the practice of psychological explanation should be confined to language-using creatures. I have so far, however, said little about precisely how these explanations should be understood. As I will show in the next section, these very general comments about the role of psychological explanations in explaining the behavior of nonlinguistic creatures leave open a range of important questions about the type of explanation at stake and the nature of the representational states that they attribute.

1.2   The Parameters of the Problem

A theorist confronting the wide range of psychological explanations applied to nonlinguistic creatures, and convinced, in the light of Morgan's canon and the general considerations brought out in the previous section, that these psychological explanations are indispensable, will find it natural to ask just how we are to understand the thoughts and types of thinking that are now being attributed to creatures not previously taken as candidates for thinking at all. Questions such as the following spring to mind.

- Can nonlinguistic creatures properly be described as having beliefs about the way the world is (or indeed, *knowledge* of how the world is)? Can they properly be described as having desires, or hopes or fears? How does the psychological vocabulary appropriate for characterizing nonlinguistic creatures relate to that which we apply to language-using creatures? What sorts

of things might nonlinguistic thoughts be? How can animals and prelinguistic infants *grasp* thoughts in a way that will influence behavior?

- Do the thoughts of nonlinguistic creatures represent the world in a determinate way (do they have determinate *contents*)? Can we characterize those
thoughts in the way we characterize the thoughts of language-using creatures, by using "that—" clauses that specify their content? Are there distinctive ways that nonlinguistic creatures classify objects in thought? Do the
thoughts of nonlinguistic creatures have any sort of determinate structure?
Should they be assimilated to sentences, or are they in fact closer to perceptual representations and mental images?
- If it is the case that nonlinguistic creatures *do* have beliefs and desires with
determinate contents, how are we to work out what those contents are? As
observers of animal or infant behavior we of course only have behavior to
go on. How are we to attribute thoughts on the basis of behavior in a way
that will explain behavior?
- Does the attribution of thoughts to nonlinguistic creatures explain their behavior in anything like the way that the attribution of thoughts explains the
behavior of language-using creatures? Can we say that a nonlinguistic creature behaves in a certain way because it has beliefs and desires that render
that particular course of action a rational one to adopt? What sort of transitions between thoughts can nonlinguistic creatures make? Are they properly
described as making inferences?

These questions, all of which will be tackled in this book, fall into four different
groups. Questions in the first group are broadly *metaphysical*. They all concern the
nature and mechanics of nonlinguistic thought. Questions about whether nonlinguistic creatures can properly be described as having beliefs and desires fall under
this heading, as does the issue of how such beliefs and desires (if they exist) might
have effects on behavior. The second group of questions concerns the *semantics* of
nonlinguistic thought. These are questions about how we should understand the
content of nonlinguistic thought and about the different types of thinking available
to language-less creatures. Under this heading fall, for example, the issue of
whether nonlinguistic thoughts are structured and the question of whether any
sorts of thoughts are in principle unavailable to nonlinguistic creatures. The third
group of questions is largely *epistemological*. Even if all the metaphysical questions are answered satisfactorily, we will still need some account of how we can
come to attribute thoughts to nonlinguistic creatures. We need to have a reliable
method for working backward from behavior to the thoughts generating that behavior. Without this we will be unable to deploy our theory of nonlinguistic
thought in explaining behavior. The fourth and last group of questions has to do
with the *practice of explanation* within which the attribution of nonlinguistic
thought is embedded. In the forms of psychological explanation with which we are
most familiar (the standard, belief-desire explanations of the behavior of language-
using, concept-possessing humans) we assume that psychological explanation is
an idealized reconstruction of practical decision-making. In a psychological expla-

nation we cite beliefs and desires such that the agent whose behavior is being explained could have reasoned (and perhaps even did reason) from those beliefs and desires to the intention to act in the way that he actually did act. So a proper understanding of the practice of giving psychological explanations of the behavior of nonlinguistic creatures must bring with it a plausible account of how nonlinguistic creatures fix on a particular course of action.

An adequate account of nonlinguistic thought must accommodate all four of these dimensions. It must

- explain the metaphysics of nonlinguistic thought
- explain the semantics of nonlinguistic thought
- explain how it is possible for us to identify the content of such thoughts
- explain the decision-making processes of nonlinguistic creatures in a way that underwrites the practice of psychological explanation

These four dimensions must, of course, be accommodated by a theory of any type of thought (linguistic or nonlinguistic), and one way of bringing out the particular difficulties posed by nonlinguistic thought is by looking at how these four sets of questions are dealt with by two prominent approaches to the nature of thought in general.[3] That will be the task of the next chapter.

The two approaches I will discuss provide very different accounts of the metaphysical, semantic, epistemological, and explanatory dimensions of thought. They both share, however, the basic assumption that the only way to understand thought is through language. One approach, with its origins in some of Frege's writings on the nature of thought, holds that we can only approach thought through natural language. The second approach, inspired by Fodor's representational theory of the mind, explains thought through the hypothesis of an internal language of thought. I will use these two accounts as foils in order to develop a sense of the challenges that face the theorist of nonlinguistic thought.

One reason for highlighting the Fregean conception of thought and the language of thought hypothesis is that they represent the extreme points on a spectrum of possible positions with respect to the question of the relative priority of thought and language. Whereas the Fregean approach to thought ties thoughts ineliminably to the sentences of a natural language and what it is to understand those sentences, the language of thought hypothesis completely reverses the order of explanation, suggesting that the very idea of understanding a natural language does not make sense without assuming a linguistically structured inner representational medium. A corollary of this is that, whereas the Fregean view stresses the distinctiveness of language in a way that makes the possibility of nonlinguistic thought seem deeply problematic, the Fodorian view goes a long way toward assimilating linguistic thought and nonlinguistic thought. In contrast to both of these approaches, the positive account of the nature of nonlinguistic thought that I will be developing in the main body of the book aims to show both that nonlinguistic thinking has significant commonalities with linguistic thought and that there are equally significant limitations to the types of thought that can be entertained by nonlinguistic creatures.

2

Two Approaches to the Nature of Thought

Our problem is finding an appropriate conceptual framework for thinking about the nature and status of psychological explanations in the study of human infants, nonhuman animals, and early hominids. I have shown in the previous chapter that such a conceptual framework needs to have four dimensions. It needs to incorporate, first, an account of the metaphysics of nonlinguistic thinking (an account of the nature of nonlinguistic thoughts and of what it is for a nonlinguistic creature to be a thinker); second, an account of the semantics of nonlinguistic thinking (an account of how the world is represented at the nonlinguistic level); third, an account of the epistemology of nonlinguistic thinking (explaining how we as observers and theorists should go about attributing thoughts to creatures that lack a language); and, fourth, an account of the psychology of nonlinguistic rationality and decision-making.

In order to appreciate in more detail the requirements imposed within each of these dimensions it is helpful to examine in some detail two prominent theories of the nature of thought. The two theories I examine in this chapter are Frege's conception of thoughts as the senses of sentences and Fodor's language of thought hypothesis to the effect that thinking should be understood in terms of the operation of sentence-like formulae in an internal language of thought. Both approaches start off from a single basic assumption, which is that the nature of thought can best be analyzed through the nature of language, but each approach takes a very different view of the essence of language. In section 2.1 I explain the key elements of Frege's conception of thoughts as the senses of sentences, using Frege as a foil to clarify the challenges that confront a theory of nonlinguistic thought under each of the four dimensions identified in the previous chapter. As I show, taking thoughts to be the senses of sentences provides a clear account of each of the four dimensions of thinking that nonetheless cannot be extended to nonlinguistic creatures. This brings into very clear focus the desiderata for a theory of nonlinguistic thinking—namely, to provide answers to those questions that, on the Fregean theory, are answered by taking thoughts to be the senses of sentences. In section 2.2 I move on to the language of thought hypothesis. This hypothesis provides an account of the nature of thought that is applicable to nonlinguistic creatures and that accommodates three of the four dimensions. As emerges in section 2.3, however, the language of thought hypothesis falls short when it comes to the epistemological dimension. For this reason, even though the language of thought hypothesis provides a worked-out account of the mechanics of thinking that can be applied to nonlinguistic creatures, it cannot as it stands serve as a fully satisfying framework for the explanatory practices of cognitive ethology, developmental psychology, and cognitive archeology.

In the final section of the chapter I explore the lessons to be learned from these two approaches to the nature of thought and suggest an alternative way to approach nonlinguistic thought. The approach that I propose in section 2.3, and that the remainder of the book develops, takes the epistemological dimension of nonlinguistic thought to be primary.

2.1   The Fregean Approach: Thoughts as the Senses of Sentences

There are genuine questions to be raised about whether the following sketch accurately represents the views of the historical Frege.[1] It is certainly the case that Frege was far more interested in mathematical, particularly arithmetical, thoughts than in those expressible by means by a natural language. It is also true that Frege had a rather dismissive attitude to natural language. Perhaps the Fregean view that I will be discussing is an artifact resulting from the tendency of some of Frege's interpreters to focus on too narrow a range of his writings.[2] I do not believe this to be the case. But even if it were it would not matter. The conception of the relation between thought and language that has emerged from reflection on Frege's writings represents a powerful and unified theory. It deserves to be taken into account irrespective of its exegetical credentials. I will begin by explaining what I take to be the essentials of the Fregean position and then go on to draw out some of the principal constraints that the Fregean account imposes on a theory of nonlinguistic thought.

By 'thoughts' Frege did not mean individual acts of thinking. He in fact had surprisingly little to say about individual acts of thinking. What he was interested in was what we now term the *contents* of individual acts of thinking—what is known, for example, in an instance of knowledge or believed in an instance of belief. A Fregean thought is not an act of thinking. Rather, an act of thinking involves a relation to a thought. In believing, for example, that Paris is the capital of France I stand in a certain relation to the thought that Paris is the capital of France—a thought to which any other thinker can become related. These thoughts are abstract objects that serve not simply as the objects of propositional attitudes such as knowledge or belief but also as the *senses* of sentences. In fact, on the understanding of Frege's philosophy of thought that I shall be putting forward, our basic understanding of thoughts comes from considering them as the senses of sentences. It is in this sense that we should understand the claim frequently made by Michael Dummett that the essence of Frege's approach is the idea that the analysis of thought can proceed only via the analysis of language.

The Fregean theory of thought is a worked-out response to a series of problems about the nature of thought that it is important to have clearly in mind when thinking both about the nature of thought and about the nature of nonlinguistic thinking. These problems can be mapped on to the four dimensions identified in the previous chapter.

Let me start with the metaphysical dimension. For Frege, as for just about every other account of the propositional attitudes, belief is the fundamental propositional attitude. To have a belief is to commit oneself in thought to a certain state of affairs holding in the world. The belief is true just if that state of affairs does hold, false otherwise. Belief itself is a psychological state, not a part of the thought but rather a relation to the thought. The thought itself is the postulate (for want of a better word) that the relevant state of affairs holds in the world. To have the attitude of belief to that thought is to endorse the postulate. To endorse it, of course, is to take it to be true—and one cannot take to be true anything that is not a candidate for truth or falsity.

Suppose now that we ask how we are to understand these postulates to the effect that a certain state of affairs holds in the world. The central idea here is that what we endorse when we take the attitude of belief to a thought is precisely what we understand when we understand an assertoric sentence (where an assertoric sentence is one that characterizes the world as being a certain way). The significance of this emerges when we consider what sort of a thing a thought must be that we can grasp it. It is no easy matter to explain what it is to grasp something as true. And yet, if thoughts are to feature in psychological explanation in the manner discussed in the previous chapter, then we clearly need an account of how a thinker can grasp thoughts. The basic idea that thoughts are the senses of assertoric sentences gives us a clear way of understanding how we might grasp thoughts. We grasp thoughts through understanding the sentences that express them. Once we have grasped a thought in this way we can simply entertain it, where this might be construed as contemplating it without assigning it a truth-value. We can endorse it as true, which can be construed as asserting it. Or we can take to it any of the other propositional attitudes, which can be construed in terms of the different types of *force* that can be attached to the sentence.[3] Frege's account, therefore, gives a clear answer to the fundamental metaphysical problem of how we can make epistemic contact with thoughts—how thoughts can be the sort of things that can feature in reasoning and have causal effects within the world.

Moving from the metaphysical dimension to the semantic dimension, the most obvious problems with which Frege is engaged have to do with the structure of thoughts, and of thought itself. The first problem is the problem of explaining the composition of individual thoughts. There is a clear sense in which thoughts *seem* to be structured entities, made up of elements that can reappear in further thoughts.

This is closely tied to the possibility of thoughts entering into inferential relations with each other (and hence directly tied to the utility of psychological explanations of behavior, since beliefs and desires stand in inferential relations to the behavior that they explain). Some inferential relations are truth-functional. They hold between thoughts in virtue of their truth-value. So, for example, we know that we can infer "Socrates is mortal" from "Socrates is mortal and the Argives defeated the Trojans" because there are no circumstances in which "Socrates is mortal and the Argives defeated the Trojans" could be true and "Socrates is mortal" false. The internal structure of the thoughts expressed by these sentences is irrelevant, which is why in explaining why these inferences are valid we can simply employ propositional variables and do not need to go into details of what the propositional variables stand for. Other inferences (those that we might model in the predicate rather than the propositional calculus) depend on the structure of the individual thought. Consider, for example, the inference from "Socrates is mortal" to "There is at least one thing that is mortal." This is a valid inference, in the sense that it is not possible for the premise to be true and the conclusion false. If Socrates is mortal then at least one thing is mortal. But the validity of the inference is not in any sense a function of the truth-values of the relevant sentences. In order to explain why the inference is valid we need to see the inference as taking the form "a is F, therefore, at least one thing is F." But this requires us to see the thought expressed by "Socrates is mortal" as having a structure that we standardly represent as "Fa" in the predicate calculus, and the thought expressed by "There is at least one thing that is mortal" as having the structure "$\exists x Fx$." We cannot understand the validity of inferences of this type without adverting to the structure (or *logical form*) of the thoughts in question.[4]

Let us suppose, then, that the possibility of inferential transitions between thoughts presupposes some level of structure, whether in the thoughts themselves or in the way they are determined. How are we to make sense of that structure? The Fregean approach to thought gives us a clear answer. Thoughts are the senses of sentences, and the structure of a thought is given by the logical form of the sentence that expresses it—where the logical form of a sentence is given by the appropriate logical regimentation of that sentence in Frege's concept-script (roughly, the second-order predicate calculus). This logical form identifies the constituents of the thought, that is, the senses of which it is composed. Consider, for example, the thought expressed by "There is at least one mortal thing." According to Frege, the proper analysis of the logical form of that sentence identifies it as expressing a thought whose constituents are (roughly speaking) a first-level functional sense (corresponding to the predicate "— is mortal") and a second-level functional sense to the effect that the first-order functional sense has at least one object falling under it. Of course, the details of Frege's positive account of the composition of thoughts can, and perhaps ought to, be challenged. Many philosophers, for example, would contest the claim that quantifiers should be viewed as functions taking first-order functions as their arguments. But it is undeniable that the basic idea that thoughts are the senses of sentences yields both a powerful account of the compositional structure of thoughts and a practical method for uncovering the compositional structure of any given thought.[5]

Still on the semantic dimension of thought, there is a further and more overarching structural isomorphism in play, not simply between a thought and the sentence expressing it but between thought as a whole and language as a whole. It is widely held that thoughts have certain structural characteristics as a matter of definition. Not only are they *compositional* (made up of recombinable constituents that can feature in a range of further thoughts in the way I have already considered) but the range of available thoughts is not in principle limited. The capacities of individual thinkers may be limited by time, computational constraints, and so forth, but in principle an indefinite number of thoughts can be constructed from a finite number of primitives. That is to say, thoughts are *generative*. An account of thought needs to provide some explanation of this phenomenon. Taking thoughts to be the senses of sentences, so that the analysis of thought proceeds via the analysis of language, offers a clear way of understanding generativity. We can quite simply point to the mechanisms that secure linguistic generativity—the mechanisms of pronominal reference that allow one sentence to be embedded within another, the logical operators that allow sentences to be combined to form complex sentences, and the ways that complex referring terms (such as definite descriptions) can be formed from simple predicates.

Let us move on to the epistemological dimension. The problem here is how we are to understand and attribute thoughts. It is obvious that the practice of psychological explanation requires the ability to identify the psychological antecedents of behavior from a third-person perspective. It requires being able to work backward from observed behavior to attribute beliefs and desires with determinate contents—being able to interpret observed behavior as intended to achieve certain specifiable ends in the light of the agent's information about the world. But once again the abstract nature of thoughts makes this enterprise seem deeply problematic. How are we supposed to be able to identify the thoughts to which an agent is related? How are we supposed to identify the contents of her beliefs and desires? If thoughts are the senses of sentences, and if belief is in some sense an interiorization of the linguistic act of assertion, then it is clear how we might proceed (when we are dealing with linguistic creatures). We can use what people say to work out what they believe, on the twin assumptions, first, that if someone sincerely assents to "p" then it is reasonable to take her to believe that p, and, second, that, if people believe that p they will generally be disposed to assent to "p." These disquotational principles are, of course, rules of thumb rather than necessary and sufficient conditions on what it is to believe that. Few would suggest that someone believes that p if and only if she is disposed to assent to "p." And in practice of course the interpretation of beliefs and the interpretation of speech go hand in hand, since we need some sort of assumptions about what a person believes before we can determine how her words might be a guide to what she believes (how else could we interpret, for example, whether she was being sincere). Nonetheless, taking thoughts to be the senses of sentences, and the structure of a thought to be given by the structure of the sentence that expresses it, yields a very clear resolution to the epistemological question of how thoughts can be identified and attributed.

The final dimension is the explanatory dimension. Models of psychological explanation go hand in hand with models of practical decision-making. The standard form of a psychological explanation as applied to language-using humans is "A ø-ed because $P_1 \ldots n$" where $P_1 \ldots n$ report certain psychological states of the subject, most standardly a belief-desire pair. The guiding assumption is that $P_1 \ldots n$ rationalize or make comprehensible why the subject should have acted the way he did. How do they do this? One standard way of looking at the matter is expressed in the following passage from Donald Davidson.

> If someone acts with an intention then he must have attitudes and beliefs from which, had he been aware of them and had he the time, he could have reasoned that his act was desirable. . . . If we can characterize the reasoning that would serve we will, in effect, have described the logical relations between descriptions of beliefs and desires and the description of the action, when the former gives the reasons with which the latter was performed. We are to imagine, then, that the agent's beliefs and desires provide him with the premises of an argument. (Davidson 1978/1980a, 85–86)

According to this view, which in fact goes back at least as far as Aristotle, a psychological explanation is informative because it points toward (although usually does not actually specify in any detail) a set of decision-making processes that could plausibly have generated the target behavior. In the case of our normal day-to-day psychological explanations it is widely held that we lean heavily on a shared 'theory of mind,' part of which spells out the inferences that we can expect to be made by other people with whom we interact and whose behavior we need to be able to explain and predict. This is why psychological explanations rarely need to spell out the actual reasoning that might have led from the relevant belief-desire pair to the action in question. It is obvious to all of us how someone with that belief-desire pair would have been led to act the way she did. This is partly because we realize that, had we had that combination of beliefs and desires in similar circumstances, we would have acted the same way. But it is also because we appreciate the inferential transitions that could have led a rational thinker from that combination of beliefs and desires to a decision to act in that particular way. Psychological explanation is in key respects the converse of practical reasoning. So we need a model not simply of how thoughts can be grasped but also of how there can be inferential relations between thoughts of the sort that might issue in behavior.

Once again, the Fregean approach to thought through language provides such a model—more accurately (since the psychology of reasoning was not Frege's concern), it makes clear how there can be such a model. The notion of logical form is at the heart of Frege's conception of thought, given that the structure of a thought is determined by the logical form of the sentence that expresses it. This is the key to a Fregean account of the psychology of inference. Although inferential relations in the strict logical sense (what Frege called the laws of thought) hold between thoughts, we grasp inferential relations between thoughts in terms of inferential relations between logical forms. These relations can be syntactic. That is to say, they can be understood in terms of rule-governed transitions applying to sequences of sentences in virtue of their formal structure. Or they can be semantic, holding between sentences in virtue of their semantic properties. Both ways of understanding inference have been well studied.

If, therefore, we take thoughts to be the senses of sentences then we have a clear account of the nature of thought that accommodates the four dimensions identified in the previous chapter. It is hard to see, however, how this account might be extended to cover thinking without words. It is true that the general proposal that the analysis of thought should proceed via the analysis of language is not directly incompatible with the existence of nonlinguistic thought. The proposal that a thought be analyzed through the sentence that expresses it does not entail that any thinker capable of thinking that thought should be able to express it. There could still be thoughts without language even if the study of thought has to proceed via the study of language. Something like this was, after all, Frege's own view. He was explicit that, although thoughts come for us "clothed in the form of a sentence," it is possible that other creatures could grasp thoughts directly (although he was doubtless not thinking about the candidate instances of thinking without words discussed in the first section of the previous chapter).

The problem comes, however, because it is not enough to provide an account of what thoughts are and how they should be analyzed. If we are interested in thoughts from the perspective of psychological explanation (as opposed, for example, to the perspective of logic) then our account of what thoughts are has to be accompanied by an account of how thoughts can be responsible for action. And this, as I have shown, seems to require developing the Fregean view in a way that is incompatible with the possibility of nonlinguistic thought. If thoughts are the senses of sentences then it is hard to see (on the assumption that the analysis of thought has to proceed via the analysis of language) how grasping a thought can be anything other than understanding a sentence, and how practical reasoning is to be understood except in terms of transitions between sentences. It is sometimes suggested that we understand a sentence in terms of an independently grasped thought, but to my knowledge no account has yet been given of what it might be to grasp a thought independently of understanding a sentence. Even if we bracket these difficulties, it seems that the relation between the structure and composition of a thought and the structure and composition of the sentence that expresses it poses an epistemological problem. We find this problem presented very clearly in the following passage from Donald Davidson's influential article "Thought and Talk," where he poses the question of why (in his view) the attribution of thoughts depends on the interpretation of speech.

> The general, and not very informative, reason is that without speech we cannot make the fine distinctions between thoughts that are essential to the explanations we can sometimes confidently supply. Our manner of attributing attitudes ensures that all the expressive power of language can be used to express such distinctions. One can be-

lieve that Scott is not the author of *Waverly* while not doubting that Scott is Scott; one can want to be the discoverer of a creature with a heart without wanting to be the discoverer of a creature with a kidney. One can intend to bite into the apple in the hand without intending to bite into the only apple with a worm in it; and so forth. The intensionality we make so much of in the attribution of thoughts is very hard to make much of when speech is not present. The dog, we say, knows that its master is at home. But does it know that Mr Smith (who is his master), or that the president of the bank (who is that same master) is home? We have no real idea how to settle, or make sense of, these questions. It is much harder to say, when speech is not present, how to distinguish universal thoughts from conjunctions of thoughts, or how to attribute conditional thoughts, or thoughts with, so to speak, mixed quantification ("He hopes that everyone is loved by someone"). (Davidson 1978/1980a, 164)

So, even though the letter of the Fregean approach does not rule out in principle the attribution of thoughts to nonlinguistic creatures, it does seem to present difficulties for the practices of psychological explanation within which those attributions are embedded.

In the light of this a theorist concerned with those practices of explanation has a choice. The first possibility is to seek an alternative account of the nature of nonlinguistic thought that will show how to answer the central questions that the Fregean account leaves open. He will need to explain how we can understand what it is to have a belief without appealing to the understanding of sentences or the linguistic act of assertion. He will need to explain how can we understand the inferential transitions by which beliefs and other propositional desires can lead to action. And he will need to explain how ethologists, developmental psychologists, and cognitive archeologists can go about identifying and attributing propositional attitudes.

In the next section I consider an account of the nature of thought that makes considerable progress in this direction. This is the complex of ideas associated with the language of thought hypothesis. The language of thought hypothesis is a hypothesis about the *mechanics* of thinking in a way that the Fregean approach clearly is not. If we follow Frege in distinguishing the logical question of what thoughts are from the psychological question of how we grasp thoughts and deploy them in reasoning, then the language of thought hypothesis most definitely addresses the second question. The central idea of the language of thought hypothesis is that propositional attitudes are relations to sentences/formulae in an internal language of thought. These sentences/formulae represent the thoughts in a way that allows them to feature in reasoning and decision-making. The language of thought hypothesis provides a clear alternative to the Fregean account. As I show in section 2.3, however, the language of thought hypothesis is seriously limited when it comes to the epistemological dimension of nonlinguistic thought and is of little practical use in grounding psychological explanation at the nonlinguistic level.

But the theorist of nonlinguistic thought does not need to accept the way the problem has so far been set up. We have been working on the assumption that psychological explanation at the nonlinguistic level is a species of belief-desire psychology, directly analogous to that which we employ in the psychological explanation of language-using creatures. But this assumption might be rejected. The theorist may seek to find differences between the type of thoughts involved in psychological explanations of the behavior of nonlinguistic creatures and the type of thoughts that we have been discussing up to now. If these differences are significant enough, then it may well be that the problems we have been considering cease to loom so large. In chapter 3 I examine a *minimalist* or *deflationary* way of understanding the thoughts that might be attributed to nonlinguistic creatures. On the minimalist view, it is perfectly correct to describe nonlinguistic creatures as thinkers, but we need to be careful about how we describe the type of thinking going on. We should not assimilate it to the thinking engaged in by language-using creatures, or think of it in terms of belief-desire psychology. When we appreciate the differences between these types of thinking we see that the apparent incompatibility with the Fregean approach does not really arise. Nonlinguistic thinking does not involve propositional attitudes— and, a fortiori, psychological explanation at the nonlinguistic level is not a variant of belief-desire psychology. So there is no need to give an account of how a nonlinguistic creature might believe something—or indeed of how it might grasp a thought at all. It is not, according to the minimalist view, appropriate to describe nonlinguistic thoughts as having determinate contents. Nor should the types of reasoning engaged in at the nonlinguistic level be modeled on those at the linguistic level. For all these reasons, then, the failure of the Fregean approach to extend to nonlinguistic creatures should not be a cause for concern. As I show in chapter 3, however, there are powerful arguments suggesting that the minimalist conception cannot be the whole story about nonlinguistic thought.

For the moment, the point to extract is that we have at least established a conditional. If it is indeed the case that psychological explanations applied to nonlinguistic creatures are broadly similar in structure and intent to psychological explanations of language-using creatures, then we will need to find answers to our four key questions. Here they are again.

1. What can we take as our paradigm for grasping a thought (if we cannot model it as understanding a sentence) and taking a propositional attitude to it?
2. How should we understand the structure of nonlinguistic thought?
3. How can we go about identifying and attributing propositional attitudes without the resources provided by linguistic interaction?
4. How can we understand the inferential transitions by which beliefs and other propositional desires can lead to action (without taking those beliefs to have linguistic form)?

Of course, it may turn out (as the minimalist view suggests) that nonlinguistic thoughts are so different in type from linguistic thoughts that these questions do not need to be answered. I turn to this suggestion in the next chapter. In the next two sections of this chapter, however, I consider the extent to which the language of thought hypothesis can deal with these four questions.

2.2   *The Language of Thought Hypothesis*

At the heart of the Fregean approach to thought is the suggestion that there exists an isomorphism between the structure of thought and the structure of language. For Frege and those who follow him it goes without saying that the language in question must be a public language. The language of thought hypothesis can be viewed in broad outline as commitment to the fundamental claim about isomorphism while lifting the restriction to public languages. The central idea is that propositional attitudes are relations to sentences in an internal language of thought—these sentences represent the content of the thought in a way that allows the content to be deployed in reasoning and decision-making.

The various problems in the mechanics of thinking discussed in the previous section can all be viewed as variants of the problem of explaining how thoughts, as abstract objects, can have effects within the physical world—how, for example, they can be believed and combine with other propositional attitudes to bring about behavior. On the Fregean view, thoughts are the senses of sentences, and we can model how they are grasped in terms of the understanding of the sentences that express them. Belief is modeled on assertion and practical reasoning on the inferential relations (whether syntactic or semantic) between sentences that are candidates for assertion. According to the language of thought hypothesis, however, this gets the direction of explanation completely the wrong way around. In order to understand how thoughts can have effects within the physical world we need to understand the role they play in the generation of behavior, and for that we need to take them first as the contents of propositional attitudes, and only second as the meanings of sentences. Propositional attitudes are mental states, presumably realized in (and perhaps even identical to) states of the central nervous system. So it is natural to think that we must understand the nature of thoughts through understanding the nature of the propositional attitude states that take them as contents. Here the distinctive proposal of the classical cognitive science approach emerges. Propositional attitudes are relations that the thinking subject bears to sentences—but to sentences in an internal language of thought rather than in a communicable public language. In the remainder of this section I explore this proposal in more detail, considering how it might be developed into a theory of nonlinguistic thought along the dimensions I have been discussing.

Versions of the language of thought hypothesis have frequently been proposed in the philosophical literature. They go at least as far back as William of Ockham in the fourteenth century (Panaccio 1992). All these versions share the same basic idea, namely, that thinking takes place in an internal representational medium that is in some sense structured like a language. The inner representational medium is the vehicle for thought. The modern form of the language of thought hypothesis, as proposed by Jerry Fodor in 1975 and defended by him in many writings since, is distinctive, however, in providing a detailed and worked-out account of exactly how thinking might take place in the linguaform inner representational medium. This account is based on a close analogy between the workings of the mind and the workings of a computer and is informed by research into the formal properties of logical systems (metalogic). The core elements of the hypothesis can be identified in three basic claims.

The first claim is that inferential transitions between thoughts can be understood in terms of causal interactions between physical structures. This claim has two dimensions worth highlighting. The first is that it reflects the robust intentional realism at the heart of the language of thought hypothesis—that is to say, the conception of propositional attitudes (and, by extension, the thoughts that are their contents) as causally efficacious entities. It may well be that the contents of propositional attitudes are abstract objects, but, according to the language of thought hypothesis, if these abstract objects are to play any explanatory role we must be able to identify physical structures that realize them. This intentional realism is already a departure from the Fregean approach. Whereas the Fregean approach has nothing to say about the causal processes that begin with grasping a thought and endorsing it in belief and end eventually in action, the language of thought hypothesis takes those processes to be the principal explanandum of a theory of thought. The second point is that the language of thought hypothesis is based on a causal conception of inference. That is, it views practical reasoning as primarily a matter of causal transitions between thoughts. Again, this is an idea that would be alien to the Fregean approach.

The distinctiveness of the language of thought hypothesis becomes clearer when we consider the second key claim, which is that the physical states that realize thoughts and that stand in the causal relations defining thought are sententially structured. This in turn can be broken down into two subclaims. The first of these is that the realizers of thoughts are *compositionally structured*—that is to say, they have separable components that can feature in a range of thoughts. The second subclaim is that these separable components stand in physical relations to each other that in some sense map onto the logical relations holding between the parts of the thought that they collectively realize. The physical structure that realizes the thought is isomorphic to the thought that it represents. It contains elements that correspond to the parts of the thought and that are connected together in a manner that directly maps onto the way the elements of the thought are connected together. The physical structure is a picture of the thought that it realizes.

In the language of thought hypothesis, as in the Fregean approach, it is at the level of logical form that we must look to identify the structure of the sentence that gives the genuine structure of the thought. In the Fregean approach the structure of a thought is given by the logical form of the sentence expressing it—in Frege's terms, by the translation of the sentence into the *Begriffsschrift*. In the language of thought hypothesis, however, there is no gap between the surface structure of the sentence and its logical form. Sentences in the language of thought represent at the level of logical form—for the following reason.

One of the key phenomena that the language of thought is called on to explain is how linguistic comprehension is possible in language-using creatures.[6] Since the general model of linguistic comprehension espoused by defenders of the language of thought hypothesis is one on which a natural language sentence is understood by being translated into a sentence in the language of thought, it is hard to see how the language of thought can admit a distinction between surface structure and deep structure. There can be no interpreter who will be able to abstract away from surface syntactical features to identify the deep structure of a sentence in the language of thought. Nor is there any further language into which such a sentence can be translated. So either language of thought sentences wear their deep structure on the surface (in the way that sentences in a formal language do) or it becomes very unclear how they themselves can have semantic properties.

This requirement that sentences in the language of thought be fully transparent at the level of logical form is related to the third basic claim in the language of thought hypothesis, namely, that the causal transitions between physical states respect the rational relations between the thoughts that those physical states represent. Inferential transitions between sentences in the language of thought are sensitive only to the syntactic features of the relevant sentences, although in a way that preserves relations of semantic consequence (Fodor 1987, ch. 1, Rey 1997, sec. 8.2). The language of thought theory lays great stress on the idea that inferential transitions between thoughts can be a function of causal interactions between physical structures (which of course is what sentences in the language of thought are when one abstracts from their semantic properties). The obvious and acknowledged inspiration for this basic idea is the metalogical fact that the first-order predicate calculus is sound and complete (see, for example, Fodor 1987, ch. 1). That is to say, in every well-formed proof in the first-order predicate calculus the conclusion really is a logical consequence of the premises, and, conversely, for every argument in which the conclusion follows logically from the premises and both conclusion and premises are formulable in the first-order predicate calculus, there is a well-formed proof. The well-formed-ness of a proof can be checked purely mechanically, since it is a function solely of the syntactic properties of the relevant formulae. The language of thought must, therefore, if it is to permit a comparable form of mapping of syntactic properties onto semantic properties, possess some analogue of at least the metalogical property of soundness.

The conception of reasoning at the heart of the language of thought hypothesis is well expressed in the following passage from Fodor that is worth quoting in full.

> Computers show us how to connect semantical with causal properties for *symbols*. So, if having a propositional attitude involves tokening a symbol, then we can get some leverage on connecting semantical properties with causal ones for *thoughts*. . . . Here, in barest outline, is how the new story is supposed to go: You connect the causal properties of a symbol with its semantic properties *via its syntax*. The syntax of a symbol is one of its higher-order physical properties. To a metaphorical first approximation, we can think of the syntactic structure of a symbol as an abstract feature of its shape. Because, to all intents and purposes, syntax reduces to shape, and because the shape of a symbol is a potential determinant of its causal role, it is fairly easy to see how there could be environments in which the causal role of a symbol correlates with its syntax. It's easy, that is to say, to imagine symbol structures interacting causally in virtue of their syntactic structures. The syntax of a symbol might

determine the causes and effects of its tokenings in much the way that the geometry of a key determines what locks it will open.

But now, we know from modern logic that certain of the semantic relations among symbols can be, as it were, 'mimicked' by their syntactic relations: that, when seen from a very great distance, is what proof theory is about. So, within certain famous limits, the semantic relation that holds between two symbols when the proposition expressed by the one entails the proposition expressed by the other can be mimicked by syntactic relations in virtue of which one of the symbols is derivable from the other. We can therefore build machines, that have, again within famous limits, the following property:

> The operations of the machine consist entirely of transformations of symbols;
>
> In the course of performing these operations, the machine is sensitive solely to syntactic properties of the symbols;
>
> And the operations that the machine performs on the symbols are entirely confined to altering their shapes

Yet the machine is so devised that it will tranform one symbol into another if and only if the propositions expressed by the symbols that are so transformed stand in certain *semantic* relations—e.g. the relation that the premises bear to the conclusion in a valid argument. (Fodor 1987, 18–19)

The overall vision is a powerful and clear account of the mechanics of thought. The account of inference can clearly be extended to yield an account of practical reasoning applicable to nonlinguistic creatures.

Moreover, the language of thought hypothesis has a clear account of the nature of belief and other propositional attitudes. Like the Fregean approach, the language of thought hypothesis views propositional attitudes as complex entities made up of an attitude and a content to which that attitude is taken. The content is not, of course, the relevant sentence in the language of thought (any more than a thought is to be confused with the natural language sentence that expresses it). Sentences in the language of thought serve as internal surrogates for the thoughts with which they are appropriate connected, and the particular attitudes one can take to thoughts (believing as opposed to entertaining, for example, or desiring as opposed to fearing) can all be understood in terms of the different functional roles that their internal surrogates can occupy in the cognitive economy. These different functional roles can be understood in terms of the different causal interactions into which that token sentence can feature. So, on the language of thought hypothesis, entertaining a thought is to be understood in terms of having it available to be used as, for example, the antecedent of a conditional or as an undischarged assumption in an argument (in the way that one might, for example, in proof by *reductio ad absurdum*), where these conditionals and proofs are to be understood as causal interactions holding in virtue of the syntactic properties of sentences in the language of thought. This is the functional role corresponding to contemplating a thought without committing oneself to its truth or falsity. Believing a thought has a different functional role. To have a belief with a particular content (the content that *p*, for example) is to be disposed to use the sentence in the language of thought that stands as a surrogate for p as a premise in practical reasoning (where practical reasoning is reasoning that feeds directly into action). It is to be disposed to take the same attitude toward any language of thought sentence that can be 'inferred' from p, and so on. Different functional roles can be identified for the other propositional attitudes.

As far as the three dimensions directly connected with the mechanics of thought are concerned, therefore, it looks as if the language of thought hypothesis is potentially very useful for thinking about nonlinguistic thought. It should be recognized, however, that the language of thought hypothesis is itself dependent on a particular way of understanding nonlinguistic thought. The basic argument for the language of thought hypothesis is that there are certain types of thinking that would not be possible unless the thoughts they involved had some sort of linguistic vehicles. The obvious response to this line of argument is to ask why the linguistic vehicles in question cannot simply be the sentences of the thinker's language. Perhaps the most promising way of blunting this objection (see, for example, Fodor 1975) is to appeal to the thoughts of creatures that do not have any sort of language.[7] So, for example, the language of thought theorist might suggest that we need to postulate an internal representational medium to make sense of practical decision-making in animals and young infants—to understand, in roughly the manner of expected utility theory, how beliefs and desires can issue in action. The point to notice, however, is that this argument only works on the assumption that psychological explanations of the behavior of nonlinguistic creatures are to be modeled on the belief-desire psychology we apply to language-using creatures. As I show in more detail in section 7.1, the conception of practical reasoning in play interprets beliefs as probability assignments and desires as a preference ordering and sees practical reasoning as the computation of the course of action with the maximum expected utility. At no stage is any argument given for the claim that this is the only way to understand intentional behavior at the nonlinguistic level. And, as I show in the next chapter, this is clearly not the *only* way that apparent thinking behavior at the nonlinguistic level should be understood.

Let us, then, draw a provisional conclusion. The language of thought hypothesis is capable of accounting for the metaphysical, semantic, and explanatory dimensions of nonlinguistic thinking, hence providing a framework for understanding the type of psychological explanations to be found in ethology, developmental psychology, and cognitive archeology, on the assumption that those psychological explanations are instances of the general pattern of belief-desire explanation. That is to say, the applicability of the language of thought hypothesis to nonlinguistic creatures rests on treating them as believers, desirers, and reasoners on an understanding of belief, desire, and reasoning that is derived from thinking about language-users. In this sense, therefore, the language of thought hypothesis is a hostage to empirical fortune.

But how are we to know whether the behavior of nonlinguistic creatures really does require belief-desire explanation? Recall that we require a conception of nonlinguistic thought that will underwrite the explanatory practices of the various disciplines exploring the cognitive abilities of nonlinguistic creatures. This means that the explanation offered of the nature of nonlinguistic thought must explain how we, as observers of animal or infant behavior or cognitive archaeologists striving to reconstruct the mental life of our early ancestors, can reliably attribute thoughts to explain the behavior of the nonlinguistic creatures we are studying. I turn in the next section to considering whether the language of thought hypothesis can satisfy this epistemological requirement.

2.3   The Language of Thought and the Epistemology of Thought without Language

At first sight the language of thought hypothesis seems impoverished from an epistemological point of view. The hypothesis that propositional attitudes are relations to sentences in an internal language of thought in such a way that the content of the thought is given by the semantic properties of the relevant sentences makes it mysterious how we can determine what that content is. Suppose, for the sake of argument, that we adopt a causal covariance account of the content of sentences in the language of thought (as suggested in Fodor 1987). Then, for a standard belief-desire explanation of behavior, the contents of the relevant belief and desire will be determined by the objects and properties in the world that covary in the appropriate way with the constituents of the relevant sentences in the language of thought (the sentence in the 'belief box' and the sentence in the 'desire box'). But it is far from clear how we as third-person observers can work out what those contents are in the case of nonlinguistic creatures.[8]

There are two distinct questions here. The first is whether the language of thought hypothesis can be of any immediate epistemological use to practitioners of the disciplines from which we are taking our lead. How might it help the cognitive ethologist in the field trying to determine the right way to characterize and explain the behavior of nonlinguistic creatures to be told that the propositional attitudes of such creatures consist in sentences in an internal language of thought? The answer is obvious: not at all. From the viewpoint of the developmental psychologist in the laboratory or the cognitive ethologist in the field, the language of thought hypothesis is of no immediate epistemological use whatsoever. Nonetheless, this leaves open the second question, which is whether the language of thought hypothesis might be of *indirect* epistemological use. It might be the case that, by studying correlations between brain states and states of affairs in the distal environment, we can work out what features of the environment a creature is capable of representing, so that we could arrive, so to speak, at an understanding of the vocabulary of a given species' language of thought. It is natural in this context to appeal to the results of magnetic resonance imaging, single neuron studies, and other contemporary methods of studying brain activity. Well-publicized studies such as those that have led to the discovery of mirror neurons in monkeys (Rizzolati, Fogassi, and Gallese 2000) might be thought to show that this goal is at least within reach. If we were able to carry out such a program then we would be able to put the knowledge thereby acquired to work in the practical business of attributing thoughts to members of the relevant species.[9] We would know what type of thoughts it would be possible to attribute to members of a particular species (or to infants at a particular stage of development).

Clearly, given the limitations of current knowledge about the brain, we are a long way from being able to provide any such theory. But equally clearly, if we have reason to think that such a theory will eventually be forthcoming, it would be foolish to condemn the language of thought hypothesis as a framework for thinking about the thoughts of nonlinguistic creatures on epistemological grounds. Unfortunately, there are powerful grounds for thinking that it is in principle impossible to work backward from brain states to states of affairs in the distal environment in the way that the language of thought hypothesis requires.

The main problem is quite simply that we have no way of accessing the sentences in the language of thought that determine the contents of the creature's beliefs and desires.[10] Proponents of the language of thought hypothesis often stress that the notion of sentences in the brain is not to be taken literally. The brain does not contain little sentences that a neuroscientist might discover by employing powerful enough equipment in the right sort of way. Formulae in the language of thought exist at a level of functional abstraction and cannot simply be read off from immediately observable patterns of brain activity. Nonetheless, these sentences are physical structures, albeit physical structures at a functional level several layers removed from brute neuronal activity. They *have* to be physical structures if the language of thought is be a form of intentional realism (that is, if it is to allow propositional attitudes to play a genuine causal role in the generation of behavior) as well as for the computationalist account of inference in terms of formal transitions sensitive only to syntactic properties to be coherent. But how are we to identify these physical structures?

There seem to be two possibilities (Braddon-Mitchell and Fitzpatrick 1990, Crane 1990). Either we identify the physical structures in terms of their semantic features or we identify them in terms of their syntactic features. The first possibility is obviously unsatisfactory. It presupposes precisely what is in question, namely, that we already have some way of working out the content of a sentence in the language of thought. Yet the second is no less unsatisfactory. Identifying the syntactic features of the physical structures that are sentences in the language of thought cannot be done without identifying their semantic features. So we end up with precisely the same circularity as on the first proposal. Let me explain.

In the case of sentences of a natural language, we can hive off syntax from semantics, and so it seems a natural thought that we can do the same for sentences in the language of thought. But in the case of natural language we can only hive off syntax from semantics because we have an understanding of the language that includes both its syntactic and semantic aspects. We can bring this out by reflecting on the project of radical interpretation—on how one might go about interpreting a completely alien language without the benefits of a dictionary, grammar book, or any relevant collateral information. No radical interpreter could formulate hypotheses about the syntax of a completely unfamiliar language without at the same time forming hypotheses about its semantics. How one takes the words to fit together depends on what one takes the words to mean. One very basic reason for this is that the syntax of a natural language involves grammatical categories. It involves certain expressions being substantives, others verbs, and others being adjectives or adverbs. One cannot decide what category a given word falls into without speculating about its semantics. It seems impossible, for example, to distinguish deciding whether a word refers to an object from deciding whether it is a noun. So we can only ascribe a given word a particular syntactic role in a language by according it a certain semantic characterization. Of course, this does not mean that we cannot have a syntactic understanding of a given language. That would be absurd. The point is rather that we can only have a syntactic understanding once we are in a position to identify the syntactic properties of sentences, and we will not be able to identify those syntactic properties without fixing at least some semantic properties.[11]

This points to an important equivocation in the concept of syntactic properties (Devitt 1990). Syntactic properties can be understood in purely physical terms, the shape of the letters in a word for example. Alternatively, we can understand syntactic properties as relational and functional, on the model of the syntactic properties of natural language, as having to do with how words are connected with each other. It is only if syntactic properties are understood in the first sense that a clean break between syntax and semantics seems appropriate.

But as far as identifying sentences in the language of thought is concerned, we must understand syntactic properties in the second rather than the first sense. The syntactic theorist is interested in the functional role of sentences in the language of thought: how they are causally connected up to each other and to sensory input in a way that explains behavioral output. The question we need to ask, then, is whether there are constraints on the 'radical interpretation' of sentences in the language of thought parallel to the constraints that clearly exist on linguistic radical interpretation, in such a way that fixing the syntactic properties of particular states will be impossible without fixing at least some semantic/intentional properties.

Two such constraints spring immediately to mind, both to do with how syntactic properties are fixed (Braddon-Mitchell and Fitzpatrick 1990, Crane 1990, Sterelny 1990). The first is that any such interpretation requires distinguishing inputs that do not have a genuine causal role to play (because they are just noise) from those that do. Some causal connections are functionally relevant, while others are not, and any satisfactory theory will have to discriminate between these. Second, since sentences in the language of thought are functional states realized in complex physical structures, we need to identify causal properties that derive from the physical instantiation/realization of a particular sentence, rather than from its functional role within the language of thought. The basic point, therefore, is that to identify sentences in the language of thought we need to distinguish relevant causal relations from irrelevant ones. It is clear that syntactic properties as narrowly construed (i.e., in physical terms) will be of no use here. There is no reason to think that there will be any brute physical characteristics demarcating causal properties that are functionally irrelevant. But syntactic properties in the broad sense will be of no use either, because we need to discriminate relevant from irrelevant causal properties in order to fix the broad syntactic properties. So, if we are to discriminate just the functionally relevant causal properties, it seems that we will have to advert to considerations of function and hence to how the animal needs to represent its environment. Either way, therefore, we will need to fix at least some semantic properties before being in a position to pick out sentences in the language of thought in terms of their syntactic properties.[12]

There is a further point to be taken into account here. In interpreting the type of correlations at the neural level that might be thought to provide our evidence base for identifying sentences in the language of thought, we need to make a principled decision about the level at which we are to look for the neural correlates of cognition. Are we to look for representation of objects and properties at the level of individual neurons, or at the level of populations of neurons? An answer to this question cannot simply be read off from patterns of activation in the brain. Let us suppose, for example, that we find a particular neuron that responds preferentially to a particular type of stimulus—say, to the face of one's grandmother, to take the classic example. As Churchland and Sejnowski (1992, ch. 4) have elegantly argued, such a preferential response would be compatible both with the hypothesis that the neuron in question is a dedicated grandmother neuron (hence can stand in a 'proper name' position in sentences in the language of thought) and with the hypothesis that it merely forms a conspicuous part of a population of neurons that collectively form a vector representation of the grandmother. It turns out that there are powerful computational reasons for thinking that neural representation is most likely to take a vector rather than a local form. The number of objects/features that can be locally represented by a particular population of neurons is a linear function of the number of neurons in that population, whereas the representative power varies exponentially with the population when the coding takes a vector form.

Let us suppose, then, that the representational primitives in the brain are vectors rather than single neurons. This means, of course, that in trying to identify the syntactic properties of sentences in the language of thought we will be operating at the level of populations of neurons (assuming that it is appropriate to think of populations of neurons as the bottom-level physical realization of sentences in the language of thought). But how can one identify a population of neurons in a way that might identify it as the constituent of a sentence in the language of thought? How can one tell, amid the chaos of simultaneously firing neurons in the brain, which neurons are firing together to provide a vector coding? The only way to identify populations of neurons is to work out how particular tasks are being performed. That is to say, by working backward from the particular processing tasks being performed (hence from what particular populations of neurons *might* be doing).[13] But this, of course, requires starting at the semantic level. It requires starting with the particular computational task being performed, moving to hypotheses about the representational tools for carrying the appropriate task out, and then testing those hypotheses against the observed patterns of activation. Once again it looks very much as if we can only fix the syntactic properties of sentences in the language of thought by starting with the semantic properties.

It looks doubtful, therefore, whether the language of thought hypothesis can help us with the epistemological issues that must be confronted by any account of thought in the absence of language. It doesn't give us any clues as to how we might go about attributing thoughts to nonlinguistic creatures. This is not, it must be stressed, an objection to the language of thought hypothesis as such. As a hypothesis about the machinery of cognition, the language of thought hypothesis is under no obligation to provide its own epistemology. What it does mean, however, is that the language of thought hypothesis cannot provide a straightforward solution to the problem of explaining the thoughts of nonlinguistic creatures. It provides an account of how nonlinguistic creatures might be thinkers. It offers a theory as to what the vehicles of nonlinguistic thought might be and meets many of the objections in principle to the idea of thought without language. But, insofar as it fails to provide an epistemology for the thoughts of nonlinguistic creatures, it cannot be the whole story.

2.4   The Road Ahead

As I showed in section1.2, there are four dimensions to an adequate theory of non-linguistic thought.

The *metaphysical* dimension of explaining how nonlinguistic thought is possible and what its vehicles might be

The *semantic* dimension of explaining the semantics of nonlinguistic thought

The *epistemological* dimension of explaining how it is possible for us to identify the content of such thoughts

The *explanatory* dimension of elucidating the inferential and decision-making processes of nonlinguistic creatures in a way that underwrites the practice of giving psychological explanations of their behavior

This chapter has explored a dialectic between two approaches to providing such a theory, deriving from two fundamentally different conceptions of thought. On the one hand, the Fregean approach, based on the principle that thoughts are the senses of sentences and hence that the study of thoughts can only proceed via the study of the sentences that express them, finds the notion of thought without language deeply problematic. Many of the problems that appear insuperable from the perspective of the Fregean approach seem less threatening if we shift paradigm and adopt a version of the language of thought hypothesis, centered on the twin principles, first, that we should study thoughts through studying propositional attitudes rather than sentences and, second, that propositional attitudes should be construed as relations to sentences in an internal language of thought. Yet the language of thought hypothesis cannot provide us with a wholly satisfactory account, for two reasons.

The first problem with applying a version of the language of thought hypothesis to nonlinguistic creatures is that it rests on an as yet unsubstantiated commitment to the applicability of belief-desire psychology to nonlinguistic creatures. The premise from which we began is that there are various types of behavior identifiable in human infants, nonhuman animals, and prelinguistic hominids that cannot be satisfactorily explained according to existing nonpsychological models such as innate releasing mechanisms, sensorimotor schemas, or instrumental or classical conditioning. It looks, for a range of complex behavior types, as if we will need to turn to psychological explanations that appeal, *inter alia*, to the way a creature represents the current environment and to the way those representations interact with past representations (and representations of the past). But it remains an open question whether these representations should be viewed as beliefs or desires, and whether the type of practical reasoning in which those representations can be deployed at the nonlinguistic level should be modeled, as Fodor suggests, on types of practical reasoning defined over beliefs and other propositional attitudes.

The second problem was discussed at some length in the previous section. The language of thought hypothesis can be of no use when it comes to the epistemological dimension of nonlinguistic thinking. It is a hypothesis about the mechanics of thinking, reached by, broadly speaking, transcendental arguments about what cognitive architecture must be like for thinking behavior to be possible. But it offers no guidance on how we might go about attributing thoughts to nonlinguistic creatures and hence cannot as it stands serve as a framework for thinking about the practice of attributing thoughts to nonlinguistic creatures.

The first of these two problems is addressed in chapter 3, where I consider what I term the *minimalist* or *deflationary* account of thinking at the nonlinguistic level. On the minimalist picture, the type of thinking available to nonlinguistic creatures is very limited. The distinction between linguistic and nonlinguistic thought is analogous to the distinction between knowing how to do something and knowing that something is the case. Nonlinguistic creatures are capable of thinking in the sense that they can perform various types of goal-directed actions involving representations of the environment, but these representations are radically unlike the thoughts available to language-using creatures. They are not compositionally structured and do not have determinate contents. In chapter 3 I present a range of arguments showing that there are important types of nonlinguistic thinking that cannot be accommodated on the minimalist approach. The upshot of this chapter is that we cannot avoid or downplay our theoretical commitment to some version of belief-desire psychology in the absence of language. In the remaining chapters of the book I offer a positive account of nonlinguistic thought.

Unlike the two approaches I have been considering in this chapter, the account I offer of thinking without words emphasizes the epistemological and explanatory dimensions of the problem. The best way of approaching the problem of thought without language is through providing an epistemological basis for the practice of attributing thoughts to nonlinguistic creatures and for the psychological explanations within which those attributions take place.

Providing this epistemological basis is a two-stage process. The first stage is fixing an ontology in a way that will allow the theorist to determine what objects a particular non-language-using creature is capable of thinking about. This is the equivalent in the realm of thought of one of the principal tasks faced by the radical interpreter confronting a completely alien language. Just as the radical interpreter has to determine the ontology of the linguistic community with which he is dealing in order to know what sort of things can be the semantic values of the expressions of the language he is trying to interpret, so too must the developmental psychologist or cognitive ethologist determine how members of a particular species, or infants at a particular stage of development, 'carve up the world' in order to determine how they think about it. In chapter 4 I suggest that we view particular ontologies in terms of different types of sensitivity to higher-order structural invariants. I show how this provides us with a way of distinguishing the ontologies of different types of nonlinguistic creature, looking in more detail at the philosophical implications of some of the important work in developmental psychology referred to at the beginning of the previous chapter.

The second stage in providing an epistemological basis is showing how complete thoughts can be attributed to nonlinguistic creatures. In chapter 5 I show, using a version of success semantics, how a semantics can be provided for nonlinguistic thoughts in a way that both does justice to philosophical constraints on acceptable theories of content and provides the ethologist or developmental psychologist with a workable method of assigning contents to the beliefs and desires of nonlinguistic creatures. Existing versions of success semantics have no way of accommodating the intensional dimension of thought attributions. They do not fix the complete content of a thought, but simply its truth-conditions. Chapter 5 shows how success semantics can be supplemented in a way that permits psychological attributions to take account of how truth conditions are apprehended by the thinker.

In the remainder of this book I do not engage directly with the language of thought hypothesis. The approach I develop is compatible with certain ways of developing that hypothesis. Supporters of the language of thought hypothesis can take the theory put forward in this book as an attempt to provide an epistemology and semantics for the application of the language of thought hypothesis to nonlinguistic creatures. But nothing that I say in the chapters that follow presupposes the truth of the language of thought hypothesis. The view I develope is that it is perfectly possible, and perhaps indeed desirable, to give an account of the epistemology and semantics of nonlinguistic thought without venturing into speculations about cognitive architecture.

Minimalist Approaches
to Nonlinguistic Thought

The problem of explaining nonlinguistic thought arises out of the deeply rooted practices of explaining the behavior of nonlinguistic creatures in psychological terms. As I showed in section 1.1, developmental psychologists are becoming increasingly happy to talk about young infants' *knowledge* of the world and their *beliefs* about how objects behave, while cognitive ethologists explain many types of behavior in the animal kingdom in terms of *desires* to bring about certain psychological states in others, together with *beliefs* about how best to satisfy those desires in a given environment. Primates and other higher mammals engage in deception behavior in which they are said to *intend* to manipulate the psychological states of their conspecifics through exploiting what they *know* of their perspective on the world. Early hominids are said to have a highly developed *understanding* of the natural world and of the dynamic properties of various types of object that could be used for tools.

It is natural to take descriptions such as these at face value, as attributing to nonlinguistic creatures psychological states rather similar to those that we readily attribute to each other on the basis of verbal and nonverbal behavior. If we do indeed take them at face value then there seems to be little difference between our everyday practices of psychological explanation and the psychological explanations that we might give of nonlinguistic creatures. Both can be viewed, simplifying somewhat, as instances of belief-desire psychology (more accurately, of propositional attitude psychology). I showed in chapter 2, however, that thinking about the thoughts of nonlinguistic creatures in these terms leads to a range of difficulties associated with the problem of explaining how nonlinguistic creatures can bear attitudes to thoughts. There are problems extending to nonlinguistic creatures the conception of propositional attitudes as attitudes to thoughts construed as the senses of sentences. The language of thought hypothesis is more suited to giving an account of the mechanics of nonlinguistic thought, provided that nonlinguistic thought is taken to be a version of propositional attitude psychology—but the language of thought hypothesis runs into problems with the epistemology of nonlinguistic thought. Both ways of taking psychological explanations at the nonlinguistic level to be applications of propositional attitude psychology are problematic.

Perhaps, though, we can avoid these difficulties by challenging the assumption that belief-desire psychology is the right way to think about psychological explanation at the nonlinguistic level. Perhaps it is a mistake to assimilate thinking at the nonlinguistic level to thinking at the nonlinguistic level. Perhaps it is a mistake to take talk of the knowledge, beliefs, desires, hopes, and intentions of nonlinguistic creatures at face value. In this chapter I will consider an approach to nonlinguistic thinking that tries to drive a wedge between the type of thinking available at the nonlinguistic level and the type of thinking that (on this approach) is the exclusive preserve of language-users. According to the *minimalist* or *deflationary* conception of thought without language, researchers in cognitive ethology, developmental psychology, and cognitive archaeology are absolutely right to describe nonlinguistic creatures as thinkers. But the type of thinking engaged in by nonhuman animals, prelinguistic infants, and the early hominids must be distinguished from the type of thinking engaged in by language-using creatures.

The minimalist approach is highly congenial to supporters of the Fregean approach and highly *un*congenial to supports of the language of thought hypothesis. As far as the Fregean approach is concerned, the minimalist approach promises a way of accommodating the need for psychological explanations of the behavior of nonlinguistic creatures without having to compromise the basic idea that the types of thoughts that can feature in propositional attitudes should be understood as the senses of sentences. As far as the language of thought hypothesis is concerned, the minimalist approach threatens to undercut a key argument in support of the hypothesis. It is crucial to the language of thought hypothesis that there should be significant commonalities between linguistic thought and nonlinguistic thought. This is the most plausible defense against the objection that participation in a public language would be quite sufficient for the tasks for which the language of thought is postulated. It is in many ways quite essential to the language of thought hypothesis that thought at the nonlinguistic level should be essentially propositional in nature—or rather, that there should be an essentially propositional component to nonlinguistic thought.

The minimalist approach has more sympathizers than systematic exponents, and much of this chapter will be devoted to trying to expound it in as plausible and noncontroversial a manner as possible. I start in section 3.1 by sketching out an intuitive contrast between two types of thinking (thinking-how and thinking-that). In section 3.2 I develop this intuitive contrast to set up the basic framework for a minimalist account of nonlinguistic thought. Section 3.3 explains how a minimalist might construe the practice of giving psychological explanations of the behavior of nonlinguistic creatures. I offer three arguments against various different components of the minimalist approach in sections 3.4 to 3.6.

3.1   Thinking-How and Thinking-That: An Intuitive Contrast

In thinking about the minimalist approach to nonlinguistic thought it is helpful to start with a distinction between what I will call *thinking-how* and *thinking-that*, by analogy with the philosophical distinction initially proposed by Gilbert Ryle between propositional knowing-that and nonpropositional knowing-how (Ryle 1949).[1]

Here are five examples of what I am calling thinking-how:

1. *Imagistic reasoning*, such as calculating whether a wardrobe will fit into the space between a chest-of-drawers and the bed. It is plausible on both introspective and cognitive scientific grounds that calculations of this sort are carried out by exercising our visual imagination.
2. *Empathetic reasoning*. This is the sort of reasoning about how people will behave that results not from applying theories to their behavior or forming predictions on the basis of their past behavior, but rather from "putting oneself in their shoes" and imagining how they will respond.
3. *Trial and error reasoning*. Trial and error reasoning is often driven by a representation of the goal, but it does not seem to involve the formulation of explicit hypotheses about how the goal in question is to be achieved.
4. *Analogical reasoning*. There is a fundamental difference between drawing an explicit connection between two ideas or two situations and perceiving an analogy between them. The first can usually be put in a propositional form. The second almost always resists being made explicit.
5. *The reasoning involved in the exercise of complex bodily skills*. The acquisition and exercise of complex skills is a highly cognitive activity, requiring precise calibration of different types of information. But the practical knowledge that it involves cannot usually be expressed linguistically by competent practitioners.

This list is not intended to be exhaustive, but it is certainly representative of a broad category of cognitive ability that has two principal distinguishing characteristics.

In the first place, the various types of thinking-how are most naturally described as abilities and skills that allow one to modify and adjust oneself to the environment—as opposed to bodies of information that one acquires about the environment. They result most typically in responses, rather than in an abstract proposition that one might take, for example, as the conclusion of an argument. The responses that emerge need not always be behavioral in a narrow sense. They can be highly cognitive—as when, for example, one uses empathetic reasoning to adjust one's social responses on the basis of how one predicts another person will behave. But thinking-how does not *seem* to take a classical inferential form. Empathetic reasoning and analogical reasoning are forms of pattern recognition that rest on perceived similarities between ideas and states of affairs, while imagistic reasoning seems to involve the manipulation of spatial images and the exercise of visual imagination. It does not seem right, at least on introspective grounds, to model the process of thinking-how in terms of inferences carried out on propositionally encoded representations of the environment.[2]

The second characteristic of thinking-how is closely connected to the first. The process of thinking-how cannot easily, if at all, be put into words. Of course, I can express in language the thought that the wardrobe will fit into the available space or that the man walking in front of me will swerve to the left, but I cannot express in language the thinking that leads up to that conclusion. It does not seem right to describe the processes of thinking-how as defined over states with determinate contents. The distinction here is in a sense grammatical (and directly analogous to the distinction initially pointed out by Ryle). The "thinking-how" construction is naturally completed by an infinitive identifying an activity or process, in contrast to the "thinking-that" construction, which requires completion by a sentence after the "that." The sentence following the "that—" picks out a specific content or proposition as that which is actually being thought. There is no such content in the various examples of thinking-how.

Let me try to make the contrast between thinking-how and thinking-that vivid with a concrete example. It is known that orangutans are fairly successful at tracking the larger of two quantities of liquid when the quantities are subjected to a variety of physical transformations (Call and Rochat 1996, 1997). For example, if presented with two quantities of water of different size that are then poured into differently shaped containers, they will reliably choose the new container with the larger quantity of water. How are we to understand the cognitive abilities manifested in successful performance of liquid conservation tasks such as these?

One might explain their success in terms of the practical application of a complex form of *propositional* knowledge—an intuitive fluid mechanics containing certain principles about the relation between volumes of liquid and the height and width of containers, together with principles about how liquids are conserved over transformations. These principles would be verbalizable (although not of course by the orangutans) and would have determinate contents. An intuitive fluid mechanics thus construed would be on a par with the broadly theoretical naive physics, naive biology, or naive psychology identified by contemporary researchers in young children, early hominids, and various sectors of the animal kingdom (particularly the great apes). It would be understood in terms of tacit mastery of a set of general principles that are domain-specific and only integrated to a limited extent with other bodies of information and naïve theories.

Alternatively, one might seek to explain the abilities in terms of complex perceptual skills. These perceptual skills might be either static or dynamic—or indeed both. They might, first, involve a perceptual sensitivity to the actual transformation and a corresponding ability to track a particular quantity over transformations. That would be a form of dynamic perceptual sensitivity. Alternatively, the orangutans' abilities might be explained in terms of a static form of perceptual sensitivity—that is, sensitivity to the correlations between quantity of liquid and the height and width of containers, correlations that allow two or more differently shaped containers to be compared. The experimental evidence produced by Call and Rochat seems to tell convincingly in favor of the static view—what they call the "direct perceptual estimation strategy." But for present purposes the important point is that understanding these cognitive skills as a form of perceptual sensitivity gives us an excellent illustration of nonverbalizable thinking-how involving the manipulation of spatial images and the exercise of visual imagination rather than anything classifiable as an inference.

The distinction between thinking-how and thinking-that has been drawn at a fairly intuitive level. But it should nonetheless be clear how it bears on the issues raised in the first two chapters. The two approaches to the nature of thought considered in the previous chapter are conceptions of how we should understand the nature of thinking-that. Correlatively, the problems we identified in extending each of those approaches to apparent instances of thinking behavior in nonlinguistic creatures arise only on the assumption that those thinking behaviors are instances of thinking-that, rather than thinking-how. Should it turn out that we could interpret those behaviors as instances of thinking-how rather than thinking-that then those problems would cease to apply. This is, in essence, the proposal of minimalist approaches to nonlinguistic thought, as I will show in more detail in the next section.

3.2   Minimalist Approaches to Nonlinguistic Thought

These approaches characterize nonlinguistic thought as a form of thinking-how. Whereas the two approaches canvassed in the previous chapter see the essence of thought in terms of taking attitudes to propositions, minimalist approaches adopt a different approach to nonlinguistic thought, taking it to be fundamentally non-propositional in nature. As remarked earlier, there has been relatively little explicit working out of alternatives to the propositional approach, either as an approach to thought in general (but see Cussins 1990 and 1992 for pioneering work in this direction) or as an approach to nonlinguistic thought in particular. I propose to proceed, therefore, by considering some of the key elements of the propositional approach to thought and indicating how a theorist might develop a nonpropositional alternative in each of these dimensions. What will emerge, I hope, is a picture of a relatively broad (though largely unoccupied) region of conceptual space. The different claims that can be identified within this general region are compatible but are nonetheless not all mutually entailing. In the final sections of the chapter I present a range of arguments against the different strands of the minimalist conception.[3]

Let us start, then, by reiterating some of the key features of propositional thinking. Recall that the standard model of the propositional attitudes imposes a sharp distinction between attitude and content—between the particular proposition that is the object of one's mental state and the mental attitude one takes toward it. This is a distinction that goes back to the beginnings of philosophical logic and the philosophy of language in Gottlob Frege's *Begriffsschrift*, and it is a distinction that appears to be completely indispensable to a proper account of thought and the mind. For one thing, as I have already shown, much of our understanding of ourselves and others rests on our being able to make sense of the idea of a particular person being able to take different attitudes to the same proposition, as indeed of different people being able to take different attitudes to the same proposition. Without this it is hard to see how we could make sense of either the fundamental continuities holding across a person's life or basic disagreements between people. Equally significant, an important element in thinking involves entertaining propositions without taking any sort of attitude toward them. The most obvious example occurs in conditional thought, which plays such a central role in practical decision-making. I might, for example, believe that if A is the case then I ought to $\emptyset$, without actually believing that A is the case. Of course, the conditional "If A then I ought to $\emptyset$" might itself feature as part of a *modus ponens* inference, combining with the premise that A is the case to yield the conclusion that I ought to $\emptyset$—in which case I would be believing that A is the case. But, on the other hand, the conditional might equally feature in a *modus tollens* inference, with the rejection of the proposition that I ought to $\emptyset$ leading to the rejection of the proposition that A is the case. In this case I would be entertaining the thought that A is the case without ever believing it.

A second key element of propositional thinking is that propositions should be independent of the particular context of thinking. That is to say, it should be possible to grasp a proposition both without knowing its truth value and without any contact with the state of affairs that proposition is about.[4] The first is one of the factors that make it possible to take a range of different attitudes to the same proposition. Some attitudes, such as the attitude of hope for example, seem in many cases only to be applicable when one does not know the truth-value of that which one hopes to be the case. As soon as one knows that something either is the case or is not the case it is no longer appropriate to hope that it is the case. The same might be said of fear. Many instances of fear involve fear that some state of affairs *might* hold, an attitude that ceases to be available if one has determined either that the state of affairs does hold or that it does not. The second is what makes it possible to think not simply about distant regions of space-time but also what one is not directly presented with.

The third characteristic of propositional thought is that, for any propositional attitude, it should in principle be possible to find a sentence that will specify the content of the attitude accurately and without remainder.[5] Propositional attitudes have contents that are linguistically expressible and that, moreover, have nothing more to them than can be linguistically expressed. This is closely related to the fourth characteristic, which is that the contents of propositional attitudes have a structure that permits them to feature in inference and that is in some sense isomorphic to one way of apprehending the structure of the state of affairs that that content represents.

It will come as no surprise that these four characteristics of propositional thought map very closely onto the four dimensions in which we have identified the most serious potential difficulties for the project of explaining the thinking of non-language-using creatures. Minimalist conceptions of nonlinguistic thought attempt to account for nonlinguistic thinking in ways that do not involve some or all of these characteristics of propositional thought and hence that, if successful, will allow us to avoid some or all of the related difficulties. Admittedly, as suggested earlier, it is possible for a minimalist to reject certain elements of the propositional conception while retaining others. The four characteristics fall naturally into two pairs—the first two have to do, broadly speaking, with the relation between content and context and the second two have more to do with the precise character of content. So a theorist might, for example, maintain that nonlinguistic thoughts are not linguistically expressible and lack combinatorial structure, while allowing that such thoughts can both support the distinction between content and force and be independent from the context of thinking.[6] It should be recognized, however, that it will be incumbent on such a theorist to give positive accounts of the content-force distinction and the context-independence of nonlinguistic thought—which will raise a good proportion of the difficulties raised in the previous chapter.

In thinking about the difference between propositional and nonpropositional thought, hence about how a minimalist approach might be developed, an obvious place to start is with the differences between propositional attitudes and perception. Although some philosophers (most prominently Armstrong 1961) have tried to assimilate perception to the propositional attitudes by analyzing perception in terms of dispositions to acquire beliefs, many philosophers take the view that perceptions represent the world in a manner fundamentally different from the way propositional attitudes represent the world (see, for example, the contributors to Crane 1992). Perceptual content is not, on this view, a species of propositional attitude content. Theorists in this area tend to stress three features of perceptual content that militate against considering it on the propositional model.

First, the content of perception seems to be analogue in nature, unlike the conceptual content of propositional attitudes, which is more plausibly seen as digital. The distinction between analogue and digital representations has (for my purposes) been most perspicuously put by Dretske (1981, ch. 6). Let us take a particular fact or state of affairs, say the fact or state of affairs that some object s has property F. A representation carries the information that s is F in digital form if and only if it carries no further information about s other than that it is F (and whatever further facts about it are entailed by the fact that it is F). But whenever a representation carries the information that s is F in analogue form it always carries additional information about s. It is plausible that perceptual states represent the world in analogue form and propositional attitudes in digital form.

Second, the content of perception seems to be unit free (Peacocke 1986). If I perceptually represent an object as being a certain distance from me I do not usually represent that distance in terms of a particular unit (in inches, say, as opposed to centimeters), even though what I represent is a perfectly determinate distance. I simply represent it as being *that* distance, where the content of my perception specifies the distance. Propositional attitudes, however, can only represent distances (and other comparable quantities) in terms of specific units.

Third, the content of perception is more fine-grained than the content of propositional attitudes. I can see far more colors than I can name, and discriminate far more shapes than I have concepts for. My belief that the grass is green has a single content—but would be the appropriate response to an enormous variety of perceptual states.

The debate about whether the content of perception is conceptual or nonconceptual centers around whether a conceptual account can be given of these aspects of perceptual content (see, for example, Peacocke 1992, McDowell 1994).[7] For present purposes, these three features of the phenomenology of perception suggest that the content of perception may be a good place to look for nonpropositional ways of representing the world. Certainly, of the examples of thinking-how discussed in the previous section several are explicitly perceptual in form, involving either occurrent perception (analogical reasoning and trial and error reasoning) or the exercise of visual imagination (image-based reasoning).

Recall that the first feature of propositional thought is that it permits a sharp distinction between content and attitude. Within a propositional attitude it is possible to distinguish the particular content from the attitude that is taken to that content, so that it is possible for different people to take different attitudes to the same content and the same person to take different attitudes to the same content over time (and indeed at a time). This sharp distinction between attitude and content is not available in the case of perception. Partly this is because the content of perception is perspectival in a way that the content of propositional attitudes (even indexical propositional attitudes) simply is not. The way that perception represents the world is so closely tied to the perceiver's particular point of view that it is difficult to see how the content of perception could be transferable and shareable in the manner required by the attitude/content distinction. Perceptions typically feed into the propositional attitudes by causing perceptual beliefs whose content bears complex relations to the content of the perceptions on which they are based. Perceptual beliefs have contents that abstract away from the perspectival nature of perception to "repackage" the information in a (digital) form that will permit integration with the main body of the propositional attitude system.

The second feature of propositional thought is that the proposition in question should be available to be thought independently of the context of thinking. So, for example, it must be possible to entertain the thought without assigning it a truth-value or having any epistemic contact with the state of affairs that would make it true. The content of perception does not have this type of context-dependence. There is no analogue in the case of perception for entertaining a thought without considering whether it is true or false. Of course, we do not always believe what we perceive, and we sometimes find ourselves in situations where we do not endorse the way perception presents the world as being. Visual illusions are an obvious example. When we know that the two lines in the Muller-Lyer illusion are in fact the same length we no longer endorse the perceptual appearance that one is longer than the other. But it would be wrong to describe this as saying that we in some sense take an attitude of suspended belief to the perceptual appearance that one is longer than the other. What happens in such cases is that our perceptual representation of the world and our beliefs about the world come apart. The normal processes by which perceptions lead to beliefs have been overridden by our knowledge of how the illusion works. Nor, of course, is it possible to perceive a state of affairs with which one is not in any direct sort of epistemic contact. Perceiving is factive because, as McDowell and others have pointed out, it is a matter of how the world presents itself to the perceiver.

The third and fourth features of propositional thinking need to be taken together. The content of perception cannot be completely and accurately reported in a sentence following a "that—" clause of the type that could give the content of a propositional attitude, for reasons discussed earlier in the context of the phenomenology of perception. Any such formulation of the content of perception would be compatible with indefinitely many fine-grained perceptual contents. What is specified by such sentences is the content of the belief to which the perception would give rise if it was taken at face value (in the way that it is not taken at face value, for example, in cases of visual illusion where one is aware of the illusion).[8] Of course, it may well be the case that the content of perception can in *some* way be specified by a suitably complex sentence—perhaps a sentence that specifies the perceptible characteristics of every discriminable point in the perceptual field for a given modality, in the way that the content of a television image might be given by a sentence that specifies what is going on in each pixel. Let us call this a *pixelization* of the content of perception. It is no part of the present argument to claim that this is impossible. My point is rather that such a pixelization would not yield a specification of the *right sort* of content, where the right sort of content is one that can feature in inferences and can be integrated with the content of propositional attitudes. A pixelization has no structure. It is not formulated at a level of description that captures even the bounded edges and segmentation of the perceptual array.

There is considerable plausibility, then, in the idea that we can develop the intuitive contrast between thinking-how and thinking-that into a minimalist account of nonlinguistic thought by starting out from the nonpropositional content of perception. In the remainder of this section I will consider how this general strategy might be implemented. We can begin with Michael Dummett's account of the types of thought available to nonlinguistic creatures—what he calls *protothoughts*.

Dummett suggests that the protothoughts of nonlinguistic creatures have a very circumscribed applicability. They can only occur as integrated with current activity:

> Proto-thought is distinguished from full-fledged thought, as engaged in by human beings for whom language is its vehicle, by its incapacity for detachment from present activity and circumstances. A human being may be suddenly struck by a thought, which might be the key to the solution of a mathematical problem or the fact that he has left some vital document at home: in the latter case he may turn around and go back for it. Our thoughts may float free of the environment: we may follow a train of thought quite irrelevant to our surroundings or what we are engaged in doing. An animal may solve quite complex problems, by a process of thinking about the solution,

as was illustrated by Köhler's chimpanzees, or by the pony which, when confronted by a cattle-grid, lay down and rolled over it: but its thought, or more exactly, protothought, cannot float free but can occur only as integrated with current activity. (Dummett 1993, 123)

Dummett's emphasis on the context-dependence of protothoughts is very much in line with the earlier characterization of nonpropositional thinking. So too is his proposal that protothoughts are essentially tied to the possibilities the environment affords for action.

> The sublinguistic level of proto-thought is essentially spatial, and therefore must be conceived as operating in our apprehension of what we perceive as having a three-dimensional shape and occupying a three-dimensional position. But it is also essentially dynamic: it involves the apprehension of the possibilities and probabilities of movement, and of the effect of impact. For this reason, it incorporates, not merely perception of position, shape and movement, but also recognition of the gross properties of material things. It is an immediate feature of even our visual perceptions that we observe objects as differentiated according to the general type of material of which they consist: whether they are rigid or flexible, elastic, brittle or plastic, cohesive like a lump of sugar or a heap of grains like caster sugar, solid, liquid or gaseous, wet or dry, smooth or rough, greasy or clean, and so forth. The reason that we use visual clues to project these properties, even though unaided vision does not disclose them, is precisely that they bear on the dynamic possibilities. (Dummett 1993, 124)

As one would expect, given their essentially pragmatic and context-bound nature, the vehicles of protothoughts are much closer to perceptual states than they are to linguistically expressible propositions. According to Dummett, the vehicles of protothoughts are "spatial images superimposed on spatial perceptions" (Dummett 1993, 123). In perceiving the ambient environment protothinkers visualize the possible ways it might be transformed, drawing on motor memories and a sense of their own possibilities for action and reaction.

Protothinkers do not come to a judgment about what the environment contains or the possibilities it affords, where coming to a judgment implies something that can be detached from the here-and-now, but nonetheless they perceive the environment in a way that involves exercising judgment. The parallel to which Dummett often returns is with the type of thinking involved in skilled behavior in humans:

> A car driver or canoeist may have rapidly to estimate the speed and direction of oncoming cars or boats and their probable trajectory, consider what avoiding action to take, and so on: it is natural to say that he is engaged in highly concentrated thought. But the vehicle of such thoughts is certainly not language: it should be said, I think, to consist in visual imagination superimposed on the visually perceived scene. It is not just that these thoughts are not in fact framed in words: it is that they do not have the structure of verbally expressed thoughts. But they deserve the name of "proto-thoughts" because, while it would be ponderous to speak of truth or falsity in application to them, they are intrinsically connected with the possibility of their being mistaken: judgment, in a non-technical sense, is just what the driver and the canoeist need to exercise. (Dummett 1993, 122)

Protothoughts can be correct or incorrect. Unlike the correctness conditions of linguistically expressed thoughts, however, their correctness conditions are ultimately to be understood in terms of the success or failure of the actions to which
they give rise.

Dummett does not go into much detail about how the content of protothoughts
should be understood. His talk of "visual imagination superimposed on the visually perceived scene" and "spatial images superimposed on spatial perceptions"
make clear that he is intending protothoughts to be understood in perceptual terms,
but he does not offer any detailed suggestions as to how the content of protothoughts should be understood. Adrian Cussins has offered some very interesting
suggestions in this area (Cussins 1990, 1992). Although Cussins and Dummett are
developing very different (and in important respects incompatible) projects, some
of the specific points that Cussins makes about how we can understand experiential content can be seen as deepening Dummett's account of protothoughts.

The central feature of Cussins's account of experiential content is that it should
be understood not in terms of notions such as truth and truth-condition, but rather
in terms of the organism's abilities to act on the perceived environment. What the
organism perceives (the content of its perception) is a distal environment structured in terms of the possibilities it affords for action.

> Contents can be canonically specified with reference to abilities of the organism,
> where the abilities are not (or need not be) part of the realm of reference. The realm
> of reference is that with respect to which the correctness (e.g. the truth-value) of the
> content is determined. Evidently, a subject in thinking of a coffee mug that is full—a
> thought which is sustained by the subject's perceiving the mug—is not *referring* to
> abilities to grasp the mug, to track it as it moves, or to be selectively sensitive to
> changes in its appearance. Nevertheless, Evans's idea was that the cognitive signifi-
> cance of the singular mug content could be captured, and could only be captured, by
> the theorist's referring to abilities to grasp the mug or otherwise locate it, to track the
> mug through space and time, and to be selectively sensitive (in judgment and action
> and memory) to changes in the mug's features. These abilities are not available to the
> subject as the content's referent, but they *are* available to the subject as the subject's
> experience-based knowledge of how to act on the object, and respond to it (Cussins
> 1992, 655)

This conception of an ability-based conception of content offers a very natural way
of developing the idea that protothoughts are context-bound and relativized to the
organism's capacities for action and reaction. On Cussins's view, moreover, this
yields a sharp distinction between the success-governed level of protothoughts and
the truth-governed level of full-fledged thought.[9] Protothought does not involve
experience of an objective world.

> An objective world is given to a subject if the content presents something as being in-
> dependent of the subject's particular abilities and particular location, in space and
> time. But given only the realm-of-embodiment-specified content, all the subject (em-
> bodied organism) has is an experiential awareness of how to move etc in response to
> local changes in its environment. If this were a subject's conception of a referent it

would be a conception of something as not independent of contingent characteristics of the subject itself. The necessary separation between subject and object would not have been achieved. (659)

The environment of the protothinker is composed of superimposed features and affordances (see further hereafter) organized in terms of the protothinker's pragmatic understanding of the environment—what Cussins terms *cognitive trails*.

A similar contrast is drawn by John Campbell, who distinguishes between two fundamentally different perspectives on the world (1993, 1994). One perspective, which he describes in terms of its employment of a primitive physics, is primarily practical and engaged. The other, which uses an explicit physics, is reflective and detached. A clearer understanding of what this distinction is emerges from Campbell's discussion of the terms that one might employ in specifying the content of a practical primitive physics. These terms are, he explains, *causally indexical*. What makes terms such as "now" and "here" indexical is the fact that their reference varies systematically in different contexts, according to the spatiotemporal location of the thinker. What makes causally indexical terms indexical is the fact that their reference varies according to the causal powers of the thinker. Examples are ". . . is too heavy to lift" or ". . . is out of reach." These terms are grasped in terms of their immediate implications for action and perception: "In these cases, it is not just that grasp of the term requires the ability to register when it applies. It is rather that one uses one's grasp of the causal significance of the term in reacting to recognition that it applies" (1994, 45). So, for example, one would just give up one's attempts to lift the object in question. A primitive physics, then, is one whose content is to be specified in causally indexical terms. The content of an explicit physics, in contrast, is to be specified in terms that are somehow independent of the practical concerns of the thinker. Campbell describes them in a variety of ways, as 'disengaged,' 'reflective,' and 'theoretical,' As in the comparable distinctions drawn by Dummett and Cussins, the level of causal indexicality is governed by the norms of successful action, as opposed to the norms of truth.

All three authors offer a broadly similar way of understanding nonlinguistic thought—as fundamentally perceptual in form, essentially pragmatic and context-dependent, and as falling short in various respects of the full-fledged representation of objects. On all three accounts the contents of nonlinguistic thought qualify as nonpropositional in the terms identified earlier and seem far more easily assimilated to what in the previous section I identified as thinking-how. We can, I think, take all three philosophers to exemplify a minimalist approach that stresses the following four features of nonlinguistic thought.

- Context-bound
- Pragmatic and dynamic
- Perceptually vehicled
- Unstructured

I shall argue hereafter that the minimalist approach cannot be fully adequate to the task of explaining nonlinguistic thought. In the next section, however, I shall explain how psychological explanation is to be understood on the minimalist approach, bringing out how the minimalist approach offers an alternative to propositional attitude psychology.

3.3   The Minimalist Construal of Intentional Action and Explanation

In order to understand the type of account a minimalist might give of psychological explanation we need to be clearer on the general structure of propositional attitude explanation when we are dealing with language-using creatures. In brief, the aim of such an explanation is to present a combination of beliefs and desires that will make it intelligible why the action in question should have occurred. The action becomes intelligible when any rational agent with those beliefs and desires and in comparable background conditions could be expected to act in the same way.

This conception of psychological explanation goes hand in hand with a particular conception of how intentional actions are generated. There are generally held to be three separable components in the generation of an intentional action. The basic motor of an intentional action is a desire (whether a desire for something or a desire that something be the case.) But a desire alone is insufficient to bring about an action. Desires feed into action when conjoined with instrumental beliefs pointing to how those desires might be satisfied. These instrumental beliefs themselves need to be "anchored" in beliefs about the environment (as well as depending on further background beliefs). Correlatively, then, it is widely held that a satisfactory psychological explanation will have components corresponding to each of these three components.

This three-component model yields the standard template of belief-desire explanation, as applicable to language-using creatures. It is almost universal among philosophers to think that all social interactions are governed by psychological explanations taking this general form—that we are only able to navigate the social world because we constantly deploy belief-desire explanations to make sense of what is going on around us. Nothing that I say depends on this claim about the scope of psychological explanation, and indeed I have argued against it elsewhere (Bermúdez forthcoming-a, forthcoming-d; see also Morton 2002). As far as ordinary social interaction between humans is concerned, I am convinced that relatively little of it is governed by any sort of folk psychological explanation, as opposed, for example, to understandings of social roles, social routines, and the direct perception of emotional states. Psychological explanation and prediction come into play only when our ordinary methods of understanding other people and coordinating our behavior with theirs break down.

For present purposes, however, we are interested not in the extent to which belief-desire psychology controls social interactions among language-users such as ourselves, but rather with its applicability to nonlinguistic creatures. Are the psychological explanations given by cognitive ethologists, developmental psychologists, and cognitive archeologists best viewed as forms of belief-desire explanation, or should they viewed in another way? The distinctiveness of the minimalist approach lies effectively in denying that there is any need to attribute beliefs when explaining the behavior of nonlinguistic creatures. We can, so it is claimed, understand the behavior of nonlinguistic creatures solely in terms of the goal-directed exercise of visual imagination.

The minimalist is likely to start by pointing out that the relevant instrumental information is part of the content of one's current perception of the environment, so that there is no need for an instrumental belief. If, for example, my desire is for a drink of water and I see a glass full of a liquid that looks like water in front of me well within arm's reach, then my reaching out toward the glass will not always depend on a separate instrumental belief to the effect that I will be able to obtain the glass if I reach out for it. Often I will just be able to see that the glass is within reach and act accordingly. The possibilities for action are part of what is perceived, as is stressed in Campbell's notion of causally indexical comprehension and in Cussins's ability-based specifications of content.

The thesis, associated with J. J. Gibson and the ecological approach to visual perception, that the content of visual perception includes what Gibson termed *affordances* offers a further way of extending this basic idea (Bermúdez 1998, Gibson 1979). An affordance is a resource or support that the environment offers a particular creature—such as the possibility of shelter or the availability of food. Although affordances are relativized to particular species, so that the same region of the environment might offer different affordances to different species, they are nonetheless objective features of the environment and exist as a function of the physical properties of the environment. The basic idea behind Gibson's theory of affordances is that the environment is not perceived in neutral terms. What are perceived are the possibilities that the environment affords for action and reaction, including the potential of various locations for providing shelter, concealment, or nourishment. These affordances are directly perceived in the patterns of light in the optic flow[10]—although, of course, creatures need to become "attuned" to the relevant features of the environment. The perception of affordances is a perception of the instrumental properties of the environment that, the minimalist is likely to claim, effectively makes the appeal to an instrumental belief nugatory. The explanatory framework of affordances is not compulsory for the supporter of the minimalist approach to nonlinguistic thought, but it does offer a powerful tool for making sense of instrumental perception.

So the minimalist account of the intentional actions of nonlinguistic creatures will see these actions as being brought about by a simple combination of a perceptual state and a desire. The animal or infant whose behavior is being explained mediately perceives an instrumental property that would allow it to attain a goal—it perceives, say, not simply the lever but the fact that the lever pressing affords the possibility of gaining food. Dummett's phrase "the superposition of spatial images on spatial perceptions" is an apt way of capturing what is going on here. Given that the animal desires the goal in question, it acts on the mediately perceived instrumental property. The animal is hungry and therefore presses the lever.

The minimalist account will be incomplete, however, without some character-ization of what it is for a nonlinguistic creature to be in a given motivational state. We should start by noting that motivational states in general can have two different types of object. That is, one can desire a particular thing, or one can desire that a particular state of affairs be the case. We can label this the distinction between *goal-desires* and *situation-desires* (with a corresponding distinction between *goals* and *goal-situations*). At the level of verbalizable thought, the distinction can be marked in terms of two different ways of completing the sentence "X desires —." When the sentence ascribes a goal-desire it is completed by the name of an object or by the name of a kind of stuff (e.g., "food"). But when the sentences ascribes a situation-desire, the sentence is completed by a "that—" clause in which a com-plete sentence specifies the state of affairs in question.

Goal-desires are more basic than situation-desires. There are many types of goal-directed behavior that can be interpreted in terms of goal-desires but where it would be inappropriate to look for a situation-desire. Consider, for example, a bird returning to a stored cache of seeds. It is known from both ethological studies and laboratory experiments that species such as chickadees and marsh tits are capable of hiding extraordinary numbers of seeds in a range of different hiding places and then retrieving them after considerable periods of time have elapsed (Sherry 1982, 1984). This seems to be goal-directed behavior. It is hard to see, for example, how it can be attributed to the operation of innate releasing mechanisms, trial and error learning, or reinforcement learning. The behavior of a marsh tit returning to one of its many food caches is driven by the combination of a motivational state and a memory of the particular location and how to get to it.[11] But it seems wrong to hold that what drives the marsh tit is a desire for the food that is in the cache (which would be a situation-desire). It is driven by a far more general desire for food. There is no difference, for example, between the desire that drives it to go to one food cache and the desire that drives it to go to a different one. Nor need it be a desire for any particular one of the different types of seed or nut from which it de-rives nourishment. (But see Clayton and Dickinson 1999 on scrub jays.)

Goals are not structured, whereas goal-situations are. Goals are simple ob-jects, features, or kind of stuff. Qua goals they do not contain distinct parts. Goal-situations, in contrast, are always complexes, such as facts or states of affairs, where a complex is an ordered n-tuple of objects, properties, and/or relations. The simplest sorts of goal-situations are objects possessing particular properties (X de-sires that it be the case that such-and-such is so-and-so) or objects standing in rela-tions (X desires that *?* stand in relation *R* to *?*).

It is open to the minimalist, therefore, to adopt a very low-key approach to psy-chological explanation. The minimalist might suggest that a creature's behavior could be fully explained in terms of a goal-desire and the content of its occurrent perceptions. This means that all that is really required for a satisfactory psycho-logical explanation from the minimalist point of view is a specification of the rele-vant goal-desire. Since one can expect the creature to be suitably perceptually sen-sitive to its distal environment and the possibilities the environment presents for action and reaction, there is no need to specify the content of the creature's perceptual state. The simple fact that the creature acted in the way it did is a sign that it perceived the relevant instrumental property. The minimalist will be in a position, therefore, to work back from the attained (or striven-for) goal to the relevant desire. Once the desire is specified the explanation is complete. What makes the intentional actions of nonlinguistic creatures intentional, on this view, is that they are minimally goal-directed. Consequently, all an explanation needs to do is to find the goal. The differences between the minimalist conception and standard belief-desire models of psychological explanation should be clear.[12]

It will be helpful to compare the minimalist account as I have developed it with two earlier accounts of psychological explanation explicitly directed at the project of explaining the behavior of nonlinguistic creatures and equally intended to be alternatives to standard belief-desire psychology. Charles Taylor has suggested that the alternative to mechanistic explanation (in the form, say, of appeals to classical conditioning or innate releasing mechanisms) is what he calls teleological or purposive explanation, the characteristic of which is that events are held to occur because of what results from them. Here is what Taylor says about the form of a teleological explanation.

> To say that the behavior of a given system should be explained in terms of purpose is, in part, to make an assertion about the form of the laws, or the type of laws that will hold of the system. But qua teleological these laws will not be of the kind which makes behavior a function of the state of some unobservable entity; rather the behavior is a function of the state of the system and (in the case of animate organisms) its environment; but the relevant feature of system and environment on which behavior depends will be what the condition of both makes necessary if the end concerned is to be realized. Thus for instance, we can say that the conditions for a given action, say a predator stalking his prey, are (1) that the animal be hungry and (2) that this be the "required" action, i.e. the action in his repertoire which will achieve the result—catching his next meal. *The condition of an event B occurring is, then, not a certain state of P* [an inner purpose], *but that the state of the system S and the environment E be such that B is required for the end G, by which the system's purpose is defined.* (Taylor 1964, 9-10; my italics)

Taylor is at great pains to show that purposive explanations can be formulated in ways that do not leave them open to the sorts of criticisms that made behaviorism seem plausible. But his urge to keep teleological explanations at the level of the observable and verifiable leaves him with a very impoverished conception of psychological explanation—one that can only be distinguished with difficulty from certain forms of behaviorism. It is mildly troubling that there is no account of what makes it the case that a system has a certain end as its goal. It also seems wrong to demand that a behavior be *required* to attain the relevant goal. The behavior must be (perceived to be) a sufficient condition of attaining the end, but it seems unreasonable to demand that it be a necessary condition. There might, after all, be different ways of attaining the relevant end in a given environmental situation.

But the real problem is that Taylor's account does not explain how a creature moves from being in a certain environmental situation to engaging in a particular behavior. Even if we assume that a particular behavior is required (in those particular environmental circumstances) to achieve a goal that we have independent reasons to believe the animal has, we still have no understanding of why that behavior should have emerged at that moment. The animal will only embark on the behavior if it somehow apprehends that a goal is realizable through that behavior. Or rather, those behaviors in which we are interested (those for which we are compelled to offer psychological rather than mechanistic explanations) are precisely those in which the behavior is not environment driven—and it is precisely these non-environment-driven behaviors for which Taylor's account leaves an explanatory gap.

Jonathan Bennett has offered an extension of Taylor's theory that employs the concept of registration to fill this explanatory gap (Bennett 1976). The basic form of a teleological law for Bennett is as follows:

(For all x) ((Rx & x registers at time t that F/Gx) $\rightarrow$ Fx at time $t + d$)

Rx is to be read as the claim that suitable enabling conditions are satisfied; F/Gx as the claim that x is so structured that performing action F at a later time $t + d$ is causally sufficient for x's obtaining goal G at a still later time. The concept of registration is offered as a surrogate for perception—as a way of capturing, without the theoretical baggage that comes with the notion of perception, how features of the immediate environment might be epistemically accessible. According to Bennett, a creature C registers that P just if C is in a sensory state that is sufficiently like some P-operative state, where a P-operative state is one that implies that C's acting on P is noncoincidental (Bennett 1976, 56). The basic idea is that C is perceptually sensitive to P in a core set of environments and acts accordingly. The P-operative states are those that resemble the sensory states underpinning C's perceptual sensitivity in the core environments.

The concept of registration thus understood fills the gap in Taylor's account. It gives us a way of understanding why the creature should embark on the relevant behavior when it does—because it registers the contingency between acting in a certain way and realizing a certain goal. Whereas on Taylor's account a psychological explanation should cite simply the relevant goal and the fact that the behavior is a way of bringing about that goal, Bennett more plausibly demands that the agent register this fact. It is also clear that Bennett's account dovetails very nicely with the proposal that the instrumental component of intentional action be understood in terms of the perception of affordances. The theory of affordances gives us a way of understanding just what it would be for a creature to register that performing action F at a later time $t + d$ is causally sufficient for x's obtaining goal G at a still later time.

Nonetheless, Bennett's basic account must be modified before it gives us an adequate way of spelling out how a minimalist should understand psychological explanations. It cannot generally be the case that a creature acts on every affordance that it perceives—but this is clearly the consequence of the basic account.

We need some way of accommodating the thought that a creature might choose between different affordances as a function of the different goals that it has. Bennett himself recognizes this and suggests that the basic account be supplemented with a further clause in the antecedent specifying, essentially, that there is no F^*/G^* such that the creature prefers F^*/G^* to F/G—where preferring F^*/G^* over F/G would not simply be a matter of preferring the first outcome to the second, but rather involve a comparison of what Bennett calls "means and goal complexes." Again, the basic idea is very congenial to the theory of affordances. If the instrumental component of an intentional action is in fact to be understood in terms of the perception of an affordance then it seems absolutely right to hold that, when there is something like choice going on, the choice is between what we might term courses-of-action-leading-to-goals, rather than between goals per se.

Let us suppose that all instances of thought without language of the sort identified by developmental psychology and the other disciplines we are considering can indeed be accommodated according to the minimalist conception, as instances of thinking-how rather than thinking-that. This would be a way of doing justice to the widespread experimental evidence that nonlinguistic creatures are capable of genuinely thinking behaviors, while still preserving the distinctiveness and indeed uniqueness of thought with linguistic vehicles. Only language-using creatures would be capable, on this view, of thinking that fits the specification of thinking-that: compositionally structured thoughts with determinate contents would only be available to creatures who possess a language.

Unfortunately, the minimalist approach of nonlinguistic thought is unsatisfactory—or rather, it cannot provide a sufficient account of nonlinguistic thinking. In the remaining sections of this chapter I will present three arguments directed at various strands of the minimalist approach as I have sketched it out. From these arguments there will emerge certain features of nonlinguistic thought that any adequate theory must be able to accommodate. In particular I will argue for two theses. The first thesis is that the instrumental component of intentional action cannot always be understood at the level of perceptual content. As I will show, in at least some instances, nonlinguistic creatures behave in ways that involve complicated instrumental reasoning about the possible consequences of different courses of action. This conclusion is argued for in section 3.4 in the *argument from planning*. The second thesis is that the representational states of nonlinguistic creatures need to be viewed as structured states. This conclusion is drawn in the *argument from intelligent action* in section 3.5 and in the *argument from psychological explanation* in section 3.6.

3.4   The Argument from Planning

The minimalist position, as outlined here, is committed to a relatively circumscribed conception of nonlinguistic thinking behavior. It is integral to the minimalist position that a nonlinguistic creature's thoughts cannot be divorced from the here-and-now of the perceived environment. In the words of Michael Dummett, the thoughts of nonlinguistic creatures "cannot float free but can occur only as integrated with current activity." (Dummett 1993, 123). To say that protothoughts can occur only as integrated with current activity is rather metaphorical, however. It clearly cannot be right that a nonlinguistic creature can act only on a visible goal—although the anecdotal examples that Dummett gives of Köhler's chimps and a horse rolling over a cattle grid both happen to be ones in which the goal is visible. Animals can clearly act on goals that they cannot perceive—the predator lying in wait for prey is an obvious example. In section 3.3 I presented a model of psychological explanation that tries to do justice to this while adhering to the basic minimalist claim that the thoughts of nonlinguistic creatures are circumscribed by their perceptions of the immediate environment.

The key point is that the content of perception can include factors that are not themselves directly perceived. For present purposes it will suffice to understand a creature C immediately perceiving an object O in terms of C standing in such a relation to it as to enjoy an experience as of an O being present in the relevant sensory modality, where an experience as of O being present is an experience that would allow O to be discriminated from other elements in the perceptual field.[13] In the case of vision the holding of the relevant relation would obviously require that O was within C's field of vision; that there be no obstructions between O and C; that C's perceptual apparatus be functioning properly; that environmental conditions be more or less normal; and so forth. It is often correct to describe a creature as perceiving an object even when there can be no question of immediate perception. In an important group of cases it is possible to detect the presence of an object that one cannot immediately perceive from the behavior of things that are immediately perceptible—as when a creature is alerted to the presence of a predator by the behavior of conspecifics in a flock. In another important group of cases creatures can perceive what Jonathan Bennett calls instrumental properties (that is to say, the fact that the environment is such that a particular course of action will lead to the satisfaction of a certain goal) even when the goal is not immediately perceptible. The natural way to understand what I am calling nonimmediate perception is in inferential terms—and this is certainly how it has been understood by many philosophers who have considered the matter.[14] Clearly, no defender of the minimalist theory of nonlinguistic thought can accept such an interpretation of mediate perception. It is hard to see how the notion of inference can be accommodated within the minimalist framework, since it seems clearly to fall on the thinking-that rather than thinking-how side of the distinction with which I began the chapter. But, as I pointed out in section 3.3, Gibson's theory of the direct perception of affordances gives us a good way of understanding how mediate perception might occur noninferentially.

An illustration of this type of noninferential mediate perception of instrumental properties can be found in some of the studies Marc Hauser has carried out on the perception of the functional properties of objects in cotton-top tamarin monkeys (Hauser 1997). The experiments involved offering the monkeys a series of choices between two different tools, each of which could be used to access food. The tools were all cane-like objects with hooks at the end, but they varied across a range of dimensions. Some of these variations were functional. So, for example, in one experiment the monkey had to choose between a cane with food located on the inside of the hook (hence easily accessible) and a cane with the food less easily accessible on the outside of the hook. The tamarins quickly learned to select the tool yielding the greater affordance of food. This choice pattern was preserved when the properties of the two canes were systematically varied. Tools with alterations in noninstrumental properties such as color or texture (which would not affect the usefulness of the tool for securing the food) were systematically preferred over tools with alterations in properties such as size or shape, which rendered the tool less appropriate for securing the food. It looks very much as if the cotton-top tamarins (who do not use tools in the wild) are learning to become perceptually sensitive to instrumental properties/Gibsonian affordances.

These brief reflections illustrate how the minimalist is committed to the following restrictive thesis about the nature of nonlinguistic thought. Whenever the thinking behavior of a nonlinguistic creature is directed at something that is not immediately perceptible, the instrumental representations driving its behavior cannot be anything more complicated than mediate perceptions. This is a function of the minimalist emphasis on the content of perception rather than on propositional attitude content.

Clearly, then, we will have an argument against the minimalist interpretation of nonlinguistic thought if we provide examples of behaviors in nonlinguistic creatures that do not seem to be interpretable at the level of perceptual content, whether that content is understood in terms of affordances, or some other form of noninferential mediate perception (which might, for example, involve the exercise of visual imagination in reconfiguring the elements of the perceived environment). Of course, no individual example can be definitive, but it seems to me that there are enough broad areas in which it is plausible to identify such examples for the minimalist claim to be seriously threatened.

Let us start with the notion of an affordance. Although minimalist approaches are not compelled to employ the notion of an affordance, it is a very natural way of developing the basic minimalist claim that what a creature perceives are its possibilities for action and reaction in the perceived environment. It is an important part of the theory of affordances that affordances should reflect what is sometimes called the "animal-environment fit." It is an ethological commonplace that particular species (indeed, particular communities within individual species, not to mention individuals at different stages of development) occupy distinct environmental niches. If explanations appealing to affordances are to be more than just-so stories there must be a significant correlation between the affordances that a creature can perceive and relatively stable features of its environment. The perception of affordances is one of the ways that animals become attuned to their environmental niches. It would seem, therefore, that explanations of behavior appealing to the perception of affordances will be of limited use when the behavior in question occurs in highly unfamiliar surroundings unrelated to the creature's environmental niche. Yet much of the evidence for thinking in the absence of language is derived from studying how nonhuman animals and human infants behave in precisely such unfamiliar surroundings.

The *dishabituation* paradigm in developmental psychology is a case in point. The basic reasoning behind dishabituation experiments is that infants look longer at events that they find surprising and hence one can read back from what they find surprising to the expectations that they have about how events should turn out. So by habituating infants to a given event and then presenting them with events that differ from that event in specified ways one can detect those features of events to which they are sensitive. This allows one to identify the general higher-order physical principles that the infants can detect perceptually. The dishabituation paradigm has produced much of the evidence of cognitive sophistication that has revolutionized the study of early infancy (Baillargeon 1995, Gopnik and Meltzoff 1997, Spelke 1990). But many, if not most, dishabituation experiments proceed by showing infants events that appear to be physically impossible. In Baillargeon's well-known drawbridge experiments, for example, infants are presented with a state of affairs that seems to involve a solid drawbridge passing through a solid object. What in the 3-month-old infant's environmental niche corresponds to such an event?

The same holds for much of the laboratory-based research that has been done in animal learning theory. There is a direct analogy with the infant case, given that animal cognition is now being studied through versions of the dishabituation paradigm (Hauser 1998, Munakata et al. 2001).[15] Although the behavior of animals in the wild, as studied by cognitive ethology, is very much suited to explanations of behavior that stress the ways that animals resonate to features of their environment, it is much harder to offer genuine explanations of the behavior of animals in highly artificial environments such as mazes and Skinner boxes. The extensive research that has been carried out on trying to teach animals artificial communication systems provides an even clearer example. Appeals to the perception of affordances or to any type of mediate perception would seem to be completely vacuous when trying to explain how a dolphin can learn to respond to sequentially complex gestural commands (Herman 1980, 1986) or how a pygmy chimpanzee can spontaneously start to use lexigrams to communicate after having watched experimenters trying and failing to teach his mother to communicate with them (Greenfield and Savage-Rumbaugh 1990, Savage-Rumbaugh, Shanker, and Taylor 1998).

Versions of the minimalist approach that depend on the perception of affordances are difficult to apply, therefore, to types of thinking behavior that emerge in highly unfamiliar environments.[16] This is not, of course, an argument against those versions of the minimalist approach that do not deploy the concept of an affordance. But there is a second problem—one that is not tied to the notion of an affordance. Many types of animal behavior involve acting on goals that are not even mediately perceptible. Many of these behaviors are not thinking behaviors at all. So, for example, the minimalist should not be troubled by the fact that birds build nests to shelter young that have not yet been born or that individual salmon engage in large-scale migrations. But some are thinking behaviors. Technological manipulation in the higher primates and in the early hominids provides good examples.

Wild chimpanzees, for example, make two different types of wands for dipping into ant and termite nests from different types of branches. Wands for dipping into ant swarms are made by stripping the side leaves and leafy stem from a stick several feet long. The wands constructed for dipping into termite nests, on the other hand, are made from vines or more flexible twigs and are considerably shorter. They also have a bitten end, unlike the ant wands. These tools are extremely specialized and, as Byrne notes (1995, 97), the wands are often constructed some time in advance and a considerable distance away from the place where they are going to be used. Even better evidence for instrumental thinking in tool construction comes from the archeological record. Complicated tools were being constructed long before the emergence of language (Gibson and Ingold 1993, Mithen 1996).

As I show in much more detail when I come to consider the nature of nonlinguistic reasoning and rationality in chapter 6, examples such as these of technological manipulation reveal a distinctive type of instrumental thought. In sophisticated forms of tool construction and manipulation a creature is representing the outcomes of particular courses of action in a manner that we would most naturally model in terms of a sequence of instrumental statements. In the terms I have been using, the instrumental properties are perceived in inferential terms as the likely consequences of a particular course of action. The minimalist account does not seem able to accommodate this, however. As I have shown, the minimalist is committed to an account of the perception of instrumental properties in terms of noninferential mediate perception.

Nor is tool construction the only area that presents problems for the minimalist approach. There is a basic type of practical decision-making that the minimalist approach finds very difficult to accommodate. As I shall show in more detail in chapter 6, all decision-making involves a selection between different courses of action. But there are two different ways in which different courses of action can be compared. On the one hand, they can be compared simply qua courses of action. That is to say, an animal might compare the action of fighting with the action of fleeing. On the other hand, however, an animal might compare *the consequences* of the action of fighting with *the consequences* of the action of fleeing. These are two very different types of representation. One involves representations of actions. These representations are not very complex. They can plausibly be understood at a purely perceptual level. The other, however, involves representations of contingencies between actions and outcomes. It involves choosing a course of action *because* it will lead to a particular goal. This is a far more sophisticated type of representation that it does not seem possible to understand in terms of noninferential mediate perception at all.[17]

It is arguable that many instances of instrumental conditioning fall into this category (Dickinson and Balleine 1993, Heyes and Dickinson 1993, 1995). A related example comes with Rescorla and Skucy's discovery that rats trained to press a lever for food will cease to press the lever when the schedule is changed so that the food is delivered whether they press the lever or not (Rescorla and Skucy 1969, Hammond 1980). This seems to involve recognition that the contingency between lever pressing and food delivery no longer holds. The rats had initially been pressing the lever in virtue of an instrumental belief that lever pressing would result in the appearance of food. When the correlation tracked by the instrumental belief ceased to hold the associated behavior also ceased.

It looks, therefore, as if the minimalist account runs into clearly defined empirical problems. Nonlinguistic creatures are capable of forms of instrumental reasoning considerably more complex than the minimalist account can allow. The conclusion to draw from the argument from planning and instrumental belief is that thinking at the nonlinguistic level cannot be driven by, and limited to, the immediate environment in the manner prescribed by the minimalist view—even taking into account the availability on the minimalist construal of a notion of noninferential mediate perception. The upshot of the argument from planning is that it looks very much as if psychological explanations of the behavior of nonlinguistic creatures will at least sometimes have to approximate to standard belief-desire explanations by including the ascription of an instrumental belief and/or the assumption that nonlinguistic creatures engage in inferences about what is not immediately present.

3.5   The Argument from Intelligent Action

The second argument for the insufficiency of minimalist approaches to nonlinguistic thought starts from the adaptive requirements of the thinkers of such thoughts. What benefits accrue to a creature in virtue of its capacity to represent the environment and hence to behave in a thinking rather than unthinking way? The most obvious answer is that the power to represent the environment bestows a flexibility and range of response that would not otherwise be available—and it is, as I showed in section 1.2, precisely in order to explain such flexible responses that we need to appeal to psychological explanations of behavior. But when we think more carefully about how the capacity to think generates this flexibility and range of response it becomes apparent both that the types of thinking attributed to nonlinguistic creatures must have a distinctive internal structure (Horgan and Tienson 1996) and that these types of thinking involve a type of *reification* that is not available at the purely perceptual level.

The essence of learning is the capacity to extrapolate from previously experienced situations to situations that have not previously been experienced. Such extrapolation involves identifying the salient respects in which two situations are similar and to strip away the inessential features. The particular features that are salient will vary, of course, depending on the activities in which the creature is engaged and its particular interests at that moment. With respect to one set of activities and interests the most salient similarity between two states of affairs might be that the same individual features in both of them. With respect to a different set of activities and interests the salient similarity might be that similar properties are instantiated in the two states of affairs. The creature's actions in the second (later) situation will of course vary depending on which similarities are salient. This is what generates the flexibility of response characteristic of thinking behavior. A thinking creature will not always respond to the same situation in different ways, because its response will depend on which aspects of the situation are perceived as relevant.

Frequently this flexibility will come only because the creature is capable of representing and keeping track of the separable components of the perceived environment and, subsequently, of acting in ways that reflect this capacity. When this is the case the creature's representations of the environment must be structured so as to have separate components that can reappear in, and be extrapolated from, a range of further representations of the environment. The relevant distinction can be made in terms of the initial characterization of thinking-how at the beginning of the chapter. It will be recalled that reasoning by analogy was a prime candidate for thinking-how—a form of reasoning that is not verbalizable, does not have linguistically expressible structured contents, and is context-bound. The essence of the argument from intelligent action is that the simple perception of analogies and similarities across different environments and situations is not always sufficient for the flexibility of response characteristic of thinking behavior. Intelligent action often requires keeping track of differentially represented features and objects in the perceived environment (see Horgan and Tienson 1996, ch. 3, for a similar argument).

One way of developing this point would be in terms of the level of detachment from the current context involved in nonlinguistic thought. The essence of the minimalist approach is that nonlinguistic creatures need only represent the environment perceptually, where the content of perception is understood solely in terms of the possibilities that the environment affords for action and reaction. The three exponents of the minimalist conception that I have been considering all draw a sharp distinction between this action-based conception of the content of perception and a more objective and context-independent conception of the content of propositional attitudes. Consider, for example, this passage from Cussins:

> An objective world is given to a subject if the content presents something as being independent of the subject's particular abilities and particular location, in space and time. But given only the realm-of-embodiment-specified content, all the subject (embodied organism) has is an experiential awareness of how to move etc in response to local changes in its environment. If this were a subject's conception of a referent it would be a conception of something as not independent of contingent characteristics of the subject itself. The necessary separation between subject and object would not have been achieved. (1992, 659)

A similar point is at the heart of Campbell's conception of the contrast between causally indexical thought and fully self-conscious thought paradigmatically exemplified only by language-using humans. Causally indexical thought does not support a conception of objects as individuals persisting through space and time and entering into causal interactions. Nor does it support the idea of reidentifying an object (as opposed to recognizing a particular feature or a particular possibility for acting).

Let us locate this aspect of the minimalist approach in a wider context. In the broadest sense, to perceive the world as a structured entity is to perceive it as composed of bodies interacting according to certain basic principles within a unified spatial framework (Strawson 1959). We can follow Quine (1995, ch. 3) in describing the process of arriving at this sort of perception of the world as one of reification. In order to get clear on how this process might work we need to understand the alternative to a fully reified perspective on the world. One distinction here is between the recognition of bodies and the recognition of recurrent circumstances or features. It is possible for a creature to be in a position to recognize that it is once again in the presence of certain features that it has previously encountered (such as food or water or danger or shelter) without being able to parse the perceptual array into genuine bodies. Let us suppose that the creature encounters a tree that affords shelter. Then the creature could perceive the tree as affording shelter without perceiving it as a tree. To perceive a tree as affording shelter one need only recognize its similarity to other things that have afforded shelter and to act accordingly. All that is required here is appropriate action grounded on some form or other of perceived similarity. It is often thought that perceiving the tree as a tree requires no more than this. Some such idea is behind most empiricist theories of concept formation and learning. But this neglects an important distinction. Being able to respond appropriately to the presence of treeness is a matter of appropriate action based on perceived similarity. But to perceive a tree as a tree is to perceive it as an individual thing, as something that persists over time and can be encountered at different times and in different sensory modalities. It is to be able to reidentify the tree; to be able to pose the question, for example, whether the tree in front of one is the same tree one perceived earlier; or to be able to select one tree out from a group of perceptually similar trees; or to be able to count the number of trees in one's immediate vicinity.

We can follow Strawson in terming this the distinction between the feature-placing level of experience and the particular-involving level of experience (Strawson 1959). At the feature-placing level of experience there is no distinction to be drawn between one instantiation of, say, foodness and another. A creature at this level inhabits a world composed of different kinds of stuff. These different kinds of stuff can be encountered at different places, at different times, and in different combinations. Some of these encounters and combinations are predictable, and the creature best able to make these predictions will flourish. But the regularities on which these predictions are based are simply conjunctions of features—associations of food with a particular perceptual Gestalt associated with a certain combination of leaves and branches, for example. In contrast, the creature that operates at the particular-involving level is able to detect regularities of a completely different order—regularities that govern the behavior of persisting bodies. Many of these regularities will be causal, governing the interactions between persisting bodies. Others will be kinematic, governing the possible movements and behavior of any given body.

The three versions of minimalism that we have been discussing (those offered by Dummett, Campbell, and Cussins) are all committed to locating nonlinguistic behavior at the feature-placing level. This follows from the different ways they develop the idea that nonlinguistic thoughts are constrained by the here-and-now and immediately integrated with action. Types of thinking that are constrained in this way do not need the mechanisms of individuation and identification that emerge with the particular-involving conception,. The regularities that drive nonlinguistic behavior on the minimalist construal are conjunctions of features and circumstances, rather than regularities holding over the behavior of persisting bodies. The particular-involving conception of the world comes with detachment from the here-and-now and the capacity to represent the world in a manner that is not constrained by the requirements of immediate action. The point of the argument from intelligent action is that many examples of intelligent action in the nonlinguistic realm require thought at the particular-involving level. Some examples are discussed in subsequent chapters.

Thinking at the particular-involving level places significant constraints upon how we think about the content of thought at the nonlinguistic level. The contrast with perception becomes even clearer. If a creature is representing particulars that can be individuated and reidentified at subsequent times, then we will need to attribute to it thoughts that have a character much closer to the subject-predicate character of the thoughts that we attribute to nonlinguistic creatures—thoughts in which, to take the simplest example, there is a representation of an object in the subject position and the representation of a property in the predicative position. This goes far beyond the way in which nonlinguistic thoughts are construed on the minimalist conception. In particular, and this is a theme that will recur both in the next argument against minimalism and in the remainder of the book the thoughts attributed will have an internal structure that perceptions do not have. The ability to represent a given object as having a given property goes together with the ability to represent that object as potentially having a range of properties and, moreover, with the ability to represent that property as holding of a range of further objects. The stable representations involved are far from the perceptual and sensori-motor representations postulated by minimalism.

As will emerge in the next two chapters, it is no easy manner either to understand what such thoughts might consist at the nonlinguistic level, or to identify the grounds on which they can be attributed to nonlinguistic creatures. However, there are three points that need to be born in mind. The first is that structured thoughts of this type cannot be accommodated within the minimalist conception of nonlinguistic thinking. The second is that such structured thoughts will need to be attributed when what is being explained is behavior that rests upon a particular-involving conception of the world. The third is that nonlinguistic creatures are capable of such behaviors.

3.6   The Argument from Psychological Explanation

A similar conclusion about the need for structured thoughts at the nonlinguistic level can be reached by arguing not from the practical requirements of the thinking creature but instead from the requirements of psychological explanation. In making sense of the behavior of a nonlinguistic creature we are often required to attribute to it structured thoughts with a determinate and linguistically expressible content (or, at least, a content no more indeterminate than we find acceptable in dealing with language-using creatures).

It is a constraint on explanations in general that they support counterfactuals (statements about what *would* happen, or have happened, in different circumstances). Let us suppose that the presence of an F-type event is appealed to in order to explain the occurrence of a G-type event within the context of a particular set of background conditions that we can term C. Any such putative explanation is subject to the following explanatory adequacy constraint (EAC):

> (EAC) An occurrence of an F-type event in conditions C (causally) explains the occurrence of a G-type event if and only if the following two conditions are met: (1) had the F-type event not occurred the G-type event would not have occurred; (2) in any comparable situation in which an F-type event were to occur a G-type event would also occur.[18]

Clause 1 is intended to rule out the possibility that the occurrence of the F-type event is an accidental concomitant of the occurrence of the G-type event that did not genuinely contribute to its occurrence. If it were an accidental concomitant then one would expect the G-type event to occur even if the F-type event did not occur. The second clause is intended to secure some sort of lawlike connection between the occurrence of F-type events and the occurrence of G-type events, again to rule out a merely coincidental juxtaposition of F- and G-type events.[19]

Let us assume (as we need to do even on the minimalist construal) that we are attributing a desire to explain a particular behavior. The content of the desire we attribute must satisfy the two clauses of EAC. That is to say, it must be the case both that had the creature in question not had a desire with that content, the behavior being explained would not have occurred and that in a suitably similar situation in which the creature has a desire with the same content it would behave in the way it actually did behave. Suppose we ask how one might go about determining whether or not clause 1 of the counterfactual constraint is satisfied.[20] What would make it the case that, had the agent not had the hypothesized desire, it would not have acted in the way it did? How could we evaluate this conditional for truth or falsity?

The content of a desire is given by the state of affairs that serves as its satisfaction-condition, and a state of affairs serves as the satisfaction-condition of a desire if its being the case would bring about (in the right way) the cessation of the behavior to which that desire gave rise. If clause 1 of the counterfactual constraint does indeed hold, then the behavior would also cease (and hence the desire be satisfied) in any state of affairs that is suitably similar to the state of affairs in which the creature actually acted. I shall call these the experimental state of affairs and the candidate state of affairs, respectively. The respects in which the experimental and the candidate states of affairs are suitably similar are determined, of course, by the content of the desire. So one would test clause 1 by varying the environment in various respects and seeing whether the relevant behavior does indeed cease. If the desire-driven behavior is extinguished (in the right sort of way) by an experimental state of affairs that differs from the candidate state of affairs in one or more respects then those respects should not be reflected in the specification of the desire. But, of course, these variations between the target state of affairs and the experimental state of affairs must be variations to which the creature is cognitively sensitive. But this requirement entails that the creature possesses structured motivational states—desires with contents that are sensitive to variations in possible satisfaction-conditions.

I can illustrate this point with a simple example. Suppose that we are considering a bird delivering food to its chicks in the nest (and let us assume, purely for illustrative purposes, that this behavior warrants a belief-desire explanation). The bird lands at the edge of the nest and delivers food to the nearest chick. The question is whether the bird is motivated by the desire to give food to that particular chick (perhaps because it has kept track of how much that chick has been fed relative to the other birds) or by a desire to give food to the nearest chick—or by an even more general desire. It is clear what predictions are made when the counterfactual constraint is applied to these proposals. Clause 1, as applied to the first candidate desire, implies that in the counterfactual situation in which the chick were in a different position in the nest the parent would seek it out to give it food. Clause 1 applied to the second candidate desire implies that in that counterfactual situation the bird would behave in the same way as in the target situation. Clause 2 for both candidate desires suggests that in a situation similar to the target situation the bird would act in the same way. Clearly, however, the possibility of the counterfactual constraint applying in this way depends on the bird's desires being sensitive to separable components of the relevant situations. That is to say, the applicability of the counterfactual constraint depends on the content of the bird's desire being sensitive to variations in possible satisfaction conditions, hence on its being structured. The creature must be credited with the ability to detect and recognize common features of the situation across the experimental and candidate states of affairs.

This line of thought complements the argument from intelligent action discussed in section 3.5. The upshot of the earlier argument was that a nonlinguistic creature's successful navigation of its environment, as manifested in the ability to learn from experience and to recognize salient similarities across different situations, requires a more objective way of representing the environment than the minimalist conception has the resources to provide. It requires something much like the process that Quine has termed reification, which cannot be accommodated purely at the level of perceptual content. What I have shown in the argument from psychological explanation is that a similar approach to nonlinguistic thought appears to be built into our models of psychological explanation—and, in particular, into the way we employ counterfactual reasoning to evaluate particular attributions of desires.

3.7 Taking Stock

Chapter 2 developed some of the principal difficulties posed by the apparent need to give psychological explanations of the behavior of nonlinguistic creatures. These difficulties arise primarily because these psychological explanations are understood as applications of the same belief-desire psychology that is applicable to language-using creatures. In this chapter I have been looking at an alternative way of construing the project of explaining the behavior of nonlinguistic creatures in psychological terms. The minimalist proposal is to take the psychological states attributed in such explanations to be nonpropositional, analyzing them on the model of perceptual states rather than propositional attitude states. The thoughts attributed to nonlinguistic creatures on the minimalist approach are context-bound, essentially tied to the creature's capacities for action and reaction, perceptually vehicled, and lacking the constituent structure characteristic of propositional thought.

This approach to nonlinguistic thought allows us to avoid some of the key problems that arise in explaining how nonlinguistic creatures can have states with propositional content. And, as I showed in section 3.3, it permits a very low-key approach to psychological explanation. There can be no doubt that the minimalist account is highly profitable and that these low-key psychological explanations are frequently applicable. Many types of behavior in nonhuman animals and human infants are best understood in the, broadly speaking, sensorimotor terms proposed by the minimalist (whether this is understood in terms of Dummett's proto-thoughts, Cussins's cognitive trails, or Campbell's causally indexical thoughts—or, indeed, any other related notion). Many cases of thinking without words (no doubt, in fact, the majority of such cases) are not best described as involving structured and context-independent thoughts that are linguistically expressible. I suggested in chapter 1 that thinking behaviors are neither inflexible nor stimulus driven. This freedom from the constraints of the stimulus and from the rigidity of fixed behavioral responses can perfectly well be generated by the types of perception-based thought identified by the minimalist approach. And this perception-based type of thinking permits both the possibility of misrepresentation and the cognitive integration that, in section 1.2, I proposed as the hallmarks of the intentional states featuring in psychological explanations. I will show in more detail at later stages in the book how the minimalist approach can fruitfully be applied.[21]

Despite the obvious utility of the minimalist approach, however, I have argued that it cannot be a *complete* account of nonlinguistic thought. Various important types of thinking behavior cannot be understood in the context-bound and essentially perceptual manner proposed by the minimalist account. This is the case, for example, with those types of thinking that involve instrumental reasoning about the likely consequences of actions and about how to tailor means to ends. Moreover, we have to see nonlinguistic thoughts as structured in a way that reflects the creature's capacity to think about the different things and properties that the environment contains—both in order to understand how nonlinguistic creatures are capable of learning and adapting to different environments and in order to identify the particular beliefs and desires that it is appropriate to identify in a particular context.

In moving beyond the minimalist framework we need to pay particular attention to two dimensions of nonlinguistic thought. The first is the dimension of what, following Quine, I have termed *reification*. That is to say, the way the world is carved up in thought into reidentifiable particulars, as opposed to clusters of features. This will be explored in the next chapter, where I will develop a framework for thinking about different ontologies at the nonlinguistic level. The second is the dimension of instrumental belief. We need to understand what it is for a nonlinguistic creature to have beliefs about the consequences of its actions and about the different ways of achieving a given end. This will be considered in greater detail in chapters 6 and 7. The first step, however, is to get a clearer perspective on what it might mean to attribute beliefs and desires to nonlinguistic creatures. In the first two sections of chapter 4 I will develop a version of success semantics that will simultaneously explain what it is for a nonlinguistic creature to have a given belief or a given desire and how we might go about attributing those beliefs and desires.

4

Ascribing Thoughts
to Nonlinguistic Creatures
Toward an Ontology

It has emerged that we cannot hope to provide an adequate ground for the widespread practices of attributing thoughts to nonlinguistic creatures if we restrict ourselves to the tools offered by the minimalist approach. The minimalist account of nonlinguistic thought in terms of perceptually based protothoughts understood primarily in terms of a creature's ability to act on its environment is without doubt all that we need to understand many of the types of behaviors that were put forward in chapter 1 as candidates for psychological explanation. The upshot of chapter 3, however, was that the minimalist approach cannot be a complete account of nonlinguistic thinking. There are types of thinking behavior that require a form of explanation much closer to propositional attitude explanation—a form of explanation that will involve the attribution of thoughts. Whereas the minimalist approach attempts to specify nonlinguistic thought in terms that are fundamentally perceptual and nonpropositional, it looks as if, for at least some cases of nonlinguistic thought, we will have to engage in a limited form of propositional attitude psychology, explaining behavior through the attribution of beliefs and desires. In this chapter and the next I develop a framework for understanding such attributions.

I will be offering a version of success semantics, based on the idea that the content of a belief is its utility condition and the content of a desire its satisfaction-condition. This is outlined in section 4.1. As I show in section 4.2, existing versions of success semantics generate a significant problem of indeterminacy that is rather similar to the indeterminacy of radical translation discussed by Quine (1960). Applying success semantics does not give us any way of distinguishing between the different thoughts that could be attributed in any given situation. In the main part of this chapter (sections 4.3 and 4.4) I will be concerned with one dimension of this indeterminacy—the ontological indeterminacy arising from the need to specify how a creature carves up its environment. The issues here intersect, as I will show, with the points raised in the previous chapter about the need to explain how nonlinguistic creatures represent and identify particulars.

Section 4.3 considers Quine's account of how a creature can make the move from experiencing a world composed of features to a world composed of bodies (the process he terms reification). Quine's own account of reification is heavily language dependent. He argues, in effect, that reification is achieved through the linguistic machinery of pronominal reference and quantification. I develop an alternative account of reification based on a different understanding of what it is to perceive something as a body. The central claim is that perceiving something as a body is to perceive it as subject to a range of higher-order physical principles. In section 4.4 I show how this understanding of reification allows us to resolve the issue of ontological indeterminacy. The essential structure of a creature's ontology should be understood in terms of the higher-order physical principles to which it is perceptually sensitive.

4.1   Success Semantics: Problems and Prospects

The idea I propose in this section is that the process of ascribing thoughts to animals is a form of success semantics, based on the idea that true beliefs are functions from desires to actions that cause thinkers to behave in ways that will satisfy their desires (Mellor 1991, Whyte 1990). The basic idea of success semantics is that the content of a belief is given by its utility condition, that is, the condition that would have to obtain for the various desires with which it is associated to be satisfied. In brief, true beliefs cause actions that satisfy desires.

Success semantics originated with some fleeting comments by Frank Ramsey about the beliefs of a chicken in his 1927 article "Facts and Propositions." He commented that the chicken's belief that a certain type of caterpillar is poisonous should be equated with the chicken's "abstaining from eating such caterpillars on account of unpleasant experiences connected with them" (Ramsey 1927[1978], 46). He then went on to generalize the point: "Thus any set of actions for whose utility P is a necessary and sufficient condition might be called a belief that P, and so would be true if P, i.e. if they are useful" (46). Although contemporary proponents of success semantics tend to think that they are merely expanding on Ramsey's original insight (see, e.g., Mellor 1991, 23), this cannot be right. It is hard to see how the basic idea that true beliefs are functions from desires to actions that cause thinkers to behave in ways that will lead to the satisfaction of those desires can be extracted from Ramsey's comments. For one thing Ramsey's proposal is clearly committed to a strong form of behaviorism. Ramsey suggests that we should identify the belief that P with the set of actions whose utility condition is given by P. But this makes a nonsense out of the idea that true beliefs are functions from desires to actions. How can a set of actions be a function from desires to actions? How, for that matter, can a set of actions combine with a desire to cause an action? Nonetheless, the germ of the idea of success semantics is clearly there in Ramsey. This is the claim, first, that we need to approach the truth-conditions of beliefs through their utility conditions and, second, that these utility conditions should be understood in terms of the satisfaction of desires.

Two qualifications before going any further. First, I do not think that success semantics can be employed to elucidate the nature of truth in the way that Whyte, for example, has argued. He suggests that "truth just is the property of a belief that suffices for your getting what you want when you act on it" (1990, 149). This seems to invert the true order of explanation. We need an independent characterization of truth if success semantics is to be genuinely contentful. Second, I am not putting success semantics forward as a global semantic theory that will apply equally to the beliefs of language-using creatures and the beliefs of non-language-using creatures. This is another respect in which I differ from contemporary proponents of success semantics (although not, it should be said, from Ramsey himself). There are no prospects for giving an account of the complex belief systems of language-using creatures in terms of success semantics, for the simple reason that so many of our beliefs have little *direct* contact with actions or desires. Success semantics can only be plausibly applied to creatures of whom it is right to say that the role of doxastic states in their cognitive economy is to secure the satisfaction of their desires, and that is simply not true of language-using human beings. As I show in some detail in chapters 8 and 9, the acquisition of language opens up an enormous range of types of thinking that effectively puts the language-user beyond the scope of success semantics.

It is sometimes objected that success semantics is threatened by circularity, since it is impossible to give the contents of desires without presupposing the contents of beliefs (by holding, for example, that the satisfaction-condition of a desire is that state of affairs guaranteed to obtain if the desire combines with true beliefs to cause an action). However, there are ways of specifying the content of a desire that do not involve any such circularity, namely, in terms of the state of affairs that would cause the desire to cease.[1] In thinking about the content of a desire we need to start with the notion of a satisfaction-condition. The satisfaction-condition of a desire is a direct analogue of the truth-condition of a belief. Just as the truth-condition of a belief is the state of affairs that would make it true, the satisfaction-condition of a desire is the state of affairs that would satisfy it. And just as the content of a belief is given by the state of affairs that would make it true, the content of a desire is given by the state of affairs that would satisfy it (Whyte 1991).[2] What makes a creature's desire a desire for food is that it would be satisfied by that creature's obtaining food. What counts as satisfaction? Most straightforwardly, a desire is satisfied when the behavior to which it is giving rise ceases. Of course, not just any cessation of behavior will count as a satisfaction of the desire. The behavior to which my desire for food gives rise may well be brought to a halt if someone offers me a large sum of money to sit still, but my desire for food would not ipso facto be satisfied. The cessation of the behavior has to be brought about in the right way. I shall return to this shortly.

Dretske has objected to accounts of the content of desire in terms of their satisfaction-conditions. He takes the example of the desire that must be invoked to explain why a pet rabbit (PJ) licks the spout of a water bottle attached to his cage:

> PJ may not actually get what he wants. If the water bottle is empty, he licks the spout in order to get water, but this goal—getting water—is never reached. This doesn't prevent it from *being* PJ's purpose in licking the spout. It doesn't prevent *water*, or *getting water*, from being the goal of that internal state (D) that is now active in producing licking movements. For what makes *water* the goal of this state is not what *will* satisfy it (perhaps nothing ever will satisfy it) but the fact that it makes water reinforcing, makes water the sort of result that tends to promote the behavior that leads to it. And what makes this state, and the fact that it is, in this sense, *for* water, explanatorily relevant to PJ's current licking behavior, is the fact that D was recruited as a (partial) cause of licking movements because those movements *resulted* in water. (Dretske 1988, 128)

Dretske's objection to specifying the content of PJ's desire in terms of its satisfaction-condition is that the desire may well not be satisfied. His competing suggestion is that the content of a desire is given by the state of affairs that reinforces the actions to which that desire gives rise (provided that the background conditions are the same). But neither Dretske's objections to the satisfaction-conditions account nor his alternative are convincing. The problem with making the notion of reinforcement central to determining the content of desires is that it is very restrictive. As Dretske himself recognizes in the final sentence of the quoted paragraph, a reinforcement-based account of the content of desire can only accommodate goals that have been experienced as reinforcers in the past ("the desire that explains the behavior is a desire for whatever past result figured as a structuring cause of the behavior" [129]). This entails that new desires can emerge only by chance—when a behavior happens to give rise to a felicitous outcome and the creature in question is motivated to repeat that behavior (as in Jean Piaget's [1952] notion of a secondary circular reaction). This result should be avoided if at all possible, and it is fortunate therefore that his objection to the satisfaction-condition account is less than convincing. The undeniable possibility that a desire may not be satisfied should be no more of an obstacle to specifying its content in terms of what would satisfy it than the possibility that a belief might not be true should stand in the way of specifying its content in terms of what would make it true. The point is not what will satisfy the desire, but what would satisfy it (and not what does make it true, but what would make it true).

Yet the notion of reinforcement does have a role to play in determining the content of desire. As Whyte has noticed (1991), we can employ it to solve the problem mentioned earlier, namely, the problem of specifying the right sort of circumstances in which the cessation of desire-generated behavior will indicate the content of the desire. As he puts it, "a desire is satisfied if and only if its going away reinforces the disposition to act in the way that caused it to go away" (1991, 68). Using the notion of reinforcement in this way does not restrict the possible contents of desires to goals that have been experienced as reinforcers in the past, thus avoiding the central problem in Dretske's theory.

This account of the satisfaction-conditions of desires reveals a further reason for thinking that success semantics cannot be extended beyond the realm of the non-linguistic. The model only works for relatively simple desires. In fact it works best for basic appetites (and it is no accident of course that published discussions of success semantics tend to concentrate on these). There is a very clear sense in which we can identify when the behavior associated with the desire for food actually ceases and hence work backward to its satisfaction-condition. But one of the many cognitive advantages made possible by language acquisition is precisely that of supporting desires for which this straightforward model of cessation and satisfaction is completely inappropriate. To give just one example, I will show in chapters 8 and 9 that acquisition of a language makes possible critical reflection on one's own thinking. A creature capable of critical thinking about its own desires is, ipso facto, capable of second-order desires about the desires it should have. But only the simplest and most straightforward second-order desires can be understood in terms of the states of affairs that would bring about their cessation. Some second-order desires are targeted on specific first-order desires and hence can be understood as states that cease when the relevant first-order desires come into being. But many second-order desires are open-ended. They are desires not about the specific desires one wants to have but about the sort of person one wants to be. Second-order desires such as these do not come to a halt, and their satisfaction is not all-or-nothing.

Taken as a theory applicable solely to the behavior of nonlinguistic creatures, however, success semantics has several conspicuous advantages. The first is epistemological. Success semantics provides simultaneous answers to two questions—the question of what a nonlinguistic belief consists in and the question of how we are to go about identifying the content of that nonlinguistic belief. As I showed in chapter 2, no acceptable theory of the thoughts of nonlinguistic creatures can separate the constitutive dimension from the epistemological dimension.[3] This was one of the principal shortcomings of the language of thought theory. In contrast, the two dimensions are inextricably linked in success semantics. The utility condition of a belief in a particular situation is completely open to the third-person perspective of the ethologist or developmental psychologist. Moreover, success semantics does not fall foul of the basic difficulty that strikes competing theories such as causal covariance semantics (Fodor 1987) and teleosemantics (Dretske 1988, Millikan 1984). The characteristic of these theories is that they work backward from vehicle to content, characterizing content in terms of a relation between the vehicle and features of the distal environment in a way that requires being able to identify the vehicle independently of identifying the content. As I showed in chapter 2 (section 2.3), such theories are prone to serious epistemological difficulties, because we cannot identify a representational vehicle without fixing its semantic properties.

A second advantage of success semantics is that it provides a clear way of capturing how an adaptive creature is in tune with its environment without making implausible claims at the level of the vehicle of representation. According to the various versions of teleosemantics, for example, the attunement of a creature to its environmental niche is a direct function of the fact that various elements of the subpersonal representational system have evolved to track certain features of the distal environment. This runs into some of the problems identified in the previous chapter for the minimalist theory of nonlinguistic thought. In particular, many types of intelligent thinking behavior arise in novel situations where evolutionary notions of proper function do not seem to get a grip. Attunement to the environment arises at the level of the organism, rather than at the level of subpersonal representational vehicles. That is to say, an organism can be attuned to the environment in a way that will allow it to operate efficiently and successfully, even though there has not been selective pressure for sensitivity at the subpersonal level to the relevant features of the distal environment. Successful attunement to a particular situation can emerge from the combination of different heuristics and representational abilities for which the selective pressures were completely different. In the extreme it might be, as in the cases brought to our attention by Stephen Jay Gould, be a complete by-product of adaptation to something else (Gould and Lewontin 1979).

Perhaps the principal advantage of success semantics, however, is that it delivers truth-conditions (via utility conditions). Success semantics starts at the level of the complete thought, rather than at the level of individual content constituents. Causal covariance theories have primarily addressed the question of how individuals and properties are mentally represented, but no accounts have been offered of how these representations combine to generate a thought. The defining feature of a thought is that it is truth-evaluable. Thoughts are things that can be either true or false because they represent states of affairs as holding. These states of affairs are their truth-conditions. Yet it is clear that the simultaneous tokening in the mind of a property representation and an object representation is not sufficient to generate the thought that the object in question has the property in question—hence to determine the relevant truth-condition. This can be seen most easily when we are dealing with relational properties that are asymmetric. Simultaneous tokening of the mental representation of a two-place relational property and two object-representations leaves completely undetermined which object-representation is to occupy which place in the property-representation. This is, of course, the traditional problem of the unity of the proposition, which might be described in more up-to-date terms as the binding problem for thoughts. There is no such problem for success semantics, because it starts from complete thoughts/truth-conditions.

4.2   Success Semantics and Radical Interpretation

The utility condition of a belief, as I have so far discussed the notion, is simply a state of affairs—namely, the state of affairs whose holding will bring about the satisfaction of desires with which that belief is conjoined. The satisfaction-condition of a desire is equally a state of affairs—namely, the state of affairs that will extinguish in the right sort of way the behavior to which the desire has given rise. But identifying these states of affairs is only the first step in the process of giving a psychological explanation at the nonlinguistic level. We also need to know how the creature in question registers that state of affairs—what it takes to be the constituents of that state of affairs and how it might reidentify them in different contexts. When we are dealing with language-using creatures with whom we believe that we share a conceptual framework, we can presume that their perspective on the world is broadly similar to our own. So we are able to move without any problem from identifying the relevant utility condition or satisfaction-condition to specifying the content of the appropriate belief or desire. Our specification of the content simply employs the conceptual apparatus that we ourselves would employ to characterize the relevant state of affairs. This, of course, is because we can presume that our fellow language-users apprehend a world composed of roughly the same type of objects that we perceive and obeying the same kind of laws.

But there are no grounds for making a comparable assumption when we are dealing with the beliefs and desires of nonlinguistic creatures. An important source for the resistance that many theorists have expressed to the ascription of beliefs and desires to nonlinguistic creatures is the thought that any such ascription will inevitably and illegitimately use our own conceptual framework and ways of categorizing the world in characterizing the psychological states of creatures who may well have a completely different way of categorizing the world. And it is surely correct that even once we have identified a utility/satisfaction-condition, it will be misleading to specify the relevant state of affairs in a manner that unquestioningly presupposes our own conceptual framework. When we are faced with the behavior of nonlinguistic creatures and attempt to move backward from that behavior to what they believe and desire, we are in many respects in the position that Quine envisaged a field linguist being in when confronting a completely unfamiliar language about whose syntax and semantics he has absolutely no clue (Quine 1960).

The field linguist's task is to translate the language into his own language. He starts, of course, with sentences that seem the closest to factual observations on the perceptible environment, trying to correlate utterances with the states of affairs on which they seem to be commenting.

> The sentences first and most surely translated in such a case are ones keyed to present events that are conspicuous to the linguist and his informant. A rabbit scurries by, the native says "Gavagai," and the linguist notes down the sentence "Rabbit" (or "Lo, a rabbit") as tentative translation, subject to testing in further cases. (Quine 1960, 29)

The testing is required to rule out alternative available translations. The native might have been commenting on the presence of food, or on the presence of an animal, or on the rabbit's color. It seems plausible that these ambiguities can be resolved by considering other situations in which "Gavagai" is uttered, as well as what the native says when confronted with things that are animals but not rabbits, as well as non-rabbit-like objects that happen to be the same color as the original rabbit:

> The general law for which he is assembling instances is roughly that the native will assent to "Gavagai?" under just those stimulations under which we, if asked, would assent to "Rabbit?" and correspondingly for dissent. (Quine 1960, 30)

Quine's principal point is that there is no way of determining how to move beyond this general law. Quite apart from the local semantic indeterminacies that the radical translator can resolve in the manner I have considered, there are global ontological indeterminacies that do not lend themselves to the same treatment. The simple fact that there are certain sentences that inspire identical patterns of assent and dissent from translator and native across a range of stimulus situations (so that they are what Quine calls stimulus synonymous) does not guarantee even the coextensiveness of the relevant terms:

> For, consider "Gavagai." Who knows but what the objects to which this term applies are not rabbits after all, but mere stages, or brief temporal segments, of rabbits? In either event the stimulus situations that prompt assent to "Gavagai" would be the same as for "Rabbit." Or perhaps the objects to which "Gavagai" applies are all and sundry undetached parts of rabbits: again the stimulus meaning would register no difference. When from the sameness of stimulus meanings of "Gavagai" and "Rabbit" the linguist leaps to the conclusion that a gavagai is a whole enduring rabbit, he is just taking for granted that the native is enough like us to have a brief general term for rabbits and no brief general term for rabbit stages or parts. (Quine 1960, 51–52)

The problem here is one of whether terms are common nouns that divide their reference in a standard way (e.g., "rabbit") or whether they divide their reference in a nonstandard way or whether they fail to divide their reference at all. This is, of course, an ontological issue. The problem is how to determine whether to translate into a language reflecting a particular set of ontological categories.

Quine himself takes the view that this ontological indeterminacy cannot be resolved—and he argues from it to the general indeterminacy of linguistic meaning. There are serious questions to be asked about whether radical translation could possibly be subject to an ontological indeterminacy as radical as Quine suggests and, of course, about the inference from indeterminacy of translation to indeterminacy of linguistic meaning. Gareth Evans, for example, has argued that certain types of combination and negation of predicates would be impossible to understand in a language whose general terms failed to divide their reference over physical objects (Evans 1975; and see Wright 1997 for further discussion). Be that as it may, it is clear that a parallel set of questions is raised by the interpretation of the behavior of nonlinguistic creatures. The developmental psychologist, animal behaviorist, or cognitive ethologist is in exactly the position of an idealized radical translator, with the utility/satisfaction-condition corresponding to the field linguist's stimulus situation. There are many *stimulus synonymous* ways of specifying the utility condition—many different ways of describing the given state of affairs that are compatible with its being such as to result in the satisfaction of the creature's desires. Precisely the questions that Quine raises for the radical translator arise for the ethologist or animal behaviorist, even once a utility condition has been identified within the ethologist's own ontological framework. These are questions about how to specify that utility condition to reflect the way the creature carves up the environment it experiences—how it digitalizes the analogue information derived from perception.

The issue of ontological indeterminacy is most conspicuously a matter of the types of singular terms and common nouns that can be employed in ascribing thought-contents to nonlinguistic creatures—which will of course have ramifications for the predicational structure and compositionality of the language employed to attribute contents. The determination of an ontology will, if it is indeed possible, allow an initial removal of indeterminacy. It will place us in a position to discount as expressions of the thought in question all those sentences whose singular terms and common nouns do not pick out individuals of the appropriate ontological category. But is it really possible to determine an ontology for nonlinguistic creatures?

Competing philosophical orthodoxies push us in different directions. For philosophers influenced by Quine, there can be no such determination of an ontology—radical indeterminacy is ineliminable. For another group of philosophers, the ontology of mind-independent persisting objects standing in causal, spatial, and temporal relations is in some sense a necessary condition of genuine thought (Evans 1975, Strawson 1959). This view is essentially neo-Kantian. Both views militate against the determination of an ontology for nonlinguistic creatures—the first for obvious reasons and the second because it seems frankly incredible that animals and nonlinguistic infants should carve up the world in exactly the same way that language-using adult humans do.

As I bring out in the remainder of the chapter, however, there is a false opposition here. It is not the case that the only determinate ontologies are object-centered in the strong sense of involving mind-independent persisting objects standing in causal, spatial, and temporal relations to each other. There is a spectrum of possible ontologies approximating in different degrees to the full-fledged ontology with which we are familiar from the neo-Kantian tradition in philosophy. Different ontologies will be appropriate for different species, as well as, of course, for different developmental stages within a single species. Identifying an ontology will be the first step in capturing, at the level of sense, the determinate contents of nonlinguistic thoughts.

4.3   Two Types of Reification

As emerged in the previous chapter, there is an important distinction between feature-placing and particular-involving levels of experience. The transition from feature-placing to particular-involving experience takes place in many species, including our own. I shall, following Quine, call this transition the process of reification. The details of how this move might take place have not received much attention from philosophers, although there are important issues concerning the preconditions of reification and the cognitive abilities on which it depends. The most developed theory in this area is Quine's account in various writings (1960, 1974, 1995) of what he terms the psychogenesis of reification. Quine sketches out an account of how reification might occur in terms that are decidedly language-dependent. In this section I explore this account, explain why it raises problems for the theory of nonlinguistic thought, and then offer an alternative. As I show at the end of this section, the proposed alternative will offer a way of thinking about different ontologies at the nonlinguistic level and working toward a resolution of the indeterminacy problem identified in the previous section.

The key claim in Quine's account is that reification involves more than the perception of clusters of features. Clearly, it is a necessary condition for perceiving the world as divided up into bodies that a perceiver be capable of recognizing that features are juxtaposed in a single place—that the perceiver be capable of responding to the presence of combinations of features as well as to individual features. To perceive a body is to perceive a compact clustering of visually detectable features and to recognize that that cluster is associated with further features detectable in different sensory modalities. A body is a bundle of properties. But a body is not just a bundle of properties. A body is a thing that has certain properties. The simple clustering of colocated features can be immediately perceived, but to get genuine reification there needs to be an understanding (which may or may not be purely perceptual) of a form of coinstantiation stronger than simple spatiotemporal coinstantiation.

It might help to focus the issue here by drawing a comparison with a well-known difficulty in the neurophysiology of perception. It has been established that different perceptual features are processed in different areas of the visual cortex (Zeki 1993). This raises the question (the so-called binding problem) of how and where those different streams of processing are brought together in a way that will permit our phenomenological experience of unified objects (for a review see Treisman 1996). That the binding process can go wrong is shown by the possibility of inducing illusory conjunctions in which a feature of one object is perceived as a feature of another. Such illusory conjunctions occur when exposures are brief and subjects are prevented from focusing their attention on each object in turn. In one experiment (Treisman and Schmidt 1982) subjects were briefly presented with an array of colored letters bounded on each side by a digit and told in advance that the task would be to identify the flanking digits. The array was displayed for 300 ms— just long enough for the subjects to attend to the digits and succeed in identifying them. When the subjects are asked to report on the letters between the flanking digits they regularly mix up shapes and colors, so that the letters are correctly identified but with the wrong colors. The subjects correctly pick out all the relevant features in the perceptual array—the full range of shapes and visually presented colors. But they put them together (bind them) in the wrong way. One way of describing the distinction between a body and a bundle of properties would be to say that this featural binding problem is not the only binding problem. A solution to the featural binding problem will still only give us a bundle of features. It would not be enough to underwrite our experience of a world of objects. Something more needs to be added. A further binding problem needs to be solved.

The point emerges from a different angle if we consider the type of generalizations that can be entertained at the feature-placing level—what Quine calls *observation categoricals*: associations of features along the lines of "Where there's yellow, there's food" or "When there's growling, danger is near." It is clear, as Quine remarks (1995, 25), that observation categoricals occur at the most basic level of inductive learning—and, moreover, can be completely association-driven. There is a clear difference between these feature-based generalizations and the corresponding *particular-involving generalizations*: "Yellow things provide food" or "Growling things are dangerous." Most important, the truth of the relevant observation categorical is entirely compatible with the falsity of the associated particular-involving generalization. It may well be that the presence of yellow is an infallible sign of the presence of food, but this is perfectly compatible with some yellow things not themselves being edible but always being accompanied by edible things. Similarly, growling might reliably signal danger even though the danger does not issue from the creature that is doing the growling. Yet this distinction is unavailable to creatures operating solely at the feature-placing level. What would make it available? How might a creature make the shift from observation categoricals to particular-involving generalizations? In Quine's view the shift is made with the acquisition of the linguistic apparatus of quantification.

> The crucial leap to reification of ravens can be achieved by just improving our near approximation by changing "there" to "it": "Whenever there is a raven, *it* is a black raven"; "Whenever there is a raven it is black"; "All ravens are black".
>
> The pronoun "it" is a vital new link between the component observation sentences "Raven" or "Lo, a raven" and "Black" or "Lo, black." It posits common carriers of the two traits, ravenhood and black. The carriers are ravens, bodies. I see this pronominal construction as achieving objective reference. (1995, 27)

According to Quine, then, reification is achieved by acquiring the linguistic tools that will allow the perceiver/thinker to move beyond juxtapositions of features and to bind those bundles together into bodies. These tools are not, as one might immediately think, the apparatus of proper names and common nouns. A child can employ a proper name to refer to a feature, and mere employment of a common noun is not an index of reification—as is shown by Quine's own example of the sentence "Whenever there is a raven there is a black raven," which can be used in a way that simply associates the features of blackness and ravenhood, rather than quantifying over the domain of ravens. Proper names only achieve reification when they are brought within the ambit of pronominal reference and quantification.

Quine's suggestive remarks make very clear that the theorist of nonlinguistic thought needs at the very least to show that reification can take place in the absence of the linguistic machinery associated with pronominal reference and quantification. It is important to get clear on the precise terms of this challenge. The outcome of reification is the perception of an articulated and structured world. We need good evidence for thinking that nonlinguistic creatures can achieve this outcome—hence that it cannot be dependent on the linguistic machinery of pronominal reference, or indeed of any other type.

This might seem an impossible task. How can one tell whether a creature is perceiving an agglomeration of features rather than a reified body? The answer emerges when one reflects that reified bodies obey certain principles and behave in certain regular ways. Clearly, it is a necessary condition of perceiving the world as divided up into objects that a perceiver be capable of recognizing that features are juxtaposed in a single place—that the perceiver be capable of responding to the presence of combinations of features as well as to individual features. To perceive a body is to perceive a compact clustering of visually detectable features and to recognize that that cluster is associated with further features detectable in different sensory modalities. But perceiving objects is not just a matter of how one parses the perceptual array. It is also a matter of the expectations one has about how those compact clusters of visually detectable features will behave, both when one is perceiving them and when one is not perceiving them.

A world articulated in terms of reified bodies is a world that obeys certain basic physical regularities. The physical regularities under discussion here are not the simple particular-involving generalizations that I have already discussed. They are the higher-order physical regularities that govern, and indeed make possible, those particular-involving generalizations by circumscribing what it is for something to count as a particular or a body at all. Bodies tend by and large to have certain higher-order physical properties in common. They tend, for example, to have sharply defined edges relative to their environment. They usually maintain certain forms of perceptual constancy relative to the perceiver when the perceiver moves or when they move themselves. Their properties can be detected in different perceptual modalities. They do not pop in and out of existence but move through space-time on a single connected path. They are resistant to pressure and have a certain mass that governs their interactions with other individuals. No more than one body can be in one place at a time. They are susceptible to gravity and interact with each other through transmitting energy. And so forth. These are higher-order similarities that are not immediately perceptually salient but to which a creature must be sensitive if it is properly to be described as perceiving and acting within a suitably reified and structured world.

Earlier I suggested that a creature might be operating at what, following Strawson, I called the feature-placing level of experience even though its perceptual systems had solved the binding problem, as it is standardly understood within cognitive neuroscience. We are now in a much better position to get a grip on what this might amount to. Suppose we have a creature that perceives the world as composed of bounded segments whose boundaries map onto the boundaries of the objects in the perceived environment, and moreover that it clusters perceptible properties in more or less the right way. That is to say, to put it in Triesman's terms, the representation of redness gets bound to the representations of size and shape in a way that matches the distribution of the relevant features in the environment. It seems to me that this does not imply any perceptual sensitivity to the higher-order physical regularities that govern the behavior of objects. The binding can take place without there being any such sensitivity.

Here is a very simple illustration. One of the characteristic regularities governing the behavior of objects is that they tend to maintain their shape and size over relatively short periods of time. I shall call this the object-property of constancy

(I'll say more about this terminology shortly). It is clear what is involved in perceptual sensitivity to the object-property of constancy. The perceptual systems of normal perceivers automatically compensate for variations in the size and shape of the image on the retina produced by a particular distal object—the well-known phenomena of size and shape constancy. After a very early age, normal humans, for example, do not see a person diminishing in size as he moves away from them—what they see is a person who retains a constant size moving into the distance. Similarly, we are all capable of extracting a single perceptual form as an object's shape despite variations in its orientation. But it does not seem to be part of solving the binding problem that the perceptual system should be sensitive to shape constancy and size constancy. We can appreciate this by thinking about how we would expect a perceptual system that is not sensitive to shape constancy and size constancy to operate. We would not expect such a system to produce the totally chaotic representations that would result if it had completely failed to solve the binding problem. Nor would we expect it to come up with the sort of illusory conjunctions that we considered earlier—illusory conjunctions in which, say, color features and size features are mismatched. All we would expect is that the system would not make the sort of compensations that we make. An organism with such a perceptual system would not see a retreating object as retaining its size—nor would it perceive a rotating object as retaining its shape. Nonetheless, it would still see a persisting cluster of coinstantiated features.

An example will help make the point. There is strong experimental evidence that size constancy is an acquired feature of infant perceptual systems. The experimental paradigm was originally developed by Thomas Bower (1964, 1966), although it turned out that it proved impossible to replicate his early findings of size constancy as early as 8 weeks of age. I will briefly sketch it out, as it is important for the point I want to make. The paradigm involved operant conditioning. Infants were conditioned to respond to visually presented cubes of a particular size. The reinforced behavior was head movement, and the reinforcing was the appearance of the infant's mother.

The infants were conditioned to respond when a cube 30 cm in diameter was presented 1 m in front of them (see fig. 4.1). The question that the experimenters posed was how this response would be generalized—on the standard assumption that a generalized response reflects a perceived similarity. Would the response generalize across similarities in retinal image size? Or would it generalize across similarities in real size, thus showing that the infants were compensating for differences in size of the retinal image and deploying a form of size constancy? It turns out (McKenzie, Tootell, and Day 1980) that size constancy is present at 6 months although not much before.

Consider what happens in experiments that *fail* to detect size constancy in young infants, such as those of McKenzie and Day (1972). Using a version of the paradigm just described, McKenzie and Day conditioned infants between 6 and 20 weeks to one object at a set distance. They found that infants failed to generalize their response when an object was presented at a different distance. The simple

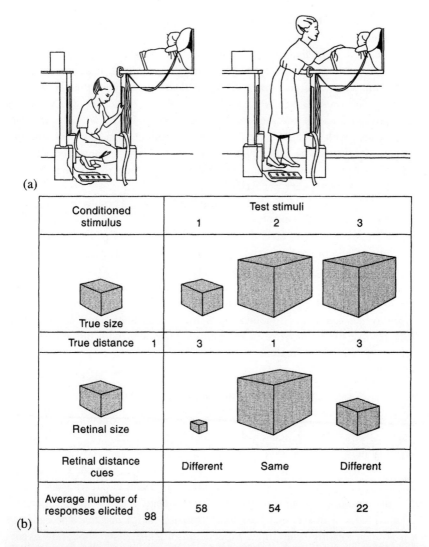

Figure 4.1 (a) Apparatus used by Bower (1964, 1966) to test for depth perception and size constancy. *(b)* Test stimuli showing true sizes, distances, and corresponding retinal image. Reproduced by kind permission of Blackwell Publishers from Bremner 1988, p. 78.

point I want to extract is that the original process of conditioning would only work if the infant perceptual system had solved the binding problem—that is to say, if the features of the cube were all represented in a suitably integrated cluster. The very possibility of showing that infants fail to detect shape constancy requires assuming that the infant perceptual systems have solved the binding problem. Yet, since perceptual sensitivity to shape constancy is integral to the perception of an object, it seems clear that solving the binding problem does not guarantee object perception. There is more to perceiving an object than perceiving clusters of coinstantiated features.

What we need to do, therefore, to test whether reification can emerge in the absence of the linguistic machinery of quantification, is to investigate the extent to which nonlinguistic creatures can properly be described as perceptually sensitive to reified bodies. As Quine's work shows, one way of understanding the move from bundles of features to reified bodies is through the idea that bodies are bundles of features with a single common bearer. We might term this the traditional metaphysical approach to individuation, in honor of its distinguished ancestry within philosophy. If we adopt the metaphysical approach then something like Quine's account seems very persuasive, because it is hard to see how a creature might get a grip on the idea of a bundle of features having a common bearer without explicitly positing the existence of a common bearer—and hard to see how such explicit positing could take place without the machinery provided by the linguistic tools of pronominal reference and quantification. But Quine's thesis looks less compelling if we shift from viewing reified bodies as bundles of features with a single common bearer to viewing them as bundles of features that obey certain general higher-order physical principles. I will term this the higher order principles approach to individuation. In the next section I will show how this can be put to work to resolve the ontological indeterminacy associated with the ascription of thoughts to nonlinguistic creatures.

4.4 Dishabituation and Higher-Order Principles

How might we employ the higher-order principles approach to individuation to investigate the process of reification in nonlinguistic creatures? The dishabituation paradigm in developmental psychology has produced striking and suggestive results in the study of nonlinguistic infants (Baillargeon 1995, Gopnik and Meltzoff 1997, Spelke 1990) and nonhuman animals (Hauser 1998, 2001, Munakata et al. 2001). The reasoning behind dishabituation experiments is that nonlinguistic creatures look longer at events that they find surprising and hence that one can read back from their looking-times to the expectations that they have about how events should turn out. So, by habituating nonlinguistic creatures to a given event and then presenting them with events that differ from that event in specified ways, one can detect those features of events to which they are sensitive. What has emerged from experiments with the dishabituation paradigm on very young infants (long before even the first stages of language acquisition) is that sensitivity to certain very basic physical principles starts at birth. The process of reification is far advanced long before the acquisition of language. The dishabituation paradigm has also been used to investigate the perceptual expectations of higher primates, particularly rhesus monkeys and cotton-top tamarins (Hauser et al. *forthcoming*). The results of these experiments provide strong evidence that reification precedes language acquisition in phylogenetic as well as ontogenetic terms (Munakata et al. 2001). In this section I will explore some of the key findings about infant cognition achieved through the dishabituation paradigm. The extension of these findings to nonhuman animals will be considered in the next section.

Elizabeth Spelke has suggested that human infants perceive individuals as spatially connected bodies that retain their connectedness as they move. She maintains that the perceptual universe of infants as young as 3 months is governed by what she calls the *principle of cohesion*, according to which surfaces lie on a single body if and only if they are connected (Spelke 1990, Spelke and Van de Valle 1993). It is evidence for the principle of cohesion, for example, that infants do not appear to perceive the boundary between two objects that are stationary and adjacent, even when the objects differ in color, shape, and texture. Spelke's dishabituation experiments have shown that infants perceive two objects as one if they are spatially contiguous, even if they do not display the sort of Gestalt properties that adults take to define the boundaries of stationary objects—such as color similarities, smoothness of edges, and so forth. That is, in experimental set-ups such as those in figure 4.2 young infants find the righthand scenario in the two test conditions more surprising than the lefthand scenario.

This is particularly striking in condition (d), where the conflicting visual properties in the two halves of the stationary object might suggest to many adult viewers that the righthand scenario is more likely.

Infants seem perceptually sensitive to principles governing the movement of bodies. Unsurprisingly (since contiguity and connectedness dominate in their perception of stationary objects), infants perceive a single object moving when two adjacent objects move together (Spelke, von Hofsten, and Kestenbaum 1989). It

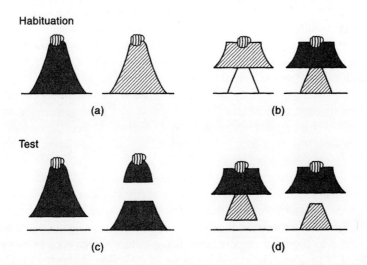

Figure 4.2 A schematic depiction of displays from an experiment on infants' perception of object boundaries. Reproduced by kind permission of Blackwell Publishers from Spelke and Van de Walle 1993, 135.

also follows from the cohesion principle that infants will not amalgamate two objects separated by a visible gap even if they are moving together. They do, however, perceive a single object when the two objects are separated in depth. Spelke explains this by suggesting that infant perceptions are governed by the *principle of contact*, according to which surfaces move together if and only if they are in contact. So, if two partly hidden surfaces move together and there is no visible gap making it impossible for them to be in contact, the infants will expect them to continue to behave as if they were two surfaces of a single object.

It is another basic principle governing the behavior of enduring bodies (as opposed to sensations or sounds, for example) that they should continue to exist when unperceived. There is some evidence from infant behavior that they have at least the beginnings of a grip on this principle. Some of this evidence is anecdotal. One might think that infants reveal sensitivity to this higher-order principle when they move their head one way to regain sight of an object they lost sight of when they moved their head in the opposite direction. Some of it is more experimental. For example, 5-month-old infants will continue to reach for a previously seen object when the room lights are put out (Hood and Willats 1986), although this may well be due to an executive inability to inhibit an already launched prepotent response. Experiments have also shown that infants will look in anticipation toward the far end of a screen when an object disappears at the other edge, and will show surprise when it does not appear at the appropriate time (Moore, Borton, and Darby 1978). But perhaps the most clear-cut evidence in this area has come from a famous set of dishabituation experiments carried out by Renée Baillargeon (1987). In one experiment, Baillargeon habituated 4.5-month-old infants to a screen rotating 180° on a table, rather like a drawbridge. She then, in full view of the infant, placed a stationary object behind the screen so that it was completely occluded by the time the screen had been raised 60°. She was interested in whether the infants would show surprise at trials on which the screen rotated 180° even though the object had been placed behind it, as opposed to the trials in which the screen came to a halt just at the point where it would be expected to encounter the invisible object. It turned out, and has proved to be a very robust finding, that the infants were more surprised by the first type of trial. It appears that they have some expectations about the physical properties of objects even when those objects are currently invisible. Moreover, the drawbridge experiments show an appreciation that objects have properties of solidity and impenetrability.

The dishabituation paradigm was deliberately designed as an alternative to the more traditional Piagetian methods of testing infant's cognitive capacities as a function of their motor capacities. It was felt that these methods could not adequately distinguish performance failures due to lack of sensorimotor coordination from those due to cognitive capacities not being sufficiently developed. Nonetheless, looking at infants' actions and reactions can provide rich evidence for the richness of their perceived environment. The idea that individuals are bundles of features that can be detected in different sensory modalities emerges very early on, for example, and is manifest in infant behavior. Almost as soon as they are capable of coordinating their movements, infants will move an object they hold into their line of sight (Piaget 1954). Also appearing very early on in infancy is the capacity for fairly accurate perception of whether objects are in reach, something that clearly depends on perceiving the object as a locus of both visually and tactually identifiable properties (Field 1976, Von Hofsten 1982).

A final source of evidence in this area comes from experiments on infant perception of shape and size constancy. Bodies tend to preserve their shape and size over relatively short time intervals. Since bodies move relative to perceivers (and perceivers relative to bodies) the size of the retinal image is no index of the real size of the body. The way perceptual systems automatically correct for this is known as size constancy. Shape constancy is a similar phenomenon. Clearly, if infants are to be properly described as perceiving a world articulated into bodies they must be sensitive to the constancies that govern object perception in adults. As I have noted, there is evidence that infants are sensitive to size constancy by about 6 months (McKenzie, Tootell, & Day 1980). Shape constancy, in contrast, has been demonstrated not simply in young infants (Bower 1966, Caron, Caron, and Carlson 1979) but also in newborns (Slater and Morrison 1985).

The experimental evidence clearly suggests, therefore, that even young infants are perceptually sensitive to a significant proportion of the higher-order physical regularities to which bodies are subject. It seems right to conclude from this that they inhabit a reified and articulated perceptual universe. The immediate conclusion to draw is that nonlinguistic creatures are perfectly capable of perceiving a structured world. It seems unlikely that the perceptual universe of young infants is structured according to criteria of identity that are at all comparable to those employed by adult humans. It looks very much as if the principles of individuation that young infants employ are criteria of identity for bodies in general, rather than criteria of identity for particular bodies. This is consistent with experimental evidence showing that, although infants younger than 9 months will show surprise when a body disappears behind a screen and fails to emerge on the other side, they seem unmoved if a different object emerges on the other side (Bower 1982). This is not particularly surprising. But it does highlight the importance of clarifying the differences between the way linguistic creatures apprehend the world and the way nonlinguistic creatures do. I shall return to this in chapters 8 and 9, where I will argue that there are radical differences between linguistic and nonlinguistic cognition.

There is a further conclusion to draw from this examination of reification in human ontogeny, and this brings me back to the discussion at the end of the last section. I proposed there that we must be sensitive to the range of different ontologies that exist throughout the animal kingdom and through the course of infant development. There is no one way that nonlinguistic creatures carve up the world. What is now emerging is a way of making this basic thought concrete and determinate. We can understand variations in ontology across the animal kingdom and the course of infant development in terms of differential sensitivity to the set of basic physical principles that govern the behavior of objects. What makes the ontology of one species different from that of another, what makes it the case that they carve the world up in different ways, is that they are sensitive to different higher-order physical principles. In the next section I turn to making this basic thought more precise.

4.5   From Object-Properties to Ontology

In the previous section I argued in support of the higher-order principles approach to individuation. What makes it the case that a creature perceives agglomerations of spatiotemporally coinstantiated properties and features as bodies is that it perceives them as subject to certain higher-order physical principles. The results of the dishabituation experiments surveyed in the previous section give us a clear illustration in the case of human infants of what this perceptual sensitivity amounts to. In this section I will explore how this conception of individuation can be employed to determine the ontology of nonlinguistic creatures, thus allowing us to take the first step in resolving the indeterminacies of success semantics. The basic idea is that we can understand a creature's ontology in terms of the particular set of physical principles to which it takes bodies to be subject. The problem, of course, is how we are to go about identifying the relevant set of physical principles—the physical principles that form what I will term the *physical parameter set*. The easiest case is one in which, as with the infant example, the relevant physical parameter set is largely a subset of our own physical parameter set. In this case we can simply work backward from our own case, employing what I will term the *canonical object-properties strategy*—essentially subtracting from our own physical parameter set. But, as I have already shown in passing and will explore further below, the infant physical parameter set contains higher-order principles that do not feature in our own. So the canonical object-properties strategy needs to be supplemented what I term the *deviant object-properties strategy*.

I shall start with the canonical object-properties strategy. The basic idea here (as I discussed in *The Paradox of Self-Consciousness*) is to start with the properties that are constitutive of something qualifying as an object. These are what I will call canonical object-properties. The following are plausible candidates for the status of canonical object-properties:

- The property of following a single continuous trajectory through space-time
- The property of continuing to exist when unperceived
- The property of having a determinate shape
- The property of being internally unified
- The property of only being able to undergo a fixed set of changes
- The property of being impenetrable
- The property of being apt to fall when unsupported
- The property of being internally causally connected
- The property of having mass

- The property of posing resistance to the touch
- The property of having its state of motion or rest explicable in terms of mechanical forces acting on it
- The property of causally influencing other objects

The list of canonical object-properties is not fixed and rigid. There may well be some objects that lack one or more object-properties, and it is possible that certain object-properties will be reducible to others (as the property of presenting resistance to the touch might be reducible to the property of impenetrability). Some of the candidate object-properties might not be expected to apply to all objects at all times. Objects that are lighter than air, for example, will not be apt to fall when unsupported. Even more borderline are those objects, such as birds, that are capable of overcoming the effects of gravity. Yet part of what it is to be perceptually sensitive to an object-property is to be perceptually sensitive to the exceptional cases in which certain object-properties cease to hold.

To each of these object-properties there obviously corresponds a higher-order physical regularity of the type discussed in the previous section. So, for example, in virtue of the fact that having a determinate shape is an object-property, there is a higher-order physical principle that bodies have determinate shape. The proposal I made in *The Paradox of Self-Consciousness* was that we can understand the way prelinguistic infants carve up the world in terms of the object-properties (and correlative higher-order physical principles) to which they are perceptually sensitive. How might perceptual sensitivity to these higher-order physical principles be manifested? Some will be directly manifested in the manner revealed by the dishabituation experiments. So, for example, perceptual sensitivity to the object-property of being apt to fall when unsupported (and correlative physical principle that bodies tend to fall to the ground when unsupported) might be manifested in surprise if an object resting on a supporting surface stays where it is when the supporting surface is removed. Sensitivity to other object-properties will be manifested indirectly. Consider the object-property of having a determinate shape. One would not expect an infant sensitive to this object-property to be surprised by a thing that lacks it. After all, they might regularly be expected to encounter smoke rings, shadows, clouds, and the like. But they might manifest their sensitivity to the object-property by showing surprise when an object that lacks it nonetheless appears to possess other object-properties, such as, for example, the object-property of impenetrability.

It seems possible, therefore, to construct an account of the ontological development of the human infant in terms of perceptual sensitivity to an increasing range of object-properties. That sensitivity to certain object-properties emerges at more or less constant stages in human ontogeny seems undeniable. It would appear, for example, that sensitivity to the object-property of causally influencing other bodies emerges in some form at around the age of 7 months (Leslie 1984). However (and this is something I failed to realize in *The Paradox of Self-Consciousness*), this account cannot be a complete account, even in the case of infants. Not all the "properties" to which infants are perceptually sensitive are canonical object-properties.

What is sometimes called the infant's naïve physics is not simply an impoverished version of our own. This is stressed in recent work by Alison Gopnik and Andrew Meltzoff on the development of physical knowledge during infancy and early childhood (Gopnik and Meltzoff 1997, particularly ch. 4).

Gopnik and Meltzoff identify a crucial difference between the criteria that young infants (before the age of about 9 months) and adults deploy to determine object continuity. For infants, movement information dominates information about features and properties, so that their principal criterion for whether or not something is the same object is simply that it should maintain a single observable trajectory, irrespective of any alterations that there might be in its general appearance. This is one important reason why infants will not show surprise when one object disappears behind a screen and a completely different object emerges on the other side. For adults, on the other hand, as Gopnik and Meltzoff elegantly point out, featural constancy can frequently trump continuity of trajectory in determining whether or not two perceptions are taken to be perceptions of a single object:

> As adults we individuate and reidentify objects by using both place and trajectory information and static-property information. We also use property information to predict and explain appearances and disappearances. If the same large, distinctive white rabbit appears in the box and later in the hat, I assume it's the same rabbit, even if I don't immediately see a path of movement for it. In fact, I infer an often quite complex invisible path for the object. If I see the green scarf turn into a bunch of flowers as it passes through the conjuror's hand while maintaining its trajectory, I assume it is a different object. On the other hand, if an object changes its trajectory, even in a very complex way, while maintaining its properties, I will assume it is still the same object. (Gopnik and Meltzoff 1997, 86)

This example shows that it is a matter of some delicacy to characterize exactly what object-property the infants are tracking. They are not tracking the object-property of following a single, continuous trajectory through space-time. Rather they are tracking a deviant object-property of spatiotemporal continuity that can be best identified through its associated higher-order physical principle, namely, that everything following a single trajectory through space-time is a continuously existing body. This is in contrast to the higher-order physical principle associated with the canonical object-property of spatiotemporal continuity, which is that all continuously existing bodies follow a single trajectory through space-time.

In the example just considered there is a canonical object-property on which the deviant object-property can be modelled. The difference between them is essentially one of direction of entailment. But there are more extreme examples of deviant object-properties elsewhere in the animal kingdom, where one might expect to find an almost complete divergence from canonical object-properties. Some of these will be a function of radically different sensory modalities—echolocation in bats and dolphins, for example, or electric field sensitivity in various species of freshwater and marine fishes or magnetic field sensitivity in pigeons. Others will be a function of the different weightings between sensory modalities that hold for other species. The overwhelming importance of olfaction in the cognition of canines and rodents is a case in point. Different species have evolved to be sensitive to different types of information, and there is serious work to be done identifying the relevant types of object-properties in a way that will allow us to move toward an understanding of their ontology.

Most approaches to studying object representation in nonhuman animals have understandably been based on search- and behavior-based criteria. An elegant experiment recently carried out by Marc Hauser and collaborators (2001) has offered very suggestive evidence that cotton-top tamarins have a "gravity bias" analogous to that of 2.5- to 3-year-old human infants—that is to say, they expect objects to fall down in a straight line irrespective of their trajectory. An adult cotton-top tamarin was presented with an opaque S-shaped tube arranged so that the bottom opening was significantly horizontally displaced from the top opening and with a box directly beneath each opening. The experiment was to drop an object down the tube in order to see where the monkey would search for it. It turned out that the monkey consistently searched in the box beneath the top opening (the entry point) rather than that beneath the bottom opening (the exit point)—even immediately after having seen the experiment carried out with a transparent rather than an opaque tube. When the tube is transparent the monkey searches in the correct box (presumably because it has been able visually to track the object as it falls through the tube), but as soon as the opaque tube is reinstated the original behavior reappears.

A different set of experiments has illustrated that rhesus monkeys possess this gravity bias to an extent that overrides sensitivity to the object-properties of solidity and impenetrability (Hauser 2001). In these experiments rhesus monkeys are placed in front of a table with two boxes, one of which is on top of the table and the other below it (see fig. 4.3, step 1). The setup of boxes and table is hidden by an occluder (as in step 2) and a food reward is dropped behind the occluder. The aim of the experiment is to see where the monkey searches for the food. The food reward has of course ended up in the top box, but it turns out that rhesus monkeys almost invariably search in the lower box—even though to have ended up in that box the food reward would have had to pass through both the upper box and the table-top.[4]

There is considerable scope for applying the dishabituation paradigm to nonlinguistic creatures. Steps have already been taken toward using preferential looking time to tap into the perceptual expectations of free-ranging rhesus monkeys. Munakata and collaborators (including Elizabeth Spelke) have explored the expectations that rhesus monkeys have about object motion. It turns out (Munakata et al. 2001) that monkeys appear to be more surprised by distinct objects moving together than they are by distinct objects moving conjointly. Just like human infants, they do not amalgamate together objects between which they can see a spatial gap, even when those objects are moving together.

Another potential model for sensitivity to object-properties in nonhuman animals is provided by research into the visual discriminatory abilities of pigeons using the familiar paradigm of conditioning to color slides containing a variety of visual scenes (see Walker 1983, 254–266, for a brief survey). It has been found

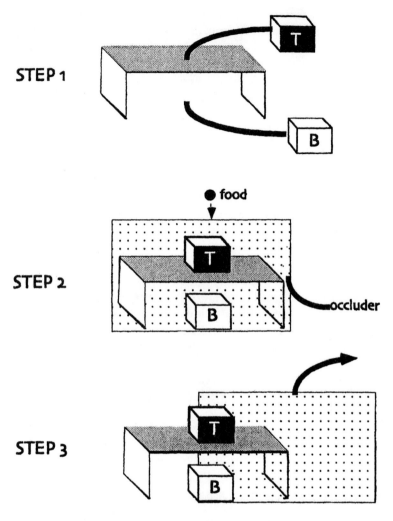

Figure 4.3 A schematic depiction of an experimental paradigm testing gravity bias in rhesus monkeys. Reproduced by kind permission from Hauser 2001, 86.

that pigeons are able to distinguish scenes containing people from scenes not containing people (Herrnstein and Loveland 1964); scenes with a particular individual from scenes without that individual (Herrnstein, Loveland, and Cable 1976); scenes with trees from those without trees (Cerella 1979); scenes with pigeons from scenes with other birds (Poole and Lander 1971). It would be interesting to investigate whether these experimental techniques might be adapted to plot discriminatory abilities at the level of object-properties.

It is useful to draw a parallel with what Thomas Nagel termed *objective phenomenology* in his well-known article "What is it like to be a bat?" Philosophical attention has focused on the negative claims that Nagel makes in that article—claims about the inadequacy of science for explaining conscious experience, whether our own or that of other species, "from the inside"—neglecting the positive suggestions that he makes about the possibility of delineating the general structural features of experience in a way that will allow them to be scientifically illuminated.

> At present we are completely unequipped to think about the subjective character of experience without relying on the imagination—without taking up the point of view of the experiential subject. This should be regarded as a challenge to form new concepts and devise a new method—an objective phenomenology not dependent on empathy or the imagination. Though presumably it would not capture everything, its goal would be to describe, at least in part, the subjective character of experiences in a form comprehensible to beings incapable of having those experiences. (Nagel 1979, 178–179)

Objective phenomenology is not concerned with the individual what-it-is-likeness of experience, but rather with the general structure of experience shared by members of a given species at a particular stage of development.

The strategy I am proposing in this chapter provides a concrete way of implementing Nagel's proposal in this passage. Nagel calls for a way of understanding how things are from a creature's point of view that does not depend on being able to imagine how things are from that perspective. One way (the only way?) of doing this is to work out the object-properties to which a creature is perceptually sensitive. The developmental psychological work on object perception gives us an insight into how the world is experienced from the infant's point of view, but it neither depends on nor brings us one iota closer to an understanding of what it is like to be a 6-month-old human infant. The same point holds with even more force in the case of creatures that are far more exotic relative to adult language-using humans than young infants are. We can, I think, get some sort of a grip on the object-properties to which dolphins are sensitive, even though we will never be able to imagine what it is like to be a creature that navigates the world primarily through echolocation. To take a simple example, it is known that harbor porpoises (*Phocaena phocaena*) and Amazon river dolphins (*Inia geoffrensis*) can avoid submerged wires that are only 1 mm in diameter (Evans 1973). Clearly some sort of sensitivity to the object-properties of impenetrability and determinate shape is implicated here. Further research will no doubt be able to tell us more.

Ascribing Thoughts to
Nonlinguistic Creatures
Modes of Presentation

There is a problem of indeterminacy in ascribing thoughts to nonlinguistic creatures. There seem in any given situation to be indefinitely many different thoughts that could be attributed to the nonlinguistic agent. How are we to narrow them down to get either a unique content-ascription or, more plausibly, the sort of localized indeterminacy that is perfectly permissible in our normal interactions with other linguistic creatures? According to the approach I have adopted, the content of a belief is determined by its utility condition, where a utility condition is a state of affairs in the distal environment. But there are indefinitely many different ways in which that utility condition can be described. Which description should we take as the correct specification of the content of the belief? The problem of "narrowing down" has several dimensions. One problem derives from ontological indeterminacy. This was discussed in the previous chapter, where I showed how we might go about attributing different ontologies to different categories of nonlinguistic creature. The proposal that has emerged is that we can make progress calibrating a creature's ontology in terms of the particular set of higher-order physical principles that it takes to govern the behavior of bodies to which it is perceptually sensitive. This gives us the resources with which to start narrowing down the range of possible content specifications.

Determining an ontology, however, can be no more than the first stage in resolving the problem of indeterminacy. At several points in this book I have emphasized the importance of distinguishing the level of sense from the level of reference. At the level of reference a utility condition is essentially a state of affairs. A single state of affairs can be apprehended by a creature in many different ways, and in order to explain how its representations of the environment cause it to behave in the way it does, we must specify not simply the state of affairs it is representing but also how it apprehends that state of affairs. Success semantics, as so far formulated, offers us no way of choosing between the different modes of presentations under which a single state of affairs can be apprehended. If all we have to go on is the idea that a belief is a function from desires to actions that tends to ensure the satisfaction of desires with which it is associated, the best that success semantics can offer us is a range of sentences reflecting the different ways that single state of affairs might be apprehended. If we are to use success semantics as a tool to capture the content of nonlinguistic thoughts, it needs to provide us with a single sentence—a sentence that gives the determinate content of the belief in question.[1] The question, therefore, is: How are we to go about eliminating those sentences that do not correctly specify the mode of presentation under which the utility condition is apprehended?

I shall term this the *mode of presentation problem*. This is, in effect, the problem of explaining how we can give a canonical specification of a utility condition, where a canonical description is one that reflects the way the utility condition is apprehended by the creature in question. Such a canonical specification will be a specification of a complete thought. The simplest type of thought is one that can be specified in an atomic sentence. We can term this an atomic thought. It is a thought to the effect that a certain individual (relative to a particular ontology) has a certain property. In the case of atomic thoughts there will be two aspects to the canonical specification of the utility condition, corresponding to the nominative and predicative thought-constituents. Correspondingly, there will be two dimensions to the mode of presentation problem. The first dimension is specifying a notion of mode of presentation that can be deployed in giving the nominative element of a thought-ascription—that is, to spell out what it is for a nonlinguistic creature to apprehend a reified particular under one mode of presentation rather than another. This is the topic of section 5.1. The second dimension of the mode of presentation problem is explaining how the notion of a mode of presentation might be applied in the predicative element of a thought-ascription—that is to say, how a given property can be apprehended in different ways. This is explored in section 5.2. In the final section of the chapter I provide an overview of how success semantics can be deployed to make sense of the attribution of thoughts to nonlinguistic creatures.

5.1   Individuals, Modes of Presentation, and the Sortal Problem

The utility condition of a belief is a state of affairs construable in purely extensional terms. It can be adequately specified even though it does not reflect the organism's perspective on the world. Yet, although the extensional utility conditions of a belief might be what secures the satisfaction of the desires with which that belief is associated, we cannot understand why a creature acts the way it does, or predict how it will act, simply with reference to a purely extensional utility condition. The notion of a belief's utility condition has two roles. On the one hand it has to be such that true beliefs will cause actions that satisfy desires. For this the purely extensional notion will do. On the other hand, it has to explain why the believer acted the way it did (or to predict the way the believer will act). And for this a purely extensional characterization will not suffice. It is clear that a creature might see an object one way and not be impelled to act, whereas seeing it in a different way leads immediately to action. The same animal can be seen as a threat or not. A water hole might be an affordance of water at one time of day and an affordance of danger at another. Different actions will be appropriate to different ways of apprehending the animal or water hole.

Authors who have proposed versions of success semantics have tended not to address this problem. We can take Robert Stalnaker, whose version of success semantics (1987) is put forward with particular reference to the scope it offers for explaining the behavior of nonlinguistic creatures, as a stalking horse. Here is Stalnaker's account of desire and belief

> To desire that p is to be disposed to act in ways that would tend to bring it about that p in a world in which one's beliefs, whatever they are, are true. To believe that p is to be disposed to act in ways that would tend to satisfy one's desires, whatever they are, in a world in which p (together with one's other beliefs) were true. (1987, 15)

Stalnaker's comments elsewhere in the chapter make clear that he is not adopting a purely dispositionalist, or behaviorist, account of belief and desire. Beliefs and desires are the internal states, whatever they might be, that cause the appropriate type of actions. So, for Stalnaker, as for the version of success semantics spelled out in the previous chapter, true beliefs cause actions that satisfy desires, and desires cause actions, which are successful when beliefs are true.

Stalnaker's version of success semantics is linked to a particular version of possible worlds semantics. In straightforward possible world semantics the content of a belief is given by the possible situations in which it is true, so that the contents of beliefs are functions from possible worlds to truth-values. In the success semantics version, the content of a belief is given in terms of the possible situations in which the relevant desires with which it is conjoined are satisfied. This will be its utility condition. In psychological explanation, therefore, specifying the content of a belief is specifying the range of possible situations that collectively make up the utility condition of the belief. But Stalnaker is explicit that, in specifying this utility condition, we do not need to make any reference to how that utility condition is apprehended by the creature whose behavior we are trying to explain:

> It is essential to rational activities such as deliberation and investigation that the participants represent alternative possibilities, and it is essential to the role of beliefs and desires in the explanation of action that the contents of those attitudes distinguish between the alternative possibilities. The particular ways in which alternative possibilities are represented, or the particular means by which distinctions between them are made, are not essential to such activities and explanations, even if it is essential that the possibilities be represented, and the distinctions be made, in some way or other. (Stalnaker 1987, 23)

It is a crucial element in Stalnaker's possible worlds approach to propositional attitude explanation that we as theorists should distinguish between the nature of a proposition and the way that proposition is determined. So, what makes it the case that a particular set S of possible situations is the utility condition for a belief is that the believer is somehow capable of representing the set of relevant possible situations (which need not, of course, be all the situations that *could* arise) and dividing that set into two parts, one of which corresponds to S. Stalnaker is clear that there is some psychological story to be told about how the set of possible outcomes is partitioned into the two subsets that jointly determine the utility condition. He is equally clear, however, that the psychological mechanisms that will be appealed to in explaining how this partitioning takes place do not form part of the belief. The belief is simply a function from possible states of the world to truth-values.

In fact, Stalnaker maintains that this (broadly speaking) extensional approach to belief-content yields particular advantages for psychological explanations of the behavior of nonlinguistic creatures. It allows it to be the case, for example, that two creatures with wildly differing conceptual repertoires could entertain the same proposition, provided that, for some limited subset of the total possible ways in which things could turn out, they both partition that subset in the same way. There is no requirement that they partition the subset in the same way *for the same reasons*. And this means that we can deploy our own highly complex language and the conceptual scheme that goes with it to characterize the beliefs of creatures whose cognitive perspective on the world might be vastly more primitive than our own:

> When we ascribe attitudes to an animal, what we presuppose is simply that it has *some* mechanism for representing and distinguishing between alternative situations. It may be a very crude one, recognizing only gross differences, and containing no representation at all of possible situations radically different from the way things are. The conceptual space necessary to account for its capacities and dispositions might consist of just a few relevantly different "ways things might be." But *our* language, with its complex structure and capacity to make more subtle discriminations and describe more distant possibilities, may be used to distinguish between the few alternative possibilities represented by the dog without thereby attributing our concepts to it. Because propositions do not mirror the structure of sentences that express them, it is possible to use sophisticated, semantically complex sentences to ascribe attitudes to creatures with very limited cognitive capacities. (Stalnaker 1987, 63)

There are clear advantages to understanding belief-contents in the way that Stalnaker understands them. If we follow him in sharply distinguishing the nature of the proposition from the way it is determined then we may well succeed in closing the gap between the beliefs of language-using creatures and the beliefs of non-language-using creatures (particularly if one follows him in holding that identity of belief-content can be determined relative to a particular set of possible worlds, rather than relative to all possible worlds).

But there is a price to pay. The notion of belief-content thus obtained is no longer a powerful tool for psychological explanation. What is psychologically motivating, what feeds directly into action (hence what needs to be identified if action is to be explained) is more likely to be found at the level at which a particular proposition is determined, rather than at the level of the proposition itself. What makes it the case that I act on the basis of my belief (in the light of my desires) is that I have a way of categorizing the relevant class of possible situations that allows me to go about working out whether or not the actual situation falls into that class. Suppose we want to explain why the gazelle acts on its belief that all lions are dangerous in a given situation. It will not be sufficient to say that the gazelle is related to a proposition that divides a range of possible situations up so that none of them contain a lion without that lion being dangerous. It might well be the case both that the gazelle is related to that set of possible situations and that the situation confronting it falls within the set without the gazelle acting appropriately. The gazelle will only act if (to put it in Stalnaker's terms) its general belief is such as to allow it to identify the situation it perceives as falling within the range of possible situations. And this is a matter of how the general belief is determined, rather than of its content. It is a function of how the gazelle represents lions and how it discriminates situations in which lions occur from those in which they are absent—and of course of how it represents danger and discriminates situations that are dangerous from those that are not.

It would seem, therefore, that our version of success semantics needs to be further supplemented by showing how it can capture the mode of presentation under which utility and satisfaction conditions are apprehended. The first stage in expanding success semantics in this direction is to explain what it might be for a non-linguistic creature to apprehend an object in a particular way. The ontological issues discussed in the previous chapter go some way toward addressing this issue. Part of what it is to apprehend an object is to apprehend it as something that obeys certain basic physical principles, and this, as I showed earlier, can be understood at least in part in terms of perceptual expectations about how that object might behave. So spelling out the particular ontology in terms of which a nonlinguistic creature carves up the world goes *some* way toward resolving the first dimension of the mode of presentation problem.

There is a problem here, however. Part of what it is to apprehend an object in a particular way is that it should be apprehended as a member of a particular category—that it should be apprehended as falling under a particular sortal. Yet it is hard to see how the ontological considerations broached in the previous chapter fully address this issue. The proposal that the object-properties to which nonlinguistic creatures are perceptually sensitive determines the way they carve up the world is directly analogous to saying that we carve the world up into objects (the difference consisting, of course, in the range of object-properties to which we are sensitive). And, while it is true that we do carve the world up into objects, it might be argued that this is an artifact of certain other principles of organization and classification rather than a bottom-level fact about our experience of the world. So, for example, it might be suggested that the concept *object* is simply not a sortal concept and hence does not give us a way of carving up the world at all. Part of what it is for something to be a sortal concept is that it should provide criteria for individuating and counting the number of objects falling under that sortal at a given moment. So anybody competent with the concept *chair* might be expected to have the resources to count the number of chairs present in a room. Yet it is often suggested that the concept *object* is not like that at all (Wiggins 1997). It is impossible to count the number of objects in a room until we know what is to count as an object, and we will not be in a position to know that until we have more determinate sortal concepts in play. The concept *object*, on this view, is no more than a pseudosortal. So, a fortiori, the nonlinguistic equivalent of the concept *object* (that is to say, the way of carving up the perceived environment determined by the range of object-properties to which a creature is perceptually sensitive) cannot function in anything like the manner of a sortal concept either. So we have not in fact got any closer at all to making progress on the mode of presentation problem.

There are several points here. First, it is clear that some sort of principle of individuation and counting is required if we are to speak of the apprehension of particulars at all. That is one of the principal differences between the feature-placing level of experience and the particular-involving level of experience. So if the argument is to be faulted, the faults must lie elsewhere. The problem comes, I think, with the argument that the machinery of object-properties does not provide us with criteria for counting and individuation. It is just false that it is indeterminate how many objects there are in a room—or rather that there is any radical indeterminacy that cannot be resolved in a principled way, depending on the requirements of the particular situation. The qualification is important. Consider a lamp—an artifact often mentioned in this context. Is a lamp a simple object? Or should we rather view it as a complex object composed of a stand, an electric bulb, and a lampshade? It is likely that there is no fixed answer. In some contexts one will answer one way and in others the second way. Everything depends on which object-properties are more salient in a particular context. It is clear, for example, that if following a single continuous path through space-time is the salient object-property then the lamp will count as a simple object. If, on the other hand, internal homogeneity and internal unification are the salient object-properties then one might well wish to view it as a composite object composed of three simple objects. And it is easy to imagine contexts in which one object-property would be more salient than another. So, for example, if one is preparing an inventory of the house to give to the movers, it is likely that spatiotemporal continuity would be dominant. After all, what matters is that the lamp should turn up at the end of the move, not that its three components should. But if, on the other hand, one is a lamp designer trying to perfect a lamp design and entertaining the possibility of a different combination of base and stand, it is natural to think that the lamp would be classified as a complex object and that the emphasis would be on coordinating the separate components.

The issue here is really one about the relations between parts and wholes. What in one context will be treated as parts of a single object will in other contexts emerge as objects in their own right—and, of course, vice versa. Many cases of alleged indeterminacy are ones in which we are unsure how to count objects with detachable parts. But this is properly described as context-dependence rather than indeterminacy. The appearance of indeterminacy comes about in part because, when we are invited to imagine ourselves, say, counting the objects in a room, not enough of the context is filled in for us to have a handle on how the part-versus-whole issue is to be resolved. Moreover, a form of fallacious thinking (what we might call the subtraction fallacy) increases the appearance of indeterminacy. Some objects are such that it is clear that, if a part of them is removed, one will still be left with an object. So, for example, if I remove a painting from its frame, I am left with the frame, which is, of course, an object. It would be wrong to conclude from this that it makes sense to suppose that there were two objects occupying the space on the wall where the framed painting used to hang.[2] In most contexts it would be more appropriate to think that there was one object that could come apart into two parts, each of which could in certain circumstances properly be considered an object (although neither would be identical to the original object). But, of course, if one did think that the framed painting could count as two objects, then it would be much easier to think that there would be unavoidable indeterminacy when one sets about counting the number of objects in a room.

One would expect, then, that just as the concept *object* can function in many cases as a sortal concept that would permit individuation and counting, so too can the nonlinguistic analogue of the concept *object* (that is, the implicit ontology determined by the range of object-properties to which a creature is perceptually sensitive). Nonetheless, perceptual sensitivity to a given range of object-properties is not *sufficient* to explain the particular manner in which an object is apprehended by a creature. The most primitive form of categorization is grounded in perceived similarity. Seeing an object in a particular manner (under a particular mode of presentation) is in large part a matter of seeing similarities between it and other objects. And so for a creature to apprehend an object under a particular mode of presentation is both a matter of apprehending it relative to a particular ontology (as determined by the basic processes of reification and carving up the perceived environment into discrete units obeying certain high-level physical principles) and a matter of perceiving similarities between that object and other objects.

The notion of perceived similarity here is being understood in a broad sense, to include both featural similarity and higher-level similarities of the sort that might best be captured through the concepts of instrumental properties and affordances (as discussed in chapter 3). So, for example, a nonlinguistic creature might identify a conspecific on, broadly speaking, featural grounds—that is to say, as falling within a class of creatures sharing a common set of immediately perceptible physical properties, which might be detectable in a range of different modalities. On the other hand it might be sensitive to similarities that run counter to such immediately perceptible featural similarities. Things that have no little or no immediately salient featural similarities can nonetheless resemble each other in respect of being potential prey—or for that matter potential predators. Part of what it is for a non-linguistic creature to apprehend something as a predator (under the *predator* mode of presentation) is that it should be sensitive to similarities between that thing and other potential predators, similarities that can at best only be mediately perceived. Sensitivity to these mediately perceptible similarities will manifest itself in sameness of behavioral response, so that things that are perceived under the same mode of presentation will elicit the same types of response (in appropriate contexts).

And, of course, from the third-person perspective of the ethologist or developmental psychologist, similarity of behavioral response is the principal clue to identifying the mode of presentation under which a particular object is apprehended. But it is the fact that things of a certain type (relative to the perceiver) are perceived under the same mode of presentation that grounds this sameness of response, rather than the sameness of response constituting their being perceived under the same mode of presentation.

To draw the strands of this section together, the idea of apprehending individuals under particular modes of presentation is applicable to nonlinguistic creatures to the extent that they apprehend reified individual as *objects** of certain types. The object* locution is intended to serve as a place-holder, to do justice to the fact that different types of nonlinguistic creature will carve their environment up in different ways as a function of being perceptually sensitive to different object-properties. The essence of perception under a particular mode of presentation comes because different nonlinguistic creatures will perceive different types of similarity between these objects*. Any object* can stand in a range of similarity relations, correlated with properties that are both mediately and immediately perceivable. Different such properties will be salient for a given creature at different times, or for different creatures at a given time. As a consequence, a creature will be capable of acting in different ways vis-à-vis a given object at different times, and different creatures will be capable of acting differently toward the same object at the same time. The particular way a nonlinguistic creature acts will be a function of the particular similarity-based mode of presentation that dominates at that moment. Incorporating this understanding of mode of presentation into the way we specify utility conditions brings us closer to meeting the requirements of psychological explanation. The next step is to extend the notion of mode of presentation from the apprehension of objects to the apprehension of properties, thus making available the idea of a complete utility condition being apprehended under a given mode of presentation.

5.2   Structured Thoughts and Psychological Explanation

In discussing the minimalist approach to nonlinguistic thought in chapter 3 I showed that the practice of giving psychological explanations of the behavior of nonlinguistic creatures rests crucially on those thoughts being structured. Psychological explanations can only be predictively useful and genuinely explanatory if the thoughts that they involve are composed of distinguishable thought-constituents that can feature in further thoughts. Integral to genuine explanations are predictions about how the agent would behave in relevantly similar situations, under the guiding assumption that there are significant constancies in the way the agent represents the environment across these situations. An animal will continue to pursue the same goal when it encounters it in two different environments if and only if it recognizes it—recognition that is reflected in the fact that there is a single content-constituent across the two cases. Nor, of course, do representational constancies hold simply across perceptual states. They are required if instrumental beliefs are to be anchored in perceptions of the environment, as well as providing links between motivational states and perceptual-doxastic states. Behavioral constancies and representational constancies go hand in hand. But the availability of these representational constancies is dependent on the existence of structured thoughts. The key epistemological question for the theorist of nonlinguistic thought is how one goes about attributing such structured thoughts.

The discussion in the previous section took us part of the way toward answering this question by illustrating what it might be for a nonlinguistic creature to apprehend particular objects* under distinct modes of presentation. But, although discussions of the notion of sense and mode of presentation in the context of natural language have tended to concentrate on proper names, it is clear that we will not have the materials for understanding the machinery of complete thoughts unless the notion of mode of presentation can be applied to the apprehension of properties—and hence can feature in the predicative component of a thought. In this section I will explore how this might be achieved, by working in some detail through an example of how a theorist trying to apply success semantics to explain a particular behavior might resolve a particular type of indeterminacy arising primarily with respect to the predicative component of a thought.

Let us imagine, then, an animal behaviorist or a cognitive ethologist faced with a particular action that she is trying to explain. Discussion in earlier chapters has shown how such a person might begin. We can assume that the observer has established that the behavior is indeed one that requires psychological explanation. The behavior displays an appropriate degree of flexibility of response to the immediate environment and does not seem to be an instance of a fixed behavior pattern, or the result of a straightforward pattern of instrumental conditioning. The first step would be to work out what goal the animal was pursuing when it acted the way it did. Was the animal foraging, pursuing a mate, look for a nest location, escaping a predator? Once the goal has been identified with reasonable confidence, the next step is to identify the relevant utility condition—the state of affairs whose holding would, in normal circumstances, bring about the satisfaction of the relevant motivational state. The utility condition, of course, may or may not actually hold, depending on whether the action is or is not successful. It is no use, however, describing this utility condition relative to our own conceptual scheme. It needs to be described in a way that reflects how it is apprehended by the creature in question.

Let us suppose that we have a range of possible content-ascriptions for our candidate behavior—content ascriptions reflecting what we know of the agent's ontology. These content-ascriptions are, of course, different descriptions of the relevant utility condition. The variation between them will not be at the level of the individual objects* that are picked out by the singular terms and common nouns. We can expect these to remain constant across the different descriptions. Let us suppose also that we have some understanding, along the lines suggested in the previous section, of the particular mode of presentation under which those objects* are being apprehended. In order to move beyond this to select a canonical specification of the utility condition, we need a principled way both of identifying the properties that the creature represents these individuals as bearing, and/or the relations in which it represents them as standing, and of identifying the particular way it apprehends those properties and relations.

It is at this point that we must turn back to the considerations that lead us to the need to ascribe structured thoughts—and in particular the idea that behavioral constancies require representational constancies of the sort reflected by identical content-constituents featuring in a range of different thoughts. The key idea here is that the content-constituents that reflect the properties and relations apprehended by a creature must be *projectable*. They must be capable of performing genuine explanatory work when embedded in different thoughts operative in different contexts. How can this be determined?

I will describe the procedure in the abstract and then give a concrete example of how it might be applied. We will need to identify comparable sets of sentences describing the utility conditions for other behaviors salient to the target behavior—such as, for example, how the animal acts in different but structurally similar environments, or how it acts when the instrumental contingency between behavior and goal ceases to hold, or how it acts in similar situations when it no longer has the desire in question. If the original set of sentences describing our target behavior had n different predicative content constituents, then each set of sentences describing the utility conditions of salient behaviors must also have the same range of predicative components. Clearly, all members of the original set of sentences (which we can term the *target-set*) are possible candidates for the psychological explanation of the target behavior—more accurately, they specify the content of beliefs that could have caused the target behavior. However, the same does not hold for all members of the sets of sentences describing the utility conditions of salient behaviors (the *salient-sets*). Some of these sentences will quite simply not be appropriate for the behaviors with which they are matched. Let us assume, for simplicity's sake, that the sentences in the target-set and their equivalents in the salient-sets are atomic sentences and hence differ in only one content-constituent. This will, of course, be the predicative component (since, as mentioned earlier, we can assume constant singular terms and common nouns across the target-set and salient-sets). When we have a common content-constituent across a target-set and salient-set that is potentially explanatory of the target behavior but is not potentially explanatory of the salient behavior, we shall say that the content-constituent fails to project. Conversely, of course, content-constituents that project are ones that are common to the target-set and the potentially explanatory subset of a given salient-set.

In order to determine which of the descriptions of the utility condition of the target behavior captures how that state of affairs is apprehended by the agent, we look for the member of the target-set that has the most projectable content-constituent. That is to say, we look for the member of the target-set that has the greatest number of genuinely explanatory counterparts in the salient-sets. This will give us the mode of presentation of the relevant property or relation in virtue of giving the simplest and most powerful explanation of how the animal behaves.

For a simplified illustration of how this might work, suppose that our target behavior is a rat's success in retrieving food in a cross-shaped maze. The rat has succeeded in learning how to run the maze and retrieve the food. Applying our standard methodology, we begin by identifying the motivational state driving the rat's behavior. Pretty obviously this will be a desire for food—a goal-desire rather than a situation-desire, in my earlier terminology. The next step is to identify the utility condition of the accompanying belief. The desire for food is satisfied because the food is in the location in which it in fact is. I shall call this location P. The utility condition, therefore, is that there be food at location P. As far as the utility condition of the belief is concerned it is immaterial how this location is coded and described. Any frame of reference can be used to fix its location. Hence there will be a range of different sentences correctly describing that location by plotting it relative to different coordinate systems. These sentences will be atomic sentences, essentially attributing to the food the property of being at a particular location.[3] The sentences will differ only in their predicative components, and these differences will reflect different ways of coding the location of the food. Each different coding will reflect a difference at the level of sense, rather than at the level of reference. The actual spatial location of the food is constant, but there is a range of different ways that the rat might have grasped it. It is clear that we do not apprehend spatial locations *tout court*. We apprehend them relative to different frames of reference and coordinate systems. So too for the rat. The rat has learned how to navigate the maze and remembers the way through. Only one of the atomic sentences correctly captures the way the rat's memory codes the spatial location of the food. How are we to identify which sentence it is?

The rat might be coding the location of the food as the end-point of a particular series of bodily movements. That is, the rat might remember the particular set of movements that took it to the food originally. This would not, strictly speaking, be coding the location of the food in spatial terms at all, since there is no question of identifying coordinates relative to a frame of reference. It would, however, be the interpretation of the rat's behavior favored by hard-line behaviorists. There are further distinctions that might be made deriving from different ways that a sequence of movements might be apprehended—in terms of joint torques and muscle flexions and contractions, for example, as opposed to a succession of individual movement end-points. We can put these to one side.

Suppose, on the other hand, that the rat does code the location as a place defined by its geometrical relations to other places. In this case there are different coordinate systems it might be employing. It might, for example, be employing a coordinate system based on an egocentric frame of reference whose origin is given by its own bodily position when it originally began to run the maze. So it might fix the location of the food using egocentric spatial predicates such as "to my right," "in front of me," and so forth. This type of coordinate system is similar to the coding of spatial location in terms of a chained sequence of bodily movements in at least the following sense. However the maze is moved relative to the environment, the coded spatial location of the food within the maze will remain constant relative to the rat's starting point. Nonetheless, one would expect the two ways of coding to lead to different behaviors if, for example, some of the spatial distances involved were changed. Consider a very simple cross-shaped maze, and suppose that the food is hidden in the eastern branch while the rat starts from the end of the southern branch. Would a rat that has learned to retrieve food in this maze be able to retrieve food hidden in the same maze location in another cross-shaped maze in which the southern branch happened to be twice as long? It seems likely that if the rat were coding in terms of a sequence of bodily movements, it would not succeed. Repeating the sequence of bodily movements will not get it to the food, since those movements would take it only halfway up the southern branch. This would not hold, however, for a rat that had coded the requisite lefthand turn at the end of the southern branch in a body-relative coordinate system. The actual distance to be traveled down the branch is of secondary importance on the egocentric system in comparison with the body-relative direction of the turn at the end of the branch.

If the rat is not using an egocentric coordinate system and is not coding the location in terms of a chained series of movements then it must be employing an allocentric frame of reference, a frame of reference centered on fixed points in the environment rather than on its own body. There seem to be two types of allocentric coordinate systems it might be employing. It might be employing a coordinate system centered on points external to the maze that can be seen from within the maze. Or it might be employing a coordinate system centered on points internal to the maze. The first, but not the second, allows the coded spatial location of the food to vary with certain movements of the maze relative to the extramaze environment. Both coordinate systems differ from the first two ways of coding spatial location by allowing the coded spatial location of the food relative to the rat to remain constant when the rat's starting position is changed. If the rat codes the location of the food relative to, say a light bulb hanging over the section of the maze where the food is, then it will still be able to find the food when it starts from a different part of the maze. The same can hold if the rat has coded the location of the food relative to a set of landmarks within the maze. In contrast, if the rat's spatial coding takes the form either of a chained sequence of bodily movements or of a body-centered coordinate system then changing the starting point of the maze will render it incapable of returning to the location where it originally found the food.

The difference between these four different ways of understanding the predicative component of the thought should be understood at the level of sense. At the level of reference there is just one property—namely, the property of being located at the relevant point in space.[4] The utility condition of the belief (that is, the state of affairs whose holding would secure the satisfaction of the rat's hunger) is the state of affairs of the food's being located at that particular place (having the property of being located at that particular place). The four different possible frames of reference in terms of which the location of the food can be coded by the rat in the maze represent four different modes of presentation under which the rat can apprehend the property of an object's being located at that place. The point here is that thinkers and agents can only think about and act on points in space relative to a frame of reference on which they are able to locate themselves.[5] A location needs to be represented in a way that will allow the agent to act relative to that location. Descriptively adequate and predictively powerful psychological explanations need to take account of the particular frame of reference employed by the thinking agent whose behavior is being explained.

At the level of sense, therefore, there are four different ways of apprehending the property of being located at that particular place—the property such that the fact that it holds of the food determines the utility condition of the belief.[6] This gives us four different candidate beliefs about the location of the food, roughly along the following lines:

(1a) Food is located at the end-point of movements $M_1 \ldots n$
(1b) Food is located at coordinates (x, y) in egocentric space
(1c) Food is located at coordinates (x', y') in maze space
(1d) Food is located at coordinates (x'', y'') in environmental space

We can break these four down to yield four possible content-constituents, corresponding to the following four relational predicates:

(a') ``—located at the end-point of movements—''
(b') ``—located at egocentric coordinates (x, y)—''
(c') ``—located at maze coordinates (x', y')—''
(d') ``—located at environmental coordinates (x'', y'')—''

The simple behavior of the rat in the cross-shaped maze is neutral between all four descriptions. The rat that learns to run the maze and successfully retrieves the food when placed at the beginning of the maze could be employing any one of these different ways of coding the location of the food.

If we are to discriminate between them, we need to manipulate the parameters to try to find out which specifications of the utility condition are suitably projectable, in the sense discussed earlier. We need to identify a further set of navigation behaviors (what I earlier termed salient behaviors) that modify some of the relevant parameters in a way that will discriminate between the different ways that the rat might be apprehending spatial location. The guiding assumption here, of course, is that the rat will employ the same general means of coding the location of the food in the salient behaviors as in the target behavior. This seems plausible, and allows us to capitalize on the fact that each sentence in the target-set generates different predictions about how the rat will behave if, once it has learned to run the maze, it is then placed in a differently configured maze. According to the chained motor program interpretation, corresponding to sentence (1a) and content-constituent (a'), the rat will make the same series of movements that had taken it to the food in the original maze. According to the egocentric coordinates interpretation, as reflected in sentence (1b) in the target-set and corresponding content-constituent (b'), the rat will move to the same position relative to its starting-point as in the original maze. The maze space view—in sentence (1c) and content-constituent (c')—predicts that the rat will go to the same position in maze space, while the environmental space view—(1d) and (d')—predicts that the rat will go to the same position in environmental space.

What we need to do, therefore, is modify the maze in a way that will generate a series of further salient behaviors and allow us to see which of the four content-constituents (a')–(d') is suitably projectable. There is, in fact, a relatively well understood experimental literature that can be interpreted as doing precisely that (Gallistel 1990). In the following I shall adopt a slight simplification in describing the experimental work on the coding of spatial location in rats. The experiments depend on comparing performance in different mazes. Performance can be calculated in terms of the number of trials required to learn how to run the maze—or as a function of the percentage of successful trials. It is essentially a statistical measure calculated on the performance of groups of rats, not always involving the same rats in different mazes. Some experiments involve training rats to run a particular maze and then either changing the configuration of the maze (by blocking some of the routes, for example, or by rotating the maze as a whole) or starting the rats off in a different section of the maze from the one they started from in the training runs. Other paradigms train groups of rats to run mazes in ways designed to draw on different ways of coding spatial location. In this second type of experiment what is important is the relative speed with which the respective groups of rats learn to run the maze. I shall describe the experiments, however, as if they involved simply training a single rat in one maze and observing its performance on a single trial in another maze—even though it is highly unlikely that any single rat has ever been run through the all of the mazes I am about to describe.

Recall that the behavior we are trying to explain is the successful performance of a rat in a cross-shaped maze. The rat starts in one of the four arms of the maze, while the food is located in a different arm. One obvious modification of the experimental setup would be to keep the location of the food constant while starting the rat from a different arm. This experiment was famously carried out by Tolman and collaborators in one of the first experiments to present a significant challenge to behaviorist theories of location coding. Their variation was to train the rat starting from one branch of the maze and then to observe how it behaved when started from the opposite branch of the maze (Tolman, Ritchie, and Kalish 1946). I shall term this the reversed start paradigm. As is well known, the rat successfully reached the goal. Clearly, the rat would not have succeeded had it been coding the location of the goal in terms of a chained motor program. Nor would it have succeeded if it had been coding the location of the food in egocentric behavioral space coordinates. Let us suppose that in the original maze the rat began from the southern arm, with the food reward located at the eastern arm. To obtain the reward the rat must turn to the right at the center of the cross. In the experimental situation, in contrast, the rat begins at the northern arm and to obtain the food has to make a left turn at the center of the cross. On both the motor program and behavioral space views, the rat would not turn left when coming from the north but would repeat the original right turn, ending up at the western arm. Both of these codings would have the rat making, from its own point of view, the same turn from the opposite branch of the maze as it did from the original branch, and this would place it in the wrong branch for the food.

In terms of our original candidate beliefs, the content constituents in (1a) and (1b) fail to project to the reversed start paradigm. This leaves us with the two remaining beliefs. So, the candidate beliefs here are as follows.

(2c) Food is located at maze coordinates (x', y')
(2d) Food is located at environmental coordinates (x'', y'')

The predicative component in each of these candidate beliefs does indeed project to the reversed start paradigm. We have already succeeded, therefore, in making a preliminary separation of our four original candidate content-constituents. Yet we still need to disambiguate between the two candidates that remain in play.

A further classic parameter variation is to alter the shape of the maze. So, instead of starting the rat off from the opposite point of a cross-shaped maze, one might train the rat in a T-shaped maze and then see how it performs when the maze is shifted 180° (Tolman, Ritchie, and Kalish 1947). Extrapolating from behavior in the cross-shaped maze, one might expect the rat to turn in the opposite direction to the training schedule in order to return to the same "place." But this is not what happens. The rats tend to make the same turn as in the training schedule. So it might be appropriate to think that the rats are merely repeating the same sequence of bodily movements. This supports the following.

(3a) Food is located at the end-point of movements $M_1 \ldots n$

They could also be returning to the same point in behavioral space, which supports:

(3b) Food is located at egocentric coordinates (x, y)

But it could of course be that the rats are returning to the same maze-location. Turning the maze around 180° does not alter any of the geometrical relations internal to the maze. This would support:

(3c) Food is located at maze coordinates (x', y')

The rats cannot, however, be returning to the same location in environmental space, because the geometrical relations between points within the maze and points outside the maze *are* altered by moving the maze 180°. In this third behavior, therefore, we have identified three projectable content-constituents.

For each of these behaviors we can, in our simplified paradigm, identify the possible content-constituents. We can plot them out and make a table as follows.

Behavior 1	(a)	(b)	(c)	(d)
Behavior 2			(c)	(d)
Behavior 3	(a)	(b)	(c)	

So, we have four possible ways of spelling out the utility condition of the rat's behavior in the first maze, depending on how we take the rat to be coding the location of the food. We assume that the rat's coding of the place where the food is located remains constant. As the table shows, there is only one way of spelling out the mode of presentation under which the rat is apprehending the target place that projects successfully across all three of the behaviors. We should conclude, therefore, that the rat is coding the location of the food within a coordinate system whose frame of reference is determined by fixed points within the space of the maze.

This gives us the resources to identify the content-ascription in the first behavior that projects in an explanatory way. The sentence expressing a thought containing content-constituent (c′) should be taken to express *the* determinate content because it allows the identification of a common content-constituent across the range of behaviors—and we need a common content-constituent because the relevant desires and cognitive background conditions remain constant across the behaviors.

Some caveats should be registered at this point. There is no reason to think that a rat will always code locations in the same way. It is well documented, for example, that rats can orient themselves in mazes by using nongeometric cues (Cheng 1986). Rats learn surprisingly quickly to run a radial maze in which the arms are randomly permuted between each trial, provided the arms are featurally highly distinct. Similarly, it seems that the salience of landmarks in the nonmaze environment affects whether rats code locations on a maze-centered or environment-centered frame of reference (see Cheng 1986, Gallistel 1990, ch. 6). The experimenter needs to ensure as close a match as possible between the target behavior and the experimentally induced salient behaviors. Only thus can genuine projectability be established.

Nonetheless, and bearing these caveats in mind, working through this example, in conjunction with the discussion in the previous section, shows how a theorist might go about resolving the inevitable indeterminacies generated by applying success semantics to a target behavior. These indeterminacies arise at the level of sense. They derive from the different ways a creature might apprehend a given utility condition. Success semantics alone cannot provide a determinate specification of a utility condition. At best it will leave us with a choice between different descriptions of the relevant state of affairs. Unless we break these descriptions down into separable content-constituents and consider which of those content-constituents are projectable in the manner described in this section, we will be unable to narrow the list of candidate beliefs down in the way required to respect the requirement that a psychological explanation reflect the way a creature apprehends its environment.

It should not be thought, however, that this type of disambiguation is possible only in a laboratory environment. I have concentrated on the example of experimental work on rat navigational abilities because it presents in particularly clear form the basic structure of the strategy to be adopted in specifying a utility condition at the level of sense. But there is no reason at all why a similar strategy should not be adopted in a more ecologically valid context to attribute beliefs to animals in the wild. What I am calling salient behaviors can be identified by observation.

Salient behaviors involve the variation of parameters, and this is of course possible without actively manipulating those parameters. Equally, it is likely in practice that mixed strategies can be profitably pursued, deploying research done in experimental contexts on conspecifics to guide the attribution of thoughts to animals in the wild. Indeed, it should be possible to deploy the salient behaviors of members of other species, either in captivity or in the wild—provided that due account is taken of the possibility that cross-species generalizations may be invalid.

5.3   Success Semantics and Nonlinguistic Thought: An Overview

The upshot of the discussion of minimalism in chapter 3 was that an important class of nonlinguistic behavior requires explanation in terms of propositional attitude psychology. The types of nonpropositional thinking explored by different forms of the minimalist approach cannot explain all types of nonlinguistic behavior. In this context, then, it is important to stress that success semantics is intended to provide a means of extending propositional attitude psychology to nonlinguistic creatures. It is proposed as a way of attributing beliefs and desires in the absence of language, and as such, of course, it needs to satisfy the basic desiderata that hold for any theory of propositional thinking, as opposed to the more imagistic and nonpropositional types of thinking discussed in the context of the minimalist conception in chapter 4. I considered four such desiderata in 3.2.

> Propositional thinking involves a sharp distinction between attitude and content—between the particular proposition that is the object of one's mental state and the mental attitude one takes toward it.

> Propositions must be independent of the particular context of thinking. A theory of propositional thinking must make it possible for a thinker to have, for example, mistaken beliefs and to entertain a thought without knowing its truth-value.

> For any propositional attitude, it should in principle be possible to find a sentence that will specify the content of the attitude accurately and without remainder.

> The contents of propositional attitudes have a structure that permits them to feature in inference and that is in some sense isomorphic to one way of apprehending the structure of the state of affairs that that content represents.

It will be helpful to use these four characteristics of propositional thinking to structure an overview of success semantics.

Success semantics, unlike the two models of propositional thinking considered in chapter 2, is driven primarily by the relation between thinking and behavior. As such it can be viewed as a form of philosophical functionalism.[7] Beliefs, according to success semantics, are causal functions from desires to actions. The content of a belief is its utility condition, where a utility condition is the state of affairs whose holding would result in the satisfaction of desires with which that belief is associated. True beliefs are such as to cause actions that satisfy desires. Clearly, desires cannot on pain of circularity be understood as functions from true beliefs to actions, and success semantics has a different account of the content of desires. A particular desire has the content that it does in virtue of its satisfaction-condition, where the satisfaction-condition of a desire is the state of affairs whose holding leads to the cessation of the behavior to which the desire gives rise. The state of affairs has to be such, moreover, as to bring about the cessation of the relevant behavior in a manner that will make the creature more likely to pursue that behavior in the future.

Nonetheless, even though success semantics offers different accounts of the content of belief and the content of desire, it is able to satisfy the first two desiderata of a theory of propositional thinking. It is clearly the case that a creature can bear different attitudes to the same content, since a single state of affairs can be both the utility condition of a belief and the satisfaction-condition of a desire. Moreover, the accounts of what it is to have the attitude of belief to that state of affairs and the attitude of desire toward it are distinct, though related. As far as the second feature of propositional thinking is concerned, the thoughts attributed through success semantics are both susceptible to error and divorced from the immediate context of thinking. Whereas the minimalist approach to nonlinguistic thinking has difficulty explaining how there can be thoughts about states of affairs that are not in some sense part of the "here-and-now," success semantics faces no such restriction. The characterization of belief and desire is not in any sense context-bound or limited to states of affairs that can be mediately or immediately perceived. All that is required for a state of affairs to be the object of a belief or a desire, respectively, is that its holding should result either in the satisfaction of the desire(s) with which that belief is conjoined, or that it should be such as to extinguish in a reinforcing manner a particular pattern of behavior. There are no constraints of either spatial or temporal contiguity. Nor, of course, are beliefs guaranteed to be true or desires guaranteed to be satisfied. The satisfaction-condition of a desire is the state of affairs that *would* satisfy it, and the utility condition of a belief is the state of affairs that *would* result in the satisfaction of desires with which it is conjoined. Success semantics allows us to work backward from behavior to beliefs and desires without assuming that the behavior is always successful.

It would seem, then, that success semantics offers a way of understanding the propositional attitudes that respects the basic features of the distinction between content and attitude. As such it provides a response to some of the potential problems that emerged in the context of the Fregean conception of thoughts as the senses of sentences. It will be remembered that these problems were also addressed by the language of thought hypothesis. However, as I showed in chapter 2, the language of thought hypothesis has difficulties with the epistemological dimension of an account of thought. It provides no guidance on how we might go about attributing thoughts to nonlinguistic creatures in the context of psychological explanation. The discussion of success semantics in the previous two chapters should have brought out, in contrast, the extent to which success semantics provides not simply an account of the nature of propositional attitudes but also a practical framework for the attribution of those thoughts. Understanding the contents of beliefs in terms of utility conditions and the contents of desires in terms of satisfaction conditions clearly offers a way of working backward from behavior to the thoughts that gave rise to it, since the content of any given propositional attitude is determined by its behavioral ramifications. The constitutive account of what nonlinguistic thoughts are yields a method for identifying and attributing such thoughts.

However, there is a significant problem in applying the method of success semantics. The objection that is perhaps most frequently raised to the ascription of thoughts to nonlinguistic creatures, hence to the practices of psychological explanation within which such ascriptions take place, is that it is impossible to ascribe thoughts with suitably determinate contents (Davidson 1975). This is linked to the third and fourth features of propositional thinking identified earlier. Together these add up to the requirement that, for any propositional attitude, it should in principle be possible to find a sentence that will specify the content of the attitude accurately, without remainder and in a way that makes clear the structure of the thought and hence its potential inferential role. How are we to do this for success semantics? The guiding idea in success semantics is that the content of a belief is to be given in terms of the state of affairs that would bring about the satisfaction of desires with which it is associated. But there are indefinitely many ways that such a state of affairs can be characterized. How are we to identify the correct specification (or group of specifications)? This is the principal epistemological challenge confronting the theorist of nonlinguistic thought. Most of my discussion of success semantics has been devoted to showing how this epistemological challenge can be met.

In the previous chapter I considered the first stage in meeting this challenge—the stage of working out how the creature in question (or rather, the species and stage of development of which it is a representative) carves up the world in perception and thought. I suggested that this might be done by working out the higher-order physical principles to which the creature is sensitive, hence demarcating an ontology for the creature whose behavior one is trying to explain, interpret, or predict. I showed in chapter 4 that different species (and individuals at different stages of development within a given species) will *reify* the distal environment in different ways, where a reified environment is one that is parsed into clusters of features that the perceiver/thinker expects to behave in certain ways. We can, therefore, make a start on resolving the indeterminacy by identifying the expectations that the creatures will have about the behavior of bodies in its environment. This will allow us to have a much clearer sense of the vocabulary in terms of which thoughts should be attributed—and in particular, how the singular terms and common nouns in thought ascriptions should be understood.

This can be no more than the first stage, however, because it reflects only the way a particular type of creature carves up its environment. This ontology will, of course, be shared by all conspecifics at the appropriate stage of development. This is not enough for a resolution of the indeterminacy. Such a resolution will come only if we have a way of obtaining a canonical description of a utility condition, where a canonical description is one that reflects the way the utility condition is apprehended by the particular creature in question. Such a canonical description will be a specification of a complete thought, of the sort that can feature in psychological explanations of why that particular creature behaved the way it did in a particular context. A complete thought specified in this way will incorporate considerations of *cognitive significance*.

Let us assume that we are dealing with the simplest type of thought, namely, an atomic thought that can be specified in an atomic sentence. These are thoughts to the effect that a certain individual (relative to a particular ontology) has a certain property. In the case of an atomic thought, there will be two aspects to the canonical specification of the utility condition, corresponding to the nominative and predicative thought-constituents. The first will be a specification of how the individual in question is apprehended by the thinker—the mode of presentation in terms of which it is given. And the second will be a specification of the property that is being attributed to the individual. Once these two components have been specified, then we can properly be described as having provided a canonical specification of a utility condition.

As far as the nominative component of the structured thought is concerned, it is not enough simply to pick out an object (or what I termed an object*) in terms of its general ontological characteristics. In order to explain the role that propositional attitudes play in psychological explanation, we also need to specify the mode of presentation under which that individual is apprehended. The general ontological framework within which a creature experiences the world forms part of its perspective on the world, but it does not provide the full explanatory power of the notion of a mode of presentation. In particular, it does not help us to understand how two different creatures might react differently to the same situation, or how a single creature might react differently to the same situation at different times. We need some sort of analogue at the nonlinguistic level of the notion of cognitive significance as it features in psychological explanations of the behavior of language-using creatures. I suggested in section 5.1 that we could move toward resolving the mode of presentation problem by considering perceived similarities—in particular the similarities that a creature perceives between the individual in question and other individuals. The cognitive significance attached to an apprehended individual can be understood in terms of the similarity-classes within which that individual features. Different creatures will have different similarity-spaces, hence different ways of grouping things as, say, predators. Such perceived similarities (or, for that matter, failures to perceive similarities) will manifest themselves in behavior and are a crucial part of explaining what is distinctive in each individual creature's way of apprehending the world.

The notions of mode of presentation and cognitive significance are not only applicable to the nominative component of a thought, however. We also require some understanding of how we might go about determining how a given property can be apprehended in different ways—of how the notion of a mode of presentation might be applied to properties. The principal issue here is how we interpret the way a nonlinguistic creature apprehends the structure of a state of affairs. The strategy I propose for thinking about how this extension might be achieved picks up on a theme that has recurred at several points during this book—the interdependence between the possibility of psychological explanation and the ascription of structured thoughts. The guiding idea is that the description of a utility condition can be effected in different ways to yield a range of different predicative content-constituents—that reflect different ways that a creature might be apprehending the relevant properties in a state of affairs. The "correct" content-constituent is the one that best projects across an appropriate range of actual and counterfactual patterns of behavior. In the previous section I showed in some detail how this method might be applied to explain the particular mode of presentation under which a rat in a maze apprehends the property of being located at a particular place.

In terms of the overall project of providing a framework for understanding the practices of giving psychological explanations of the behavior of nonlinguistic creatures, I have reached the following position. The discussion of the minimalist account in chapter 3 pointed the way toward an important way of understanding many types of thinking behavior in nonlinguistic creatures. We can formulate the majority of our psychological explanations at the nonlinguistic level in terms of the sort of context-bound and perception-based representations of the environment developed in, for example, Dummett's conception of protothoughts, Cussins's cognitive trails, or Campbell's causally indexical thoughts. But, as I showed in chapter 3, the minimalist approach does not have the resources to accommodate all the types of psychological explanation required at the nonlinguistic level. Some such explanations will need to couched within the framework of propositional attitude psychology. It is the problem of how to understand this type of explanation that I have been pursuing in this and the previous chapter. The success semantics approach has shown what it is to attribute beliefs and desires at the nonlinguistic level and how we should understand the contents of those beliefs and desires. I have, therefore, made considerable progress on what in chapter 1 were identified as the metaphysical, semantical, and epistemological dimensions of an account of nonlinguistic thinking. I have, however, only made partial progress on what I termed the explanatory dimension, namely, the task of elucidating the explanatory practices in which the attribution of those beliefs and desires is embedded. What, if anything, are the analogues in the nonlinguistic case for the considerations of rationality that operate so centrally in psychological explanations of the behavior of language-using creatures? How do beliefs and desires in nonlinguistic creatures translate into action? What, if any, processes of practical reasoning are we supposing at the nonlinguistic level? These and related questions will be addressed in the following two chapters.

6

Rationality without Language

In the previous two chapters I proposed a way of attributing thoughts to non-linguistic creatures. This has taken us a considerable way toward addressing the problems identified in earlier chapters. It is becoming clearer how nonlinguistic creatures might have, and how we might go about, identifying thoughts that have determinate contents, are genuinely structured, and reflect the way the relevant state of affairs is apprehended by the creature in question. But this still leaves us some way short of an adequate theoretical framework for the practices of psychological explanation that we find in, for example, contemporary developmental psychology, cognitive ethology, and cognitive archeology. In this chapter and the next I complete the account by considering how we should understand the twin notions of rationality and practical reasoning at the nonlinguistic level.

I begin in section 6.1 by explaining why it is imperative to give an account of rationality at the nonlinguistic level and why the task is a difficult one. The problem is that the standard, inference-based models of rationality that seem appropriate at the linguistic level are not applicable to nonlinguistic creatures. In sections 6.2 to 6.4 I distinguish three different ways that behavior at the nonlinguistic level can be characterized as rational. In 6.5 I discuss the implications of this tripartite distinction for psychological explanation at the nonlinguistic level.

6.1 Theoretical and Practical Rationality

A successful practice of psychological explanation requires more than the simple attribution of thoughts. Psychological explanations operate by attributing propositional attitudes (typically a combination of beliefs and desires) that rationalize the behavior being explained (Davidson 1963). The governing principle of the explanation is that it would be rational for a creature with that combination of beliefs and desires (and no significantly countervailing beliefs and desires) to act in the way that it did in fact act.

The requirement here is not, of course, that the relevant action be *completely* rational in a full or everyday sense of the term. What matters is that it be rational from the point of view of the agent. That is to say, the performance of the action should make sense in the light of the agent's beliefs and desires. But it may be that those beliefs, or some subset of them, are irrational in a way that makes the action itself irrational. It may be helpful to distinguish explicitly between internal and external rationality. Assessments of internal rationality are relative to an agent's doxastic and motivational states, taking those states as given, while assessments of external rationality include assessments of the doxastic states underlying the action. To say that an action is externally rational is to say that it is in some sense appropriate to the circumstances in which it is performed, where those circumstances include the agent's motivational states—with different theories of external rationality interpreting the type of appropriateness involved here in different ways.

The internal rationalizing connection between beliefs, desires, and actions allows the attribution of thoughts and desires to be genuinely explanatory. Beliefs and desires cause behavior qua beliefs and desires (that is to say, in virtue of their content) because their contents rationally dictate a single course of action—or a limited number of possible courses of action. In the absence of such a rationalizing connection, there would be no reason why a belief-desire pair with *those* particular contents should cause *that* particular action.[1] Clearly, therefore, any application of psychological explanations to nonlinguistic creatures must rest on the appropriateness of applying criteria of rationality to nonlinguistic creatures. But how are we to extend the notion of rationality to nonlinguistic creatures?

The basic problem is that the models of rationality we possess are not easily generalized to nonlinguistic creatures. Consider, for example, the influential account of practical rationality offered by Donald Davidson—what we might term the inference-based conception of practical rationality:

> If someone acts with an intention then he must have attitudes and beliefs from which, had he been aware of them and had he the time, he could have reasoned that his act was desirable. . . . If we can characterize the reasoning that would serve we will, in effect, have described the logical relations between descriptions of beliefs and desires and the description of the action, when the former gives the reasons with which the latter was performed. We are to imagine, then, that the agent's beliefs and desires provide him with the premises of an argument. (Davidson 1978, 1980a, 85–86)

Let us suppose that practical reasoning is argument-like in the way that Davidson and many others have suggested. Then it straightforwardly follows that we can only explain and predict the behavior of other creatures to the extent that we can understand the inferential relations between descriptions of their beliefs, desires, and so forth on the one hand and their actions on the other. And it seems natural to think that our understanding of the inferential relations between propositional attitudes and actions depends on their conforming to the dictates of what might be termed *procedural rationality*—that is, sensitivity to certain basic principles of deductive and inductive inference (although such conformity is a necessary rather than a sufficient condition). Obvious examples are the familiar deductive principles of *modus ponens, modus tollens,* contraposition, and so forth, together with such basic principles of probability theory as that the probability of a conjunction can never be greater than the probability of its conjuncts; that the probability of a hypothesis and the probability of its negation should add up to 1; and so on.

There are two principal obstacles to extending this inference-based conception of rationality to nonlinguistic creatures. The first obstacle concerns the structure of the vehicles of nonlinguistic thought. We understand inference in formal terms—in terms of rules that operate on representations in virtue of their structure. But we have no theory at all of formal inferential transitions between thoughts that do not have linguistic vehicles. Our models of formal inference are based squarely on transitions between natural language sentences (as codified in a suitable formal language). To be clear on the problem, we need to remember that there is an important distinction between two different ways thoughts can be structured. They can be structured at the level of their vehicles or they can be structured at the level of their contents. In arguing against the minimalist conception of nonlinguistic thought in chapter 3 and in the semantics I sketched out in chapters 4 and 5, I made the case for viewing nonlinguistic thoughts as having structured contents— contents that contain distinguishable content-constituents capable of featuring in further thoughts. Clearly, it is a necessary condition on there being formal inferential transitions between contentful thoughts that those thoughts should have structured contents. Nonetheless, it is not a sufficient condition. Formal rules of inference do not operate on thought-contents but rather on the vehicles of those contents. They are syntactic rather than semantic. It is easy to lose sight of this when dealing with inferential transitions between sentences in formal languages, because there is a structural isomorphism between the logical structure of the sentence that expresses a given thought and the structure of the thought-content that it expresses. In the case of formal language sentences, it doesn't really matter whether one considers the structure of the vehicle or the structure of the content, since they are isomorphic. But in the case of nonlinguistic thought (as in the case of sentences in natural languages) the distinction becomes important. The contents of nonlinguistic thought are indeed linguistically expressible and have a commensurate degree of structure. That is what makes them instances of thinking-that, rather than thinking-how. But it is far from clear that the vehicles of nonlinguistic thought are linguistically structured in a way that would make it possible to apply formal rules of inference to them. This is a theme that will be discussed in more detail in the next two chapters.

It might be objected that "everyday rationality" of the type that psychological explanations aim to track is not in fact formal. That is to say, everyday rationality proceeds by seeing immediate connections between ideas, rather than by mechanically applying formal rules of inference. This, broadly speaking, *intuitionist* line of thought goes back to Locke and has been promoted more recently by Jonathan Lowe (1993). The development of formal codifications of reasoning, according to Lowe, involves maintaining reflective equilibrium between the deliverances of everyday rationality and the deductive consequences of particular formal systems.

Someone attracted to the intuitionist conception of everyday rationality would be quite justified in mistrusting an argument from a syntactic understanding of inference to the need for sentential vehicles for the thoughts between which inferences take place. But it is not clear that such a theorist can avoid the need for sentential vehicles altogether. What exactly are the two things between which we intuit connections, if not sentences? It is hard for us to make much sense of what Locke and his contemporaries found so easy to take for granted, namely, that we can directly perceive connections between thoughts. The most natural way to gloss the idea of directly perceived connections between thoughts is in terms of directly perceived connections between the truth of one sentence and the truth of another.[2] And with this we are back with linguistic vehicles.

In any case, as Davidson himself makes very clear, the explanatory power of the rationality connection in ordinary folk psychological explanations depends on the fact that the person whose behavior is being explained is at least in principle capable of carrying out the relevant reasoning—as he puts it, "had he been aware of them and had he the time, he could have reasoned that his act was desirable." Without this we would have nothing like a genuine explanation. But to be capable of reasoning requires mastery of the relevant inferential principles—that is to say, mastery of the canons of what I have termed procedural rationality. And it is here that the inference-based conception breaks down. Nonlinguistic creatures are not reasoners in anything like the sense required for them to be rational on the inference-based conception of rationality.[3]

Although students of animal behavior have sometimes suggested that nonlinguistic creatures are capable of mastering certain basic formal principles of inference, these claims are plausible only when the notion of mastering a formal principle of inference is taken in such an etiolated sense that it no longer really counts as inference at all. Some of the claims made about Ronald Schusterman's work with sea lions will illustrate this. It is frequently claimed that Schusterman has trained his sea lions to understand and apply the logical principle of the transitivity of identity. Here is a representative report:

> Researchers have so far discovered that the essentials of Aristotelian logic are accessible to at least one other species: the sea lion. The first task presented to the sea lions was to learn that two icons are equivalent: $X = Y$. Next they were taught that Y and Z were equivalent: $Y = Z$. Then they were asked if X and Z were equivalent: does $X = Z$? Sea lions readily mastered this logical train. (Gould and Gould 1994, 176)

When we look more closely at the experimental paradigm, however, it becomes clear that there is a certain creative license in this description. The initial training, which Gould and Gould describe in terms of teaching the animal that two icons are equivalent, really amounted only to rewarding the sea lion when it chose the second icon (Y) shortly after being presented with the first icon (X). There seems no reason why this form of learning should be described in terms of a logical concept such as the concept of identity. Not only is the learned behavior a purely conditioned response, but it is hard to know how even to interpret the suggestion that the two icons might be identical, given that the icons used in the experiment had different illustrations on them.

It is true that there is something significant going on here. The sea lions learn to associate X and Z even though they have never been exposed to the conjunction of the two icons. This is interesting because it seems clearly to contradict the basic claim of classical conditioning theory, which is that learned associations must rest on reinforcement. Classical conditioning theory predicts that the sea lions would fail the test, on the grounds that they had not been exposed to any reinforcement of the association between the first and third icons. But, understood in these terms, the sea lion performance seems much closer to the well-documented phenomenon of sensory preconditioning in rats (Rizley and Rescorla 1972). In sensory preconditioning rats are exposed to two pairings. The first pairing is of a light and a tone, while the second is of the same light and an electric shock. If, once the preconditioning has been completed, the rats are exposed to the tone on its own, they will manifest the same aversive behavior that they were conditioned to show to the light (in virtue of its association with the electric shock). Just as the sea lions had never been exposed to the conjunction of icon X and icon Z, the rats had never been exposed to the conjunction of tone and electric shock. Yet in both cases the response was generalized without further training. It might be appropriate to describe this phenomenon using some phrase such as the "transitivity of association," but there seems to be no sense in which implicit grasp of any *logical* principle is involved.

It is striking that Schusterman and his coworkers do not make any explicit claims about the concept of identity. In, for example, Kastak, Schusterman, and Kastak 2001, the experiments are described as showing that sea lions are capable of *equivalence classification*, where this is understood as the capacity to classify groups of physically dissimilar stimuli that are related by a relation R possessing the formal properties of reflexivity (i.e., every member of the group bears that relation to itself), symmetry (if a bears relation R to b then b will bear relation R to a), and transitivity (if a bears relation R to b and b bears relation R to c then a will bear relation R to c). Any relation satisfying these formal properties is an *equivalence relation*. It is true, of course, that the logical concept of identity is an equivalence relation—but it hardly follows that sea lions that have shown themselves capable of equivalence classification will ipso facto have mastered the concept of identity. There are various equivalence relations in play in the different experimental paradigms that have been taken to illustrate equivalence classification, but none of them has anything to do with the concept of identity. The simplest equivalence relation is the relation of having-the-same-reinforcement-history-as (i.e., all stimuli that have been positively reinforced will be classified together, as will all stimuli that have been negatively reinforced). Classification according to this very straightforward equivalence relation is not, in fact, unique to sea lions. It has been demonstrated in pigeons (Vaughan 1988). An example of a more complex equivalence relation would be the relation of having-the-same-function-as. It turns out that sea lions (although as yet no other species) are capable of classifying stimuli ordered by this equivalence relation. A recent survey article (Schusterman, Kastak, and Kastak 2002) suggests that sea lions are able to classify according to equivalence relations of being a conspecific or being related. None of these equivalence relations, however, has anything to do with the equivalence relation of identity, as a relation that holds between every thing and itself.

This is no place for a survey of claims that have been made for logical competence in nonlinguistic creatures, but it seems to me that all such claims can be fitted into one of either three categories. In the first category fall claims such as those made by the Goulds about Schusterman's sea lions experiments. The key characteristic here is that appeal is made to mastery of logical principles in order to explain forms of behavior that can be far more easily explained more parsimoniously. There is obviously little aid here for an extension of the inference-based conception to nonlinguistic creatures.

In the second category certain forms of cognitive ability are wrongly described as logical. As an example we can take David Premack's well-known experiments using a same-different paradigm on chimpanzees (Premack and Premack 1983). Premack trained his chimpanzees by presenting them with an initial symbol followed by a pair containing that symbol and a second, different symbol. They were positively rewarded for selecting the second symbol. Although at first reinforcement was required for each new pairing, the chimpanzees gradually began to respond correctly without any reinforcement. It may well be right to interpret this behavior in terms of mastery of the concepts *same* and *different,* but there is surely no *logical* principle involved here. The experiment says nothing about the capacity of chimpanzees to master formal principles of reasoning. Again, this will be of little use to proponents of an inference-based conception of practical reasoning.

In the third category of claims about the logical competence of nonlinguistic creatures we can place what might be termed "as-if" attributions of certain patterns of reasoning. As has become well known from studies of animal foraging behavior, it is possible to model certain aspects of animal behavior by making the heuristic assumption that the animal is performing complex cost-benefit calculations. Here is how Krebs and Kacelnik describe the bare bones of the framework they propose for studying patterns of animal behavior, such as those displayed by a foraging robin:

> We shall use the metaphor of the animal as a 'decision-maker.' Without implying any conscious choice, the robin can be thought of as 'deciding' whether to sing or to feed, whether to feed on worms or on insects, whether to search for food on the grass or on the flower bed. We shall see how these decisions can be analyzed in terms of the costs and benefits of alternative courses of action. Costs and benefits are ultimately measured in terms of Darwinian fitness (survival and reproduction), and may, in many instances, be measured in terms of some more immediate metric such as energy expenditure, food intake or amount of body reserves. Analyzing decisions in terms of their costs and benefits cannot be done without also taking into consideration physiological and psychological features that might act as constraints on an animal's performance. The fitness consequences of decisions, and the various constraints that limit an animal's options, can be brought together in a single framework using optimality modeling. (Krebs and Kacelnik 1991)

The guiding assumption of optimal foraging theory is that animals should optimize the net amount of energy obtained in a given period of time. So acquired energy is the benefit in the cost-benefit analysis. In the case of a foraging bird, for example, faced with the "decision" of whether to keep on foraging in the location it is in or to move to another location, the costs are the depletions of energy incurred through flight from one location to another and during foraging activity in a particular location. The cost-benefit analysis can be carried out once certain basic variables are known, such as the rate of gaining energy in one location, the energy cost of flying from one location to another, and the expected energy gain in the new location. It turns out that optimality modeling makes robust predictions of foraging behavior in birds such as starlings (*Sturnus vulgaris*) and blue tits (*Parus major*). Cowie's study of great tits foraging in an experimental environment containing sawdust-filled cups with mealworms hidden inside showed that the amount of time a given bird spent at a given cup could be accurately predicted as a function of the travel time between patches and the quantity of mealworms in the cup (Cowie 1977). Similarly, Kacelnik has shown that adult starlings foraging for their young behave in ways predicted by the marginal value theorem of optimal foraging theory, on the assumption that the relevant currency is net energy gain to the family (Kacelnik 1984). Foraging starlings collect a beakload of food from a foraging site before returning to their nests. Obviously, diminishing returns will set in during the foraging excursion, as the bird will be less efficient at gathering new food the fuller its beak is with the food it has already gathered. The marginal value theorem is a quantitative way of predicting the adjustments that a creature will make in its foraging behavior to compensate for these diminishing returns.

Of course, as Krebs and Kacelnik make plain in the quoted passage, there is no suggestion that the great tits or starlings really are carrying out complex calculations about how net energy gain can be maximized within a particular set of parameters and background constraints. It is a crucial tenet of optimal foraging theory that the optimizing behavior is achieved by the animal following a set of relatively simple rules of thumb or heuristics, which are most probably innate rather than learned. So, for example, a great tit might be hard-wired to move on to the next tree after a certain number of seconds unsuccessful foraging in one tree. Hence the phrase "as-if" reasoning. Evolution has worked in such a way (at least according to the proponents of optimal foraging theory) that foraging species have evolved sets of heuristic strategies that result in optimal adaptation to their ecological niches. This optimal adaptation can be mathematically modeled in terms of what is ultimately a sophisticated version of expected utility theory, but the behaviors in which it manifests itself do not result from the application of such a theory—any more than a bird's capacity to fly reflects any mastery on its part of the basic principles of aerodynamics. Once again, there is no scope here for understanding how the inference-based conception of practical rationality can be extended to nonlinguistic creatures.

It would seem, therefore, that Davidson's strategy of treating practical rationality as a form of theoretical rationality is doomed to failure. It is true that I have so far argued explicitly only for the thesis that we cannot extend a workable notion of procedural rationality to nonlinguistic creatures. Despite the views of some philosophers (Stein 1996) and many psychologists of reasoning (particularly those studying the Wason selection task and other experimental paradigms testing mastery of the rules that govern conditional reasoning), mastery of the basic principles of inference needs to be clearly distinguished from what might be termed norms of good reasoning. These are principles that govern the processes of thinking: weighing up the evidence for and against a particular proposition; judging the likelihood of a particular event; changing one's beliefs and probability assignments in response to changes in the available evidence; and so forth. The norms of reasoning go to make up what I have elsewhere termed the domain of epistemic rationality (Bermúdez 2001). It is also true, as I show in the final chapter (section 9.1), that there is some scope for the relevant types of belief formation and revision at the nonlinguistic level. But it is hard to see how the epistemic dimension of theoretical rationality can be of any use in making sense of practical rationality.

Clearly, therefore, if we are to identify a sense of nonlinguistic rationality in the practical sphere, it is no use approaching the issue via procedural rationality in the way Davidson does. We need a specific account of how nonlinguistic creatures might be practically rational. In line with the general methodology adopted in this book, I will broach the issue from an epistemological and operational dimension, starting with the following questions. In what circumstances would it be appropriate to describe the behavior of a nonlinguistic creature as rational? What operational criteria might there be for nonlinguistic rationality? In the next three sections I will identify three different types of behavior, each of which can be described as rational in a different sense. For reasons that will emerge hereafter, only the second and third of these can count as rational in the right sense to ground the practice of psychological explanation.

6.2   Level 0 Rationality

Let me start with a basic datum. There is no need for psychological explanations of animal behavior when we are dealing with tropistic behaviors such as those produced by reflexes, innate releasing mechanisms (such as imprinting mechanisms), or classical conditioning. In such situations we can explain the behavior in terms of a lawlike connection between stimulus and response. Whenever the relevant stimulus is encountered the same response will emerge. We do not need to postulate intermediary representational states between sensory transducers and behavioral output.

Nonetheless, there is a sense in which tropistic behavior of this form can be described as rational. This is the sense of the word 'rational' on which 'rational' means something like 'adaptive' or 'conducive to survival' (Dawkins 1986). There are criteria by which it is appropriate to judge the rationality of even the simplest tropistic forms of behavior. Take a behavior that has evolved as an adaptive response to potentially harmful events on the body surface, such as the eye-blink response to puffs of air. This is clearly adaptive, and the adaptiveness carries over even to behaviors in which the eye-blink response is itself part of a larger conditioned process. If there is reliable advance warning of the arrival of the unconditioned stimulus (e.g., the sound of a tone preceding the puff of air) then there are adaptive advantages in activating the response before the unconditioned stimulus actually appears.

I will call this level 0 rationality. It has two characteristic features, as follow.

1. It is not grounded in any process of decision-making.
2. It is applicable not to particular behaviors but to the presence (either in the organism or in the species) of a particular tendency or disposition.

The first feature should be self-explanatory, but some comments are required on the second feature. We can only apply the notion of rationality when there is a space of alternatives. A rational behavior has to be one that is performed rather than some other behavior that could have been performed. But of course there is no such space of alternatives at the level of individual tropistic behaviors. The space of alternatives exists only at the level of the genetically determined disposition to behave in a certain way. Putting the point in more familiar philosophical terms, level 0 rationality applies only to behavior types and not to behavior tokens.

This type of rationality is not confined to tropistic behaviors. We find it exemplified in foraging behavior. As we saw in the previous section, many species have evolved to follow simple behavioral rules when foraging for food. According to optimal foraging theory, in many cases these rules are such that individuals of the relevant species are maximally adapted to their environment. So, how might one apply the notion of rationality to the feeding patterns of a redshank (*Tringa totanus*)? Redshanks are shorebirds that dig for worms in estuaries at low tide. It has been noticed that they sometimes feed exclusively on large worms and at other times feed on both large and small worms. The hypothesis put forward by Stephens and Krebs to explain this behavior involves what they call the principle of lost opportunity (Stephens and Krebs 1986). In essence, although a large worm is worth more to the redshank in terms of quantity of energy gained per unit of foraging time than a small worm, the costs of searching exclusively for large worms can have deleterious consequences, except when the large worms are relatively plentiful. If the large worms are rare then it will obviously take much longer to find one—time during which the redshank is not only expending valuable energy but also losing opportunities to gain energy from smaller worms. So redshanks only ever forage exclusively for large worms when there are plenty of large worms around.

It seems perfectly reasonable to say that this is rational behavior on the part of the redshank. But of course this is not to say that whenever the redshank switches from a restricted search strategy (only large worms) to an unrestricted search strategy (both large and small worms) it is behaving rationally. That would not be right, because at the level of the individual foraging behavior there is no space of alternatives. The redshank is "following" a relatively simple algorithm, and there seems no sense in which it could fail to follow it—unless, of course, the foraging algorithm was trumped by another algorithm and the bird ceased foraging, as it might do if a predator was detected. The space of alternatives exists at the level of the hard-wired algorithm. What is rational is not the redshank's behavior on a particular occasion but rather the fact that it has evolved in such a way as to follow an algorithm that allows it to switch from a restricted search strategy to an unrestricted search strategy—as opposed, for example, to always following the same strategy.

As the example of optimal foraging theory makes clear, for a behavior pattern to count as rational in the level 0 sense, there must be not only a contrast space of alternative behavior patterns but also a normative standard against which those behavior patterns can be assessed. The normative "currency" by which to judge foraging behavior is some form of maximization of energy gain. But there are questions to be raised about how widely the energy calculation should extend. In certain cases (such as the redshank example just considered) it makes sense to restrict the calculation to the foraging bird. In other cases, such as that of the starlings foraging for their young, the most accurate predictions come when one works on the basis of the rate of energy procurement for the family as a whole. Nor, of course, is maximization of energy gain the only available currency. Another obvious normative standard for evaluating particular patterns is that they should facilitate predator avoidance—or that they should not hinder the animal from finding a mate.

A distinction needs to be made between short-term criteria of rationality of the type I have just been considering and long-term criteria (see Dawkins 1986 for a similar distinction between short-term and long-term rationality). Rate of energy procurement is a short-term criterion of rationality. The accepted currency for long-term calculations is fitness. There are different ways of calculating fitness. Strictly speaking, fitness is a matter of relative quantities of specific genes in the gene pool over time, but in practical terms this can often be measured in terms of the reproductive output of individual animals. This is individual lifetime fitness, calculated as the product of the length of time the animal survives and the average number of offspring it produces during each year of its life. In the not uncommon situation in which an animal sacrifices its own individual lifetime fitness in a way that increases the lifetime fitness of other animals that share many of the same genes by descent, the appropriate currency is inclusive fitness. Inclusive fitness is arrived at by adding the individual lifetime fitness of the donor animal to the sum of the individual lifetime fitness of the animals helped by the donor, each discounted by the probability of their sharing genes with the donor animal.

There are, therefore, many different criteria according to which level 0 rationality can be assessed. The basic distinction is between short-term and long-term criteria, but within each grouping there are further distinctions. This is important for the following reason. One objection likely to be raised against the very idea of level 0 rationality is that it is completely Panglossian. Every form of behavior that is best analyzed at this level will come out as rational, simply as a function of the way the notion is defined. Any suitable behavior pattern that exists does so because it has proved more adaptive than the other potential behavior patterns available to natural selection at a given moment in evolutionary time. But then, it looks very much as if any extant behavior pattern will prove to be rational in the level 0 sense simply in virtue of having been selected. This would deprive the notion of level 0 rationality of sense and point, since it would make it impossible for there to be a thing as level 0 *ir*rationality.

However, evolutionary fitness is not the only criterion by which the level 0 rationality of a particular behavior pattern can be assessed. Indeed, in many cases it seems that fitness (whether individual or group) is not really an appropriate currency. It is true that the overarching currency of natural selection is fitness—but for that reason fitness is too coarse-grained a tool for thinking about the ways that particular behavior patterns help a creature fit into its ecological niche. Short-term criteria are far more helpful than long-term criteria in that respect. It may well be the case that a particular behavior pattern is rational in the long-term sense of having been the most fitness-promoting of the alternatives available for natural selection to choose between without being rational in the short-term sense. Let us suppose that there is an optimality threshold for each of the different aspects of an animal's existence—foraging, mate selection, nest-building, rearing of young, food avoidance, and so forth. The fitness of animals of a particular species may well depend so crucially on striking the right balance between the various different activities in which it engages that performance above the optimality threshold on one dimension could not be achieved without compromising the balance. So, for example, performance above the rationality threshold on foraging might only be possible at the price of performance on predator avoidance too far below the threshold to be sustainable. This might well be a case in which, assuming that we were interested solely in short-term criteria of level 0 rationality, none of a creature's specific behavior patterns would qualify as level 0 rational. It is more likely, of course, that long-term fitness would be served by a combination of behavior patterns, some of which fall below the optimality threshold while others are safely above it.

Level 0 rationality is not always a matter of optimization or maximization. There are good examples of level 0 rationality in the signaling strategies that are widespread in the animal kingdom (Bradbury and Vehrencamp 1998) and in particular in what might be termed *two-way information transfers*. These are informational transactions in which information is transferred in two directions (as opposed to one-way information transfers such as mating displays). We find such transactions most typically in situations where animals are in conflict over food, prospective mates, or breeding sites. Rather than resort to the direct use of force to resolve the conflict, many animals employ threat-display signals to come to a nonviolent consensus as to which is the stronger. One feature of two-way information transfers is that each sender can modify its signal in the light of the signal it receives from the other participant in the exchange. Conflict resolution is not, of course, the only sphere in which we find two-way information transfers. Mating displays and territorial signaling provide examples in which, unlike many instances of conflict resolution, the signaling behaviors of the two participants are not symmetrical. One feature that all such information exchanges have in common is that they lend themselves to being modeled game-theoretically (Lewis 1969, Skyrms 1996). Evolutionary game theory can help make sense of why particular signaling exchanges between sender and recipient should have become stabilized. We can see both participants' signaling behavior as strategies adopted by particular roles within a population (where a role might be male vs. female, young males vs. older males, and so forth) that have become stabilized because each is the optimal response to the other within the range of alternatives made available by a particular evolutionary context. They are both *evolutionary stable strategies* (Maynard Smith 1982).

To summarize, level 0 rationality is a type of rationality appropriate to behavior types rather than behavior tokens. It does not involve any genuine decision-making. The behavior types that qualify for level 0 rationality will most often be hard-wired, ranging from simple reflexes such as the eye-blink response to innate releasing mechanisms. They are properly described as rational because there is a normative theory, such as for example some version or other of optimal foraging theory, under which they come out as the best response among the range of alternative patterns of behavior available at that time. There are, broadly speaking, two different ways of determining whether or not a particular strategy is a best response. It might qualify in virtue of maximizing some particular currency. Or it might qualify as being part of what game theorists call an equilibrium strategy—that is, a strategy such that neither party can benefit by deviating from it. In either case there remains the question of what the currency is in terms of which gains and benefits are being calculated, and as I have shown there are a range of potential currencies, short-term and long-term.

6.3   Level 1 Rationality

Discussions of nonlinguistic rationality, particularly on the part of philosophers, frequently assume that there is no middle ground between what I have termed level 0 rationality and the sophisticated types of rationality that we find in language-users and that can be modeled by formal logic, rational choice theory, game theory, and so forth. This does not seem right. Level 0 rationality is limited in two ways. First, it does not involve a recognizable process of decision-making. Second, it is not applicable to behavior tokens but only to behavior types. We can easily see that there is room in logical space for at least one intermediate conception of rationality. Such an intermediate form of rationality would be one that was subject to one of these limitations but not the other. The abstract possibility is illustrated in the following table.

	Applicable to Behavior Tokens	*Decision-Making*
Level 0	X	X
Level 1	√	X

Is this possibility realized? It seems to me that it is. A given tropistic behavior token cannot be rational because there is no sense in which it is selected from a range of alternatives. Consequently it cannot involve a process of decision-making. But it does not follow from this that any behavior that is properly described as having been selected from a range of alternatives must involve a process of decision-making.

Let me take a simplified example fairly common in the animal kingdom. Imagine an animal confronted with another potentially threatening animal. The animal has two possible courses of action—fight or flee. There is a clear sense in which one of the two courses of action could be more rational than the other. Roughly speaking, it will be in the animal's best interests either to fight or to flee. And it seems that in such a situation there need be no process of decision-making. The animal might just "see" that fighting is the appropriate response. Or it might just "see" that fleeing is appropriate. The theory of affordances developed by J. J. Gibson (1979) gives us a way of making sense of this as a form of direct perception. Gibson's theory is that perception is not neutral. It is not just a matter of seeing various objects that stand in spatial relations to each other. It involves seeing our own possibilities for action—seeing the possibilities that are "afforded" by the environment. If this is right then we can see how a given behavior might be selected from a range of alternatives in a way that does not involve a process of decision-making. The comparison of affordances does not require a process of decision-making. Nonetheless it is assessable according to criteria of rationality. I shall call this the sphere of level 1 rationality. I shall offer a detailed example of how the notion of level 1 rationality might be deployed in section 7.1. We will see there how different courses of action can be compared without a process of decision-making.

The principal difference between level 0 rationality and level 1 rationality is in the location of the contrast space of alternative possible courses of action. Assessments of rationality are only applicable when the relevant course of action is properly described as having been selected from a range of alternatives. In level 0 rationality the appropriate contrast space is between different behavior patterns or tropistic mechanisms that might have been selected by evolution, whereas in level 1 rationality the contrast space is a range of different possible courses of action available to the organism at the relevant time.

One would expect there to be a range of possible currencies in terms of which a particular behavior token might be assessed for level 1 rationality, much like the range of currencies operative for level 0 rationality. Level 1 rationality is subject to the same distinction between short-term and long-term criteria, and within each group there will be different criteria pushing in different directions. In the case of level 0 rationality we are considering patterns of behavior that are most probably instinctive, but the sources of behaviors assessable for level 1 rationality are far more fluid. We can imagine an animal being motivated to act in a way that would reduce its individual lifetime fitness (calculated as the product of survival and fecundity) and yet that counts as level 1 rational. The most obvious case would be one where an animal (a member of a species such as the vervet monkey, which has a highly developed system for alerting conspecifics to the presence of different types of predator) fails to signal the approach of a predator and instead flees the scene. It might well be that fleeing as opposed to warning decreases both individual lifetime fitness (by making other members of the group less likely to cooperate in future) and inclusive fitness (by decreasing that individual's chances of finding a mate) while yet counting as level 1 rational according to other criteria, such as for example the criterion of the individual's long-term survival.[4]

As with level 0 rationality, there will be two different ways that the notion of level 1 rationality might apply. A particular behavior token might qualify as level 1 rational in virtue of maximizing units of some relevant currency. Alternatively, it might qualify in virtue of being an equilibrium strategy in game-theoretical terms—although, unlike the level 0 case, the relevant strategy will be behaving in that particular way in that particular context, rather than a generalized behavior pattern. Although in practice it will not always be clear whether a given behavior is to be judged in terms of level 0 or level 1 rationality, one might expect the sort of situations in which issues of level 1 rationality arise to be correlated with greater amenability to game-theoretical analysis, for the following reason. The type of behaviors that it is appropriate to assess for level 0 rationality are highly invariant behaviors, instances of rigid behavior patterns that one might expect to be repeated whenever the environment is suitably configured. It is when this invariance breaks down that we move to assessing the rationality of behavior tokens rather than behavior types. But one would expect the invariance to break down far more frequently in cases involving interanimal interaction (such as conflict resolution) than in those where the interaction is simply between animal and environment, and it is the former that are susceptible to game-theoretic analyses.

Thinking back to chapter 3, it will be apparent that the notion of level 1 rationality is very much in the spirit of the minimalist conception of nonlinguistic thought. According to the minimalist view, the thinking of nonlinguistic creatures cannot be significantly divorced from the here-and-now of the perceived environment, and whenever the thinking behavior of a nonlinguistic creature is directed at something that is not immediately perceptible, the instrumental representations driving its behavior cannot be anything more complicated than mediate perceptions of the sort provided by Gibsonian affordances. If, therefore, a genuine notion of rationality is applicable to thinking behavior as the minimalist understands it, it can only be either level 0 rationality or level 1 rationality, depending on whether the notion of rationality is applicable at the level of behavior types or behavior tokens. As I showed in chapter 3, however, the minimalist conception of nonlinguistic thought is too restrictive. This in itself is enough to suggest that there must be a further intermediate level of rationality. That suggestion is strongly reinforced by the fact that one of the decisive arguments against the minimalist conception was essentially that there are important types of behavior in nonlinguistic creatures that cannot be understood in terms of mediate perceptions such as Gibsonian affordances. In the next section I will show how a further notion of rationality can be developed to deal with these more complex behaviors.

6.4   Level 2 Rationality

What is the next level of rationality? Clearly it will be one in which both criteria are satisfied. Thus:

	Applicable to Behavior Tokens	Decision-Making
Level 0	X	X
Level 1	√	√
Level 2	√	X

But it is not immediately obvious how such a notion of rationality can be applied at the nonlinguistic level. It is far from straightforward to see how nonlinguistic creatures can properly be described as decision-makers. There is no room for an inference-based conception of decision-making—whether inference is taken strictly as a matter of formally characterizable operations defined over syntactic vehicles, or more broadly as a matter of the immediate perception of entailment relations between thoughts.⁵ But then how else could decision-making be understood? Unless we can develop an alternative conception of decision-making, it looks very much as if we will have to restrict the notion of nonlinguistic rationality to level 0 and level 1 rationality.

Let us look once again at the requirements. I have already shown how in behaviors assessable in terms of level 1 rationality it is appropriate to describe an animal as behaving in a particular way within a contrast space of alternative possible courses of action. It is natural and convenient to formulate this in terms of Gibson's theory of affordances. So one might say that an animal perceives a range of different courses of action afforded by the environment and acts on one of these perceived affordances. Why is this not properly described as decision-making? To appreciate why not, it is important to make a distinction between two different ways that different courses of action can be compared. On the one hand, they can be compared simply qua courses of action. That is to say, an animal might compare the action of fighting with the action of fleeing. It is this sort of comparison that is at play in the forms of behavior that are assessable for level 1 rationality. The possibility of such comparison requires simply representations of actions. These representations are not very complex. They might (if some form of Gibson's theory is correct) be understood at a purely perceptual level. It is perfectly possible, and indeed highly likely, that the choice between such action-representations can be made on relatively simple and more-or-less noncognitive grounds. One way of interpreting the whole basis of instrumental conditioning is as a process of attaching a certain positive valence (through reinforcement) to the representation of a particular action, so that the animal being conditioned is motivated to act on that action-representation rather than one of the others afforded by the immediate environment. It is for this reason, I think, that the notion of decision-making is best not applied to cases in which courses of action are compared qua courses of action. Such cases do indeed involve a form of choice—or perhaps 'selection' would be a better word. But the choice or selection is not made on the right sort of grounds to qualify as decision-making.[6]

What then is involved in genuine decision-making? The minimal requirement is that the selection of a particular course of action from the contrast space of alternative possible courses of action should be made on consequence-sensitive grounds.[7] That is to say, genuine decision-making involves a selection between different possible courses of action that is grounded on an assessment of the likely consequences that those different possible courses of action will have. Deciding is not simply selecting. It is selecting for a reason. There is an important distinction here. In many cases of instrumental conditioning (but not all, as I shall shortly show) it is correct to say that the relevant action is performed because of its consequences. So, for example, what explains the pigeon's pressing the lever is that it will result in delivery of food from the cartridge. It is the association of that behavior with those consequences that has created the positive valence that leads the pigeon to carry out the action of lever pressing. But to say that an action is being performed on consequence-sensitive grounds implies far more than its simply being performed because of its consequences. It implies that the agent has made an assessment of those consequences, on the basis of a belief about the outcome that that action is likely to have (and, most likely, a comparison of that outcome with the likely outcomes of other possible courses of action). Decision-making only takes place, in other words, at a level where instrumental beliefs are available.

The distinction between simple selection (as in level 1 rationality) and genuine decision-making of the sort that only becomes available with level 2 rationality can be put in terms of the representation of contingencies. Some of these contingencies hold between an action and an anticipated outcome-situation. But there does not always need to be representation of the action itself. It is natural to think that one important factor motivating an animal to act on a particular represented contingency is its recognition that the outcome-situation would satisfy one of its desires—in the terminology introduced in chapter 3, the anticipated outcome-situation would be a goal-situation. So in level 2 rationality we encounter once again a familiar pattern of psychological explanation—that is to say, psychological explanation in terms of a belief-desire pair linked by an instrumental belief about how a desire might be satisfied in a particular context.

A consequence of this is that level 2 rationality can be assessed in a fundamentally different way from the other two levels of rationality that I have considered. Whereas both level 0 and level 1 rationality can only be understood in terms either of maximization of a given currency (such as rate of energy procurement, individual lifetime fitness, and so forth) or of strategies that are in game-theoretic equilibrium, level 2 rationality admits a fundamentally different type of assessment. Since the crucial element in level 2 rationality is the way action is grounded in instrumental beliefs about the outcomes of those actions, it is clear that in an important respect the level 2 rationality of an action will depend on the "match" between action and background beliefs. In this sense the level 2 rationality of a particular action will be a function of:

1. The accuracy of the instrumental belief
2. The extent to which the action in question is a suitable implementation of the instrumental belief

There is fortunately no need at present to explain how both criteria can be developed into a full-blown theory of level 2 rationality.[8] There is enough on the table already for the central problem to be clear.

The principal question is how we should understand instrumental beliefs and the representation of contingencies at the nonlinguistic level. It is open to a skeptic to accept the distinction between level 1 and level 2 rationality but to deny that behavior amenable to assessment in terms of level 2 rationality is available at the nonlinguistic level. How, it might be asked, can contingencies be represented and compared except through inferential processes of the sort that we have seen not to be available to nonlinguistic creatures? How can we make any sense of a creature acting on the basis of a comparison of contingencies unless we take it to be choosing the course of action with the highest likely benefits when each course of action's benefits are discounted by their probability? And surely that requires it to be representing the different potential outcomes, the utility it attaches to each of them, and its estimate of the likelihood that each outcome will occur—as well, of course, as performing the necessary calculations?

In line with the methodology adopted elsewhere in this book, I propose to make a start on this question by asking how we might understand the distinction between level 1 rationality and level 2 rationality in operational terms. What evidence might there be that a creature is representing the consequences of two or more different courses of action, rather than the actions themselves? Once we have a clear set of operational criteria in view it will be easier (in the next section) to offer a constitutive account of level 2 rationality. The particular forms of reasoning involved in level 2 rationality will be discussed further in chapter 7.

It is easiest to see how we might detect when a creature is *not* representing the contingency between action and consequence—that is to say, how we might detect when criteria of level 1 rationality should be applied rather than criteria of level 2 rationality. For example, if behavior were driven by the representation of an instrumental contingency then one would expect the behavior to cease in the face of repeated evidence that the contingency no longer holds. If the animal persists in the response then we have prima facie evidence that the contingency is not being represented. A classic experiment has been done by Hershberger (1986), who set up a graphic illustration of such a reversed contingency for chicks. In the experimental setup their food source retreated from them at twice the rate they walked toward it but advanced toward them at twice the rate they walked away from it. Even after 100 trials, the chicks only succeeded in obtaining the food 30 percent of the time, which has been taken clearly to indicate that they were failing to represent the two relevant contingencies (that walking backward causes the food to advance and walking forward causes the food to retreat).[9]

It is a minimal operational criterion, therefore, for actions being grounded on representations of contingencies that the action should not be persisted in once the animal has been confronted with evidence that the contingency ceases to hold. It is relatively easy to see what would count as evidence that this operational criterion is *not* being met. But what evidence might there be for thinking that it *is* being met? Some suggestive discoveries have been made by Rescorla and Skucy, and further developed by Hammond. They found that rats that have been trained to press a lever for food will cease to press the lever when the schedule is changed so that the food is delivered whether they press the lever or not (Rescorla and Skucy 1969; Hammond 1980). This seems to involve recognition that the contingency between lever-pressing and food delivery no longer holds. The rats had initially been pressing the lever in virtue of an instrumental belief that lever-pressing would result in the appearance of food. When the correlation tracked by the instrumental belief ceased to hold, the associated behavior also ceased.

Perhaps the most obvious source of relatively clear-cut evidence of level 2 rationality in nonlinguistic creatures is tool manufacture and tool-using behavior. The means-end domain of tool construction and use is deeply tied up with the representation of contingencies. Of course, not all such behavior is evidence for level 2 rationality. Many types of tool construction are relatively hard-wired and, although capable of refinement and improvement through learning, seem best evaluated according to the criteria associated with level 0 or level 1 rationality. The construction of dams by beavers is a case in point, much closer to nest building than to deliberate tool-based manipulation of the environment. A good example, though, of what seems to be the genuine representation of contingencies comes with the way chimpanzees in the wild manufacture tools for particular purposes (Byrne 1995, 96–97). Wild chimpanzees make wands for dipping into ant swarms by stripping the side leaves and leafy stem from a stick several feet long. The wands constructed for dipping into termite nests, on the other hand, are made from vines or more flexible twigs and are considerably shorter. They also have a bitten end, unlike the ant wands. It is sometimes remarked that such tool construction is purely innate. Gould and Gould (1998, 55) suggest, for example, that there is no genuine thought involved in what they call termite-fishing because even chimpanzees born in captivity make a habit of putting long thin things into holes. This neglects, however, the specialized nature of the different tools constructed. It is not just a matter of dipping a long thin stick into a narrow hole—the long thin stick needs to be constructed differently depending on what sort of hole it is going into. Nor, moreover, does the wand construction seem to be a form of trial-and-error learning. Byrne notes (97) that the wands are often constructed some time in advance and a considerable distance away from the place where they are going to be used.

Perhaps our best source of information for tool manufacture comes from archeological studies of the tools constructed by prelinguistic hominids. In human evolution the construction of complex tools long predated the emergence of language (Gibson and Ingold 1993). The fossil record suggests that hand-axes, the characteristic tool of early *Homo habilis,* first appeared about 1.4 million years ago—long before the evolution of language that (even on the most optimistic scenario) could not have occurred before the speciation of archaic *Homo sapiens* about one million years later. Considerable technical skill is required to make a hand-axe. Since the hand-axe is symmetrical, the flakes need to be removed from alternate sides. Each nodule is different, with different stresses and fracture lines, and the toolmaker needs to keep in mind a specific goal and adjust his blows accordingly. The force of the blows needs to be precisely calculated. The entire process is highly complicated and dependent on constant feedback and revision. A highly developed form of instrumental rationality is at work here, feeding into action.

The next major event in the early evolution of archaic *Homo sapiens* was the emergence of the Levallois flake, a characteristic tool that only emerged in the Middle Paleolithic period (Mithen 1996a). (Figure 6.1 shows the process of making a Levallois flake.) These Levallois flakes were then incorporated into more complex tools. Spears were made, for example, by hafting flakes onto wooden shafts—a process that involves the extraction of resin, the production of lashing materials, and so forth. It is hard to see how such complex forms of tool construc-

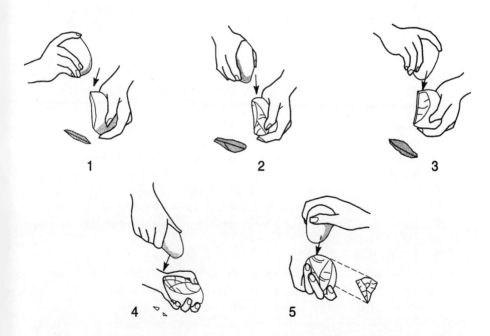

Figure 6.1 The making of a Levallois flake. To make a Levallois flake one must remove flakes from the surface of a core to leave a series of ridges on a domed surface (1–3, which will then guide the removal of the final pointed flake. A striking platform is prepared perpendicular to the domed surface of the core (4) and the Levallois flake removed by a single blow. From a drawing by Margaret Matthews in *The Prehistory of the Mind* by Steven Mithen, published by Thames and Hudson, Ltd.

tion, including the combination of tools to make further tools, could be possible without explicit representation of contingencies. Here, it seems, we are well within the realm of level 2 rationality.

6.5   Nonlinguistic Rationality and Psychological Explanation

In section 6.1 I argued that it would be futile to try to extend to nonlinguistic creatures what I termed the inference-based conception of practical reasoning. According to Davidson and many others, the rationalizing connection between the beliefs and desires cited in a psychological explanation and the action they explain is derived from the possibility of constructing an argument with those beliefs and desires as premises and a description of the action as conclusion. Of course, it is not just the abstract possibility that such an argument could be constructed that is important. It is essential that the agent should herself be capable of constructing the argument, although she need not actually have done so on the occasion in question. But, as I argued, we have no understanding of how nonlinguistic creatures can construct arguments, or assess validity in any other way. So the inference-based conception of practical reasoning has to be abandoned.

What I have shown in the last few sections is that this does not mean that the notion of rationality cannot be applied at the nonlinguistic level. Quite the contrary. There are three distinct and useful senses in which the behavior of nonlinguistic creatures can be properly assessed for rationality. The behavior of nonlinguistic creatures can be assessed according to three different sets of norms—those of level 0 rationality, level 1 rationality, or level 2 rationality. Each set of norms is appropriate for different types of behavior. Behaviors that are instances of innate releasing mechanisms and other fixed and invariant behavior patterns are best assessed according to the criteria of level 0 rationality. The assessment of rationality attaches in this case to the type under which the behavior falls, rather than to the token behavior instantiated on a particular occasion. When it makes sense to suppose that the action performed was one of a range of possible courses of action open to the creature in question, it becomes assessable according to the norms of level 1 rationality. When the criteria for genuine decision-making are met, then the norms of level 2 rationality come into play.

Two questions arise at this point. First, one might ask which of the three levels of rationality I have identified is appropriate for the project of providing psychological explanations of the behavior of nonlinguistic creatures. Are psychological explanations available all the way down the ladder of rationality, or is there a privileged level or levels of rationality below which psychological explanation is not possible? Second, one might ask what the relation is between the way rationality is assessed at level 2 and the way it is assessed according to the normative theories of rationality that might plausibly be taken as normatively binding on language-using agents. How, if at all, do the normative criteria of rationality that we apply in our everyday psychological explanations and predictions differ from those that we might apply to nonlinguistic creatures? I will take these questions in order.

It is obvious, more or less as a matter of definition, that there is no scope for psychological explanation of behaviors for which considerations of level 0 rationality are appropriate. It is equally obvious that psychological explanations can be appropriate when we are dealing with behaviors assessable for level 2 rationality. The principal question is whether we can have psychological explanations in situations where the appropriate criteria of rationality are those of level 1 rationality. There is a straightforward line of argument setting out to establish that level 2 rationality is required for psychological explanation. The argument runs as follows. Giving a psychological explanation is saying that an animal has acted in a certain way because of its beliefs and its desires. More precisely, it is to say that the *combination* of its beliefs and desires explains its actions. An animal has certain beliefs about its environment and also certain desires. But how do these come together to bring about action? Only through the representation of contingencies between actions and their outcomes. Only when an animal forms the belief that a certain course of action will lead to the satisfaction of a desire. But this is an instrumental belief about the consequences that an action is likely to have—hence the behavior to which it gives rise falls squarely within the domain of level 2 rationality.

The problem with this line of argument is that the fact that a certain course of action will bring about the satisfaction of a desire may be immediately perceptually manifest—as when, for example, a food reward is in plain view. An explicit belief is not always required. Any psychological explanation will always have an instrumental component, but that component need not take the form of an instrumental belief. In fact, to revert to some of the points that emerged in our earlier discussion of the minimalist approach, instrumental beliefs really only enter the picture when two conditions are met. The first is that the goal of the action should not be immediately perceptible and the second is that there should be no immediately perceptible instrumental properties (that is to say, the creature should not be capable of seeing that a certain course of action will lead to a desired result). The fact, however, that one or both of these conditions is not met does not entail that we are dealing with an action that is explicable in nonpsychological terms.

The basic requirement for psychological explanation is negative (as emerged in chapter 1). An action requires psychological explanation just if its occurrence could not have been predicted solely from knowledge of the environmental parameters and sensory input. That is to say, the need for psychological explanation arises only in situations where the connections between sensory input and behavioral output cannot be plotted in a lawlike manner. Clearly, however, it is perfectly possible for a situation to qualify even if the goal of the action is immediately perceptible—or, for that matter, if the distal environment contains immediately perceptible instrumental properties. In such situations the instrumental component of the psychological explanation will most likely be part of the content of perception.

It should not be thought, however, that instrumental beliefs (and with them level 2 rationality) come into play only when there is no immediately perceptible goal. It is possible for a goal to be directly in view and yet for it to be far from apparent how it is to be gained. In such a situation one would expect the instrumental component to take the form of an instrumental belief. Some of the classic examples of instrumental reasoning in animals fall into this category. Köhler's (1925) chimpanzees could clearly see the bunch of bananas that was hung out of their reach. They just could not immediately see how to reach the bunch, until they formed an appropriate instrumental belief (which, depending on the chimpanzee, was either that stacking boxes one on top of the other would bring the bananas within reach, or that two sticks could be joined together to knock the bananas down, or that standing on a box would bring the bananas within reach of the stick). Another, less anecdotal example comes from Bernd Heinrich's (2000) experiments with hand-reared ravens. Pieces of meat were hung by string from their perches, too far for them to reach from the perch and too securely tied to be accessible in flight. Four out of the five ravens eventually worked out different ways of pulling up the string and obtaining the meat. As with the chimpanzee example, the goal was clearly in view. It is tempting to think that the difference was made by an instrumental belief about how that goal might be obtained.

What is important, therefore, for the applicability of psychological explanation is that there be an instrumental component in the psychological states that give rise to the particular action. This instrumental component can be part of the content of perception (in what I have termed level 1 rationality) or it can take the form of a separate instrumental belief (in level 2 rationality). In order to appreciate the importance of this instrumental component it is helpful to return to the distinction between internal and external rationality briefly introduced earlier (see section 6.1). An action is internally rational when it makes sense relative to an agent's beliefs and desires, while an action is externally rational when it makes sense relative to a given set of environmental parameters that include the agent's desires but not his beliefs. From the viewpoint of psychological explanation the first of these is paramount. Agents often act on the basis of poorly supported inductive generalizations and inaccurate assessments of the situation. What is important in explaining their behavior is how those generalizations and assessments get translated into action. The question of how they might have acted optimally in that situation is not relevant. But assessments of internal rationality only make sense when there is an instrumental component—only with the instrumental component in play can one properly evaluate the appropriateness of an action relative to the agent's beliefs. Psychological explanation, therefore, is only applicable when we are dealing with behaviors reflecting either level 2 rationality or an instance of level 1 rationality incorporating an instrumental component.

Moving now to the second question, how are we to understand the relation between level 1 and level 2 rationality, on the one hand, and the type of rationality that we think of as governing everyday commonsense psychological explanation, on the other? There are two subquestions to be separated out here. The first concerns the norms that govern ascriptions of rationality at the different levels; the second concerns the reasoning that generates the relevant behaviors. How should we compare the reasoning implicated in behaviors assessable for level 1, level 2, and commonsense psychological rationality? The answer to the first question is relatively straightforward. There is little difference in the norms that govern and guide ascriptions of rationality at all three levels. Level 1 rationality is governed by norms of maximizing expected amounts of a particular currency, as well as by the norm of maintaining interanimal strategies that are in game-theoretic equilibrium. There is nothing here alien to the norms of folk psychological rationality— although the range of available currencies is much greater in folk psychological rationality, and there is scope for issues such as incommensurability that are hard to imagine arising at the nonlinguistic level. The difference is one of degree rather than kind. Something similar holds for the norms governing level 2 rationality. Assessments of level 2 rationality are determined by two factors, first the accuracy of the appropriate instrumental belief and second the appropriateness of the action relative to that instrumental belief. It is hard to see how the norms governing folk psychological rationality could be any different from these.

The crucial differences come, not at the level of the norms governing the ascriptions of rationality, but rather at the level of the reasoning that leads up to action. We can illustrate this by comparing level 2 rationality with the inference-based conception of practical rationality introduced through the passage from Davidson quoted at the beginning of the chapter. As just observed, the overarching norms of rationality governing ascriptions of rationality are the same at the two levels, namely, that the instrumental belief should be accurate and that the action should be appropriate relative to that instrumental belief. The difference comes in the way "appropriateness" is calculated in the two cases. In essence, the inference-based conception of practical rationality understands the appropriateness of an action relative to an instrumental belief in terms of the possibility of constructing a valid argument from the instrumental belief (and associated beliefs and desires) to a description of the action. As I showed in the first section of this chapter, no such understanding of appropriateness is available at the nonlinguistic level, because the notion of formal inference is not applicable at the nonlinguistic level. So how should appropriateness be understood at the nonlinguistic level?

It is tempting to put the point in terms of consistency, so that an appropriate action was one that is consistent with the instrumental belief, and understanding an action as appropriate is a matter of understanding it as consistent with the relevant beliefs, perceptions, and background desires, but this would be unsatisfactory for two reasons. The first is that many ways of acting in a manner consistent with an instrumental belief do not involve acting on it. Not all of these would properly be described as appropriate. Second, the notion of consistency can be viewed in two ways, neither of which is applicable at the nonlinguistic level. Consistency might be viewed as primarily an inferential matter, so that a set of beliefs, desires, and intentions is consistent just if its members do not jointly entail a contradiction. But this sort of consistency-based understanding of the appropriateness of a course of action to a set of beliefs and desires would be little improvement over an inference-based conception, which I have already shown to be inapplicable at the nonlinguistic level. Things are no better if consistency is viewed in semantic terms, so that a set of beliefs, desires, and intentions is consistent just if they can be true/satisfied together. Understanding consistency is a matter of understanding the consistency of a set of sentences—hence requires linguistic vehicles.

At the nonlinguistic level the appropriateness of a course of action relative to a set of beliefs and desires, including an instrumental belief, can really only be understood as a matter of a creature straightforwardly acting on a given instrumental belief in the light of its other beliefs and desires. It is to be assumed, in other words, that an instrumental belief will be immediately acted on, unless there are significant countervailing considerations—perhaps a potential threat from a predator, or the overwhelming energy cost of carrying out the relevant action. At the nonlinguistic level, issues of rationality get a grip, therefore, in two ways. The first way is through the accuracy of the instrumental belief—the rationality of the contemplated course of action as a means of obtaining the required goal. The second way is through the translation of the instrumental belief into action—relative to the creature's other beliefs, desires, and needs.

As far as reasoning is concerned, level 2 rationality depends on what one might term a straightforward practical syllogism—that is to say, an immediate translation of an instrumental belief into action. A preliminary answer to the second question, therefore, is that there are significant differences between level 2 rationality as applied to nonlinguistic creatures and the forms of rationality that we deploy in explaining and predicting the behavior of other language-using creatures. These are differences, however, in the types of reasoning available at the different levels, rather than in the overarching norms that govern ascriptions of rationality. The overarching norms remain constant. What varies is the complexity of the decision-making processes that lead up to the action whose degree of rationality is being assessed. The question of the specific types of reasoning available at the nonlinguistic level will be discussed in greater detail in the next chapter.

7

Practical Reasoning and Protologic

In the previous chapter I showed how the notion of rationality might be deployed in psychological explanations of the behavior of nonlinguistic creatures. I identified three different ways of characterizing behavior at the nonlinguistic level as rational. Two of these conceptions of rationality are relevant to the project of psychological explanation. These are what I termed level 1 and level 2 rationality. The distinctive feature of level 1 rationality is that, although it applies to individual behaviors, it is not properly describable as involving a process of decision-making. In this respect it contrasts with level 2 rationality, which depends crucially on the existence of instrumental beliefs about how a given end might be achieved in a particular context.

In this chapter I will complete the account of psychological explanation by exploring how the notion of practical reasoning might be applied at the nonlinguistic level. In section 7.1 I explore the idea, familiar from discussions of the language of thought hypothesis, that practical reasoning should be understood in decision-theoretic terms, both when we are dealing with linguistic and with nonlinguistic creatures. I will show that the decision-theoretic model is not required for the explanation of behaviors that are rational in either the level 1 or the level 2 sense. Nonetheless, certain forms of practical reasoning are available at the nonlinguistic level. In section 7.2 I show how it is possible to identify at the nonlinguistic level certain very basic forms of protological thinking. These basic forms of protological thinking include what I term protonegation and protoconditional reasoning. The second of these in particular can help us to understand the instrumental beliefs in behavior assessable according to the norms of level 2 rationality.

7.1 The Decision-Theoretic Model of Practical Reasoning

There is a basic distinction, drawn in this book as indeed in every discussion of nonlinguistic thought, between brute reaction and intelligent, thinking behavior.

Thinking behavior involves flexible and variable responses to the environment. It supports content-involving counterfactuals. It cannot be predicted on the basis of knowledge of what is happening at the sensory periphery. And so on. These operational criteria of course all point toward the intuitive idea that thinking behavior results from deliberation on the environment as represented in the light of background representations and motivational states.

One powerful way of fleshing out this intuitive idea is the proposal that decision-making at the nonlinguistic level might be decision-theoretic in nature. This conception of nonlinguistic reasoning has traditionally been associated with the language of thought hypothesis—on the plausible assumption that, if the actual process of decision-making is decision-theoretic, then the various components of the decision-making process (specifications of possible outcomes, calculations of preferences, assessments of probability, and so forth) will need to be represented in a language-like medium. In line with the general strategy of neutrality adopted in chapter 2, I will prescind from questions that have to do with the vehicle of nonlinguistic thinking. My concern in this section is with the basic claim that the language of thought theory sets out to explain the idea that we can only make sense of practical reasoning in decision-theoretic terms as a process of maximizing expected utility.

Fodor (1975, 28–29) offers the following schematic model of practical decision-making (see also Rey 1997).

1. A given creature finds itself in a certain situation S.
2. It believes that a certain set of behavioral options, B_1 . . . B_n, is available in S.
3. The creature predicts the probable consequences of performing each of those behavioral options by computing a series of conditionals of the form: If B_i is performed in S then consequences C_i will occur with a certain probability.
4. A preference ordering is assigned to the consequences.
5. The creature's choice of behavior is determined as a function of the assigned preferences and probabilities.[1]

There is a basic distinction to be drawn between descriptive theories of decision-making and normative theories of rationality. Descriptive theories are psychological theories about how decisions are reached and courses of action fixed on, whereas normative theories concern the rationality of the processes of decision-making and of the eventual course of action. It is clear that Fodor offers his model of practical reasoning as a descriptive psychological theory. He does not see it as providing a normative theory of rationality, since it has nothing to say about the rationality or otherwise of the creature's beliefs about possible options and outcomes; its assessments of the likelihoods of those outcomes; and its assignment of subjective utilities.

In contrast, in chapter 6 I offered an account of nonlinguistic rationality in which the theory of expected utility functioned as a normative theory. The normative criteria by which level 0 and level 1 rationality are to be judged include various versions of expected utility theory. The variation comes because of the different ways that utility can be understood at this level—in terms of rate of energy procurement, individual lifetime fitness, inclusive fitness, and so on. In neither level 0 nor level 1 rationality, however, should it be assumed that the normative criteria in any way reflect the decision-making that goes on in behavior that is assessed for rationality at the relevant level. Decision-making, properly speaking, enters the picture only with level 2 rationality.[2] There are ways of comparing possible courses of action and choosing between them that do not require anything recognizable as a process of decision-making. As I pointed out in the previous chapter, the affordances of a particular course of action can be manifest in the content of perception. The leopard does not look at the antelope and work out that if it pursues the antelope it will have a high probability of securing a considerable amount of food. When it sees the antelope it sees the affordance of food. In situations such as these, the instrumentality of a particular course of action is manifest in the content of perception—and of course a single perception can reveal several different potential courses of action.

It will be helpful to work through an example of behavior assessable according to the norms of level 1 rationality. Consider the roaring contests of red deer stags (Clutton-Brock and Albon 1979). During the rutting season red deer compete with each other for the control of groups of females. Actually fighting each other is risky and exhausting for both winner and loser. So fighting contests are frequently replaced by roaring contests, where the winner is the loudest and most sustained roarer and the loser backs down. A male's capacity for roaring is a good index of his strength and consequently of how he would have fought had he been called upon to do so. The dispute is frequently resolved by the roaring contest. However, if the roaring rates are more or less similar and fail to identify a "winner," it is usual for the contest to shift to a second stage in which the deer perform a parallel walk that seems to provide information about body height and antler size (Clutton-Brock and Albon 1979). If that also turns out equal then the deer lock antlers and proceed to fight.

In the abstract, and for the purposes of normative evaluation, the contest can be modeled as a series of choices. The behavioral options for each stag at each choice node are simple and can be represented diagrammatically (see fig. 7.1). The first choice node represents the decision to embark on the roaring contest at all and the options are: Roar or Back Down. Presumably there will be some stage during the initial roaring contest during which the stag has to decide whether to continue roaring or to back down. Hence: Continue Roaring or Back Down. If at any stage during the roaring contest the other stag backs down then the overall competition is over. If, however, neither participant backs down then at the end of the roaring contest each stag will face the choice of terminating the contest or entering the next stage: Back Down or Parallel Walk. During the parallel walk stage, each stag has to decide whether to continue walking or to back down: Continue Walking or

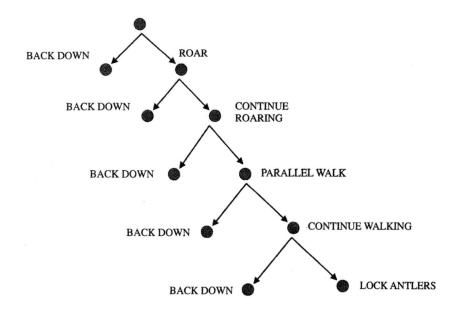

Figure 7.1 The choice nodes in a model of red deer roaring contests.

Back Down. At the end of the parallel walk stage, the choice is between retreating and progressing to the pushing contest: Back Down or Lock Antlers.

It is clear that some version of normative expected utility theory can be deployed to determine the respective payoffs at each node in the choice-tree. The stags are competing for groups of females, and it is natural to think that the relevant currency will be some form of inclusive fitness. In calculating the expected utility of the different behavioral options at each point in the choice-tree, we need to take into account the overall benefits in terms of inclusive fitness of controlling the group of females, since control of the group will be one of the two outcomes for each of what might be termed the proactive strategies: Roar, Continue Roaring, Parallel Walk, Continue Walking, Lock Antlers. For the first four of these proactive strategies, the second of the two outcomes will be straightforward—essentially a controlled retreat without physical damage. This can straightforwardly be translated into the currency of inclusive fitness. Things are slightly more complicated at the final decision-node, since the second outcome of the Lock Antlers strategy is a damaging defeat that is potentially life-threatening and definitely fitness-decreasing. The nonproactive strategies (essentially Back Down at each choice node) all have a single possible outcome, rather similar to the second outcome of the first four proactive strategies.

Once we have determined the payoffs for the different outcomes associated with each strategy available at the relevant decision-nodes, the next step is to derive an expected utility calculation by calculating the probability of each of the potential outcomes. The calculation will not be easy, since the utility of the different outcomes in the early stages is partly a function of what can reasonably be expected to happen if proactive strategies are adopted in the later stages. Nonetheless, it is manageable. It is relatively clear, therefore, how we might develop and apply a normative framework for thinking about red deer roaring contests. But recall that we are investigating whether we need to model choice behavior in a way that takes the normative theory by which we assess the rationality of a course of action as a structural guide for the descriptive theory. The question, really, is whether the applicability to the red deer stages of normative criteria based on considerations of expected utility depends on our viewing the deer as themselves making calculations of expected utility.

It is clear how we, as observers, assign probabilities to the relevant outcomes. We might employ our knowledge of the respective ages of the two stags, of how successful they have each been in previous contests, of how damaged they are from fights in the past, and so on. Obviously, in most cases neither stag has access to this type of information. So how can they calculate probabilities at all? The short answer is that they do not need to. The relevant information is directly present in the content of perception. The overarching rationale for the two early stages of the contest is that they each allow the participant to pick up information about the likely outcome of an aggressive conflict. A male's capacity for roaring is a good index of his strength, and consequently of how he would fight were he called on to do so—since roaring uses the thoracic muscles that are also employed in fighting. And, of course, it is not just that the male who roars loudest will have the greater probability of defeating his opponent in an actual physical contest than the male who loses the roaring contest. The male who roars the loudest will also have a higher probability of being able to defend the group of females. Both types of information are directly available in the content of auditory perception. The same holds for the parallel walk section of the contest, although in a different sensory modality. The parallel walk transmits information about the relative heights and muscle sizes of the two participants—information that is highly relevant to the expected utility calculation. The adaptive aim of the parallel walk section is, of course, that it allows both participants to pick up this information simply by looking—hence without having to engage in any sort of conflict.

The red deer example shows, I think, how we can place a wedge between the normative and descriptive dimensions of our theories of practical decision-making as applied to the behavior of nonlinguistic creatures. From a normative point of view we can understand the roaring contests within the framework of expected utility theory. We can also employ this framework for predictive purposes. Given our knowledge of the different possible strategies and the payoffs and probabilities of their respective outcomes, we can (on the plausible assumption that both participants are suitably sensitive to the relevant parameters) predict how far down the choice-tree each stag will be prepared to travel. But we can do this without having to say that the stags are doing anything comparable to calculations of expected utilities. For the stag the behavioral options are manifest; Roar or Back Down, and so on. The contrast-space of alternative courses of action does not need to be represented propositionally. What determines which course of action is selected? The most obvious candidate is the information about likely outcomes that is transmitted once the roaring contest has been entered into. This is information about likely outcomes, but it is not necessarily registered as information about likely outcomes. The animal just sees what to do by comparing its roar with its rival's roar, or the respective shoulder heights and musculatures revealed in profile.

It looks, therefore, as if a large category of behaviors for which psychological explanations seem appropriate, hence that involve genuine choice, can be modeled in a way that does not implicate anything like the machinery of practical decision-making envisaged by Fodor. But I have so far confined myself to what in the previous chapter I identified as level 1 rationality. Surely, the defender of the decision-theoretic model is likely to object, consequence-sensitive reasoning of the decision-theoretic type is implicated in level 2 rationality. I defined level 2 rationality as involving genuine decision-making and grounded in the representation of contingencies. Is this not decision-theoretic?

To say that the decision-making that generates behavior assessable at level 2 rationality is consequence-sensitive in form is not, however, to say that it takes the form of a calculation of expected utility in the manner implied by Fodor's psychological model. The point that I stressed in discussing level 2 rationality and the concomitant practical reasoning is that the consequence-sensitive dimension enters the picture via instrumental beliefs rather than via complex calculations of preference ordering and utility. Creatures (both linguistic and nonlinguistic) can act on the basis of a comparison of contingencies without calculating which course of action in the contrast-space of possibilities has the highest likely benefits when each course of action's potential benefits are discounted by their probability. The seductiveness of the decision-theoretic model of practical reasoning comes from the idea that consequence-sensitive comparison of alternative courses of action requires a two-stage partition of the space of possibilities—an initial partition into different available courses of action followed by a further partition, for each of those courses of action, into its different potential outcomes. But this is not, of course, the only possible model. Once again the conflation of the normative and the descriptive threatens to mislead. It is certainly true that, when we are assessing the rationality of a particular course of action, we need to consider the full range of possible outcomes. We cannot come to a view about whether a creature acted rationally in a particular situation without taking into account both the potential benefits that might have motivated it and the potentially disastrous consequences that ought perhaps to have put it off. But the creature in question does not need to make a comparable comparison and calculation. It is quite possible that all it needs to motivate its action is an instrumental belief to the effect that acting in that particular way is the only way of deriving the benefits in question.[3]

Let us distinguish then between explicit decision-theoretic reasoning and instrumental reasoning. Only the first requires the sort of comparative calculations envisaged by Fodor. The point and applicability of the contrast becomes very clear when we consider the examples of level 2 rationality put forward in chapter 6. The construction and use of tools loomed large there, and it is hard to see how these behaviors are best modeled in terms of the two-stage partition assumed in the descriptive application of the expected utility model. It seems far more appropriate to describe the chimpanzee as whittling down a twig because it believes that this will enable it to use the twig to extract termites from the termite nest than as settling on that course of action because it has calculated that it offers the highest expected utility. Again, the normative and descriptive dimensions come apart. We, as theorists, are perfectly capable of assessing the rationality of the chimpanzee's behavior by applying some form of the two-stage partition and calculating not simply the likely outcomes, costs, and benefits of the tool construction but also the likely outcomes, costs, and benefits of the other activities in which the chimpanzee could have been engaged at that time. But the chimpanzee doesn't have to do all that. The same holds for the construction of hand-axes by early hominids. The machinery that we employ to assess the rationality of tool construction and manipulation is not a reconstruction of the processes of practical reasoning implicated in those behaviors.

But why should we treat a behavior so grounded as genuinely thinking behavior and hence as a candidate for assessments of rationality at all? Do we not pay a heavy price for prising apart the descriptive and the normative by so diluting the type of practical reasoning at stake? Two points can be made in response. The first is that it is simply not the case that no comparison is involved. The environment affords many possible courses of action, and creatures operating at level 2 do indeed fix on a single member of the relevant contrast-space. Tool construction is hardly a tropistic behavior. There may even be more than one instrumental belief in play. Of course, if there is more than one instrumental belief then it is likely that some comparison of goals and outcomes will be required, but there is no reason to think that this will require complicated machinery of the sort postulated by Fodor. The second point is that, although the relevant behaviors do most likely involve comparisons of different possible courses of action, that is not why they are being treated as intentional behaviors and consequently as candidates for psychological explanation. The intentionality of the behavior derives from two considerations. The first is the creature's sensitivity to the consequences of its behavior and to the contingency (or lack of it) between behavior and desired outcome. This explains why we need to assume that the creature is genuinely representing the contingency and the instrumentality. The second factor is that the behavior does not seem to be the product of trial and error. This rules out taking the representations involved at the level of thinking-how and consequently rules out analysis in terms of the minimalist conception of nonlinguistic thought discussed in chapter 3.

It would seem, therefore, that at the nonlinguistic level we have models of practical reasoning and deliberation that do not implicate the complicated inferences and calculations that Fodor suggests are required for any form of thinking behavior. The next section will explore these models, and the types of protological thinking that they involve, in more detail.

7.2 *Inference and Protologic*

In section 6.1 I suggested that there is no hope of applying an inference-based conception of rationality at the nonlinguistic level, and in the previous section it emerged that the decision-theoretic model is equally inappropriate for characterizing the practical reasoning of nonlinguistic creatures. This poses a challenge. The notions of thought and reasoning are inextricably linked. There is no sense in which there can be thought without reasoning, and many of the arguments put forward in earlier chapters to show, for example, that nonlinguistic thoughts have genuine structure and determinate contents have hinged on claims about the role that such thoughts must play in reasoning. So we clearly need an account of the particular types of reasoning that are available at the nonlinguistic level.

The issue becomes particularly pressing when we look ahead to the conclusions of the next two chapters. In chapter 8 I show that there are definite limits to the scope of nonlinguistic thinking. Certain types of thinking are in principle only available to creatures who dispose of a language. The fundamental reason for the restriction is that, for reasons that will be explored in the final two chapters, thoughts can only be the objects of further thoughts when they are linguistically vehicled. Intentional ascent (that is to say, thinking about thoughts) requires the possibility of semantic ascent. Some thoughts that involve intentional ascent are explicitly targeted on first-order thoughts. This is the case, for example, with those forms of psychological understanding that involve attributing thoughts to others (see section 9.3). But intentional ascent is also involved (or so I shall argue) in types of thinking involving operators, such as tense operators and modal operators, that govern entire thoughts. If this line of argument is sound then it rules out thinking about the reasoning of nonlinguistic creatures in terms of elementary logical concepts. By 'elementary logical concepts' I mean those logical concepts associated with the standard connectives in the propositional calculus—the concepts of conjunction, negation, and disjunction and the material conditional. As the term "propositional calculus" suggests, these concepts are adverbial in precisely the same way as the concepts associated with modal and tense operators. They apply to complete thoughts (propositions). It is complete thoughts that are negated, conjoined, disjoined, and connected in the manner characteristic of the material conditional. Hence their application is a process of intentional ascent that requires semantic ascent.

The challenge, therefore, is to identify forms of reasoning at the nonlinguistic level and then explain them in a manner that does not require the reasoner to deploy elementary logical concepts. In identifying these types of reasoning we should be guided, as usual, by thinking both about how they might be manifested in behavior and about how they might be attributed to explain behavior. In this section I shall discuss three such basic types of reasoning that it would be natural (when thinking about language-using creatures) to characterize in terms of mastery of certain primitive basic logical concepts. As I will show, there is an alternative way of understanding them at the nonlinguistic level.

The first type of reasoning can be described as reasoning from an excluded alternative. This is the type of inference that takes a creature from recognition that one of an incompatible pair of states of affairs holds to the recognition that the other does not hold. Here is an example. Imagine a creature that has learned that the lion and the gazelle will not be at the watering-hole at the same time and, moreover, is in a position to see that the gazelle is drinking happily at the watering-hole. The creature can conclude with confidence that the lion is not in the vicinity. This type of reasoning is one of the ways a creature can learn about what is not immediately perceptible. One can see easily, for example, how this sort of inference could be life-preserving for a creature who is just as threatened by the lion as the gazelle is. It is natural to formalize it in the propositional calculus as an instance of disjunctive syllogism (the transition from "A or B" and "not-A" to "B," where A stands for "The gazelle is not at the water-hole" and B for "The lion is not at the water-hole").

A second such way of moving beyond the here-and-now comes with straightforward conditional reasoning of the form standardly termed *modus ponens*—that is, the reasoning that takes one from recognition that there is a conditional dependence between two states of affairs (the second will be the case if the first is the case) and a recognition that the first state of affairs is indeed the case to the conclusion that the second state of affairs is the case. Conditional reasoning of this type is deeply implicated in a range of different activities. The detection of patterns of behavior seems closely bound up with the possibility of conditional reasoning. A creature that knows that if the gazelles see the lion they will run away and that recognizes (on the basis of its understanding of the gazelles' visual perspective, as will be discussed in section 9.3) that the lion will shortly be detected by the gazelles is in a position to predict that the gazelles will soon take flight.

The third fundamental type of inference is also based on recognition of a conditional dependence between two states of affairs—but in this case (formalized in terms of *modus tollens*) the reasoning proceeds from recognition that the second state of affairs does not hold to recognition that the first state of affairs is not the case. So, for example, to stick with the gazelles, an observer (perhaps a fellow predator) who is too far away to have a view about the visual perspective of the gazelles can infer from the fact that they are happily feeding where they are that they have not yet seen the lion.

In standard propositional logic these three fundamental forms of inference are understood in terms of the three propositional operators of disjunction, negation, and the material conditional. What I have called reasoning from an excluded alternative is standardly understood in terms of the inference schema of disjunctive syllogism (Either A or B, not-A. Therefore B), with the relevant operators being disjunction and negation. The two types of conditional reasoning are both understood in terms of the material conditional (If A, then B). All three operators are functions from propositions to propositions and hence take complete thoughts as both arguments and values. Clearly, given my comments in the previous chapter about the inference-based conception of rationality (and anticipating the argument from intentional ascent to be given in the next chapter), if we are to find analogues of these three types of reasoning at the nonlinguistic level then we will need to find ways of understanding them on which they do not involve propositional operators.

We can make a start on this by simplifying the problem. Reasoning from an excluded alternative can be understood as a form of conditional reasoning, rather than in terms of disjunctive syllogism. Let A stand for the sentence "The gazelle is not at the watering-hole" and B for the sentence "The lion is not at the watering-hole." Then the disjunction "A or B" is truth-functionally equivalent to the conditional "If not-A, then B" (that is to say, "If the gazelle is at the watering-hole, then the lion is not at the watering-hole"). Both sentences will be true just if it is not the case that the gazelle and the lion are both at the watering-hole.[4] The process of reasoning from an excluded alternative will involve a grasp on the one hand of the conditional "If not-A, then B" and on the other of the antecedent of that conditional (where that antecedent is in some sense negative). All we need, therefore, is to find a way of understanding analogues for negation and the conditional that do not operate on complete thoughts.

Let us start with negation. Modern, that is to say post-Fregean, logic is founded on the idea that, as far as the fundamental logical form of sentences is concerned, the linguistic act of negation applies essentially to sentences—and correlatively, at the level of thought, that negation is a logical operation on propositions. It may seem that, in the sentence "Socrates is not wise" (and still more so in the sentence "Socrates is unwise"), a particular property, the property of wisdom, is being held not to apply to Socrates. However, the surface form of natural language sentences is deceptive. The negation operator actually applies at the level of the sentence "Socrates is wise" rather than at the level of the predicate "— is wise."[5] The sentence "Socrates is unwise" is a sentence that is true just if the sentence "Socrates is wise" is false. Many philosophers have thought that this obscures an important distinction. The sentence "Socrates is wise" can be false in circumstances in which Socrates does not exist—such as now, for example. Yet these are not, many have thought, circumstances in which it would be appropriate to say that Socrates is unwise. One way of putting the point would be to say that, whereas the two sentences "Socrates is wise" and "Socrates is unwise" are contraries (i.e., they cannot both simultaneously be true), the two sentences "Socrates is wise" and "It is not the case that Socrates is wise" are contradictories (i.e., one or other of them must be true). This, in fact, is how the distinction between predicate negation and sentential negation was originally put by Aristotle in the *Prior Analytics* (I.46). Aristotle insisted, and in this he was followed by almost all logicians until Frege, that there is a fundamental logical difference between negating a sentence and negating a predicate.

There is no need to go into the question of whether the distinction between predicate negation and sentential negation is a genuine logical distinction (as opposed, for example, to a distinction in the pragmatics of ordinary language best accommodated at the level of conversational implicature)—or the related question of whether a Fregean or an Aristotelian account of negation is a better way to understand the way negation operates in ordinary language.[6] For present purposes the important point is that the distinction between predicate negation and sentential negation gives us a way of understanding negation (or rather, *protonegation*) at the nonlinguistic level as involving a thought with a negative predicate (subject to the qualifications to be noted in the next paragraph)—as opposed to the truth-functional construction of a complex thought. In terms of understanding thought at the nonlinguistic level, the problem of understanding how a creature without language can be capable of negation becomes the problem of how a creature without language can think thoughts in which the predicate component is one rather than the other of a pair of contraries. The task becomes one of understanding how the nonlinguistic creature can grasp pairs of concepts that are contraries—the concepts of presence and absence, for example, or of safety and danger, or of visibility and invisibility. To return to the observer at the water-hole, we should understand the thought that the gazelle is not at the water-hole as the thought that the gazelle is absent from the water-hole—rather than as the denial of the thought that the gazelle is at the water-hole. Such a thought would be the contrary of the thought that the gazelle is at the water-hole—but it would not be constructed from that thought.

It is often put forward as an objection in principle to the idea of predicate negation that there is no principled way of distinguishing positive predicates from negative predicates. To take Frege's example, which of the pair of contrary predicates 'mortal' and 'immortal' is positive and which negative? Is 'immortal' negative, on the grounds that predicating immortality of something is denying it mortality? Or is 'immortal' positive, on the grounds that mortality is a lack of immortality? There is clearly no way of deciding this matter. But as far as protonegation is concerned, there is no need to classify one of a pair of contrary properties as positive and the other as negative. The important point is simply that it is understood (on the part of the protonegater) that no thing can simultaneously be characterized in terms of the two contrary properties. This is sufficient to permit primitive versions of the two basic types of inference involving negation that I identified earlier. The first type of inference involves reasoning from an excluded alternative. Consider the earlier example of the gazelle and the lion at the watering-hole. We are trying to characterize how a creature might reason from the thought that the gazelle is at the watering-hole to the thought that the lion is not at the watering hole. The reasoning here can be assimilated to standard conditional reasoning by treating the central premise as a conditional—namely, the conditional that if the gazelle is at the watering-hole then the lion is not at the watering-hole. The notion of protonegation shows how this can be understood without deploying propositional negation. The conditional in question becomes "If the gazelle is present (at the watering-hole) then the lion is absent (at the watering-hole)." Grasping this thought (apart from the need, to be explored further hereafter, to develop a nonlinguistic analogue of the truth-functional conditional operator) is a matter of understanding that presence and absence are contrary concepts. Any creature that understands that presence and absence are contrary concepts will also be able (again subject to a satisfactory account being given at the nonlinguistic level of conditional reasoning) to undertake reasoning approximating to *modus tollens*. Starting with the conditional "If the gazelle is present (at the watering-hole), then the lion is absent," such a creature will be able to protonegate the consequent by forming the thought that the lion is present and hence to arrive at the protonegation of the antecedent (namely, "The gazelle is absent"). This inference is not valid in virtue of its form in the way an instance of *modus tollens* is valid in virtue of its form—that is to say, it is not an instance of a valid argument-schema. But it is of course valid in the semantic sense—that is to say, its premises cannot be true and its conclusion false.

It might be objected to the proposed understanding of protonegation that the very idea of contrary properties is parasitic on propositional negation—hence that it will not be possible for a creature to grasp the idea that two properties might be contraries without a grip on the notion of propositional negation. Two properties are contrary just if it is not possible for them both to be true of a given thing at a given time—from which it appears to follow that the concept of contrariety presupposes the concept of propositional negation.[7] What this line of objection neglects, however, is that a creature can master pairs of contrary concepts (such as the concepts of presence and absence) and deploy those concepts in inferences using protonegation without a full understanding of the notion of contrariety. It is no more plausible to think that the effective deployment of contrary concepts requires a theoretical grasp of the concept of contrariety than it is to demand that the effective deployment of number concepts requires a theoretical grasp of the concept of number.

The notion of protonegation that these reflections yield is obviously very different from the truth-functional understanding of negation that dominates contemporary logic. But this is not a disadvantage. It may well be the case that, as Frege emphatically argued, there is no room in logic and the analysis of language for anything analogous to what I am calling protonegation. That would hardly entail, however, that protonegation cannot be deployed at the nonlinguistic level. Frege's arguments in his essay "Negation" (1918–19a) are all devoted to trying to show the absurdity of starting with a complete thought and then construing negation as an operation on a component of that thought. Nothing like that is involved in protonegation, however, for the simple reason that protonegation is not an operation on complete thoughts. It may be that protonegation leaves no traces at the level of full-fledged linguistic thought—that the relation of contrariety drops out of the picture in the way that certain principles of infant naive physics drop out of the picture in the normal course of development (as I showed in chapter 3). Protonegation may be a ladder that is thrown away on the way to mastery of the full-fledged concept of negation as a truth-functional operation on complete thoughts. We might take as a model Quine's proposal (1974, 89–92) that children learning the relative pronoun begin by treating relative clauses as self-contained grammatical entities (effectively complex predicables) before learning that relative pronouns in fact operate as conjunctions paired with simple pronouns.[8] Or it may be, as Aristotle originally suggested, that doing justice to the full complexity of negation requires accommodating the distinction between contradictories and contraries and hence allowing that both predicates and sentences can be negated. Were that the case, then there would less of a radical discontinuity between thought at the linguistic level and thought at the nonlinguistic level.

This discussion of protonegation still leaves us with an important challenge. We need an analogous way of understanding how some precursor of the conditional operator can operate at the nonlinguistic level. The conditional operator is a truth-functional propositional operator forming a complex thought from two thoughts in such a way that the complex thought is true in all circumstances except those in which the first component thought is true and the second component thought is false. Clearly this requires intentional ascent and hence (by the arguments to be explored in the next chapter) is unavailable at the nonlinguistic level. Equally clearly, the strategy of finding an intrapropositional precursor for the propositional operator that led to the concept of protonegation holds no promise in the case of the conditional. Conditional thought clearly links two different things. But if those things cannot be complete thoughts, then what can they be?

The proposal I would like to explore is that we look for the sources of conditional reasoning in a primitive form of causal reasoning. Whereas conditional reasoning involves a propositional operator establishing a truth-functional relation between complete thoughts, causal reasoning works on the basis of a causal condition holding between one state of affairs and another. Since causal relationships do not hold between complete thoughts, an understanding of causality presupposes no intentional ascent and hence does not require language.

Philosophers frequently reflect on the relations between causation and conditionals, and it is often suggested that a proper understanding of conditionals will be an ingredient of an adequate account of causation.[9] At the very least, a causal explanation of a particular event entails certain conditional predictions about what would happen in suitably similar situations.[10] It is clear that, in the order of analysis, thought and talk about conditionals is more fundamental than thought and talk about causation. No one has ever proposed that we understand conditionals in terms of causation. Conditional sentences and conditional thoughts assert the existence of dependence relations, and causation is just one of a range of possible dependence relations. Nonetheless, the order of acquisition frequently fails to duplicate the order of analysis. It is highly plausible on experimental and observational grounds that the capacity for causal cognition is very widespread in the animal kingdom and available at a very early stage in human development (Dickinson and Shanks 1995 and the other essays in Sperber 1995)—which is exactly what one would predict on evolutionary grounds. The ability to detect certain types of causal regularity and to distinguish genuine causal relations from accidental conjunctions has obvious survival value. Causal dependence relations are directly observable, highly salient, and pragmatically significant in a way that no other dependence relations are. It seems plausible both that causal relations should be more primitive than conditional relations and that a creature arrives at an understanding of conditional dependence by abstracting away from the more familiar and everyday relation of causal dependence. Perhaps the child's first step toward an understanding of conditional dependence is observing that a certain relation holds between the truth-values of two separate thoughts when a causal relation holds between the states of affairs that those thoughts characterize. Once this first step (which of course involves intentional ascent and hence requires language) has been taken, it is a relatively straightforward matter to notice that there are other types of situation (and correlatively other types of dependence relation) that share that feature. And thus the abstract concept of conditional dependence is grasped.

How might causality be understood at the nonlinguistic level? There are certain aspects of the full-fledged concept of causation that clearly cannot be available at the nonlinguistic level. The full-fledged understanding of causation has a modal dimension that comes with the thought that a cause is sufficient for the effect it brings about, and this is, in effect, the thought that it is not possible for the cause to occur without the effect occurring. Yet if we accept my earlier suggestion that modal thinking involves a type of intentional ascent and hence requires semantic ascent, the notion of sufficiency is not available at the nonlinguistic level. Different theorists will view this with different degrees of concern. Some analyses of causation take the idea that a cause is sufficient for its effect as central (e.g., Mackie 1965). Other accounts do not. If we follow Mellor (1995) in holding that what makes it the case that one fact c causes another fact e is that the conditional probability of e given c is greater than the conditional probability of e given not-c, then cases in which causes really are sufficient for their effects cease to be central to the understanding of causation. But there is no suggestion that nonlinguistic creatures can have a full understanding of causation. The proposal is simply that (at least some) nonlinguistic creatures have a basic capacity to track causal relationships holding between events or facts and that this basic capacity allows them to engage in a primitive form of conditional reasoning.

All accounts of causation, from David Hume's pioneering account onward, are agreed that certain forms of regularity are at the heart of the notion. And it seems overwhelmingly plausible that the core of the understanding of causation, or more accurately *protocausation*, at the nonlinguistic level will be based on the registering of regularities in the distal environment. It is easy to see where this type of understanding might originate. On the one hand, it seems plausible to take a sensitivity to environmental regularities to be a basic part of the innate endowment of any creature capable of learning about the environment. On the other, one might expect any creature to be peculiarly sensitive to regularities between its own actions and ensuing changes in its immediate environment. Of course, however, as regularity theories of causation have been forced to acknowledge, there are many regularities that are not causal, and it is in the capacity to distinguish genuinely causal regularities from accidental regularities that one might expect differences between different species of nonlinguistic creature and, for that matter, different stages of development within any given species. We know from dishabituation studies of infant perceptual expectations about object behavior that even when they are only a few months old infants show surprise at examples of "action at a distance," and many developmental psychologists have suggested that their understanding of the physical world is governed by the principle that objects can only interact causally when they are in physical contact (Spelke 1990).

The regularities to which nonlinguistic creatures are sensitive (unlike those that are usually stressed in regularity analyses of causation) need not be exceptionless. Indeed, there are very good evolutionary reasons why one would expect causal cognition to be sensitive to probabilistic regularities (Brunswik 1943). Decision-making in the wild is decision-making under uncertainty, and no creature that waited for an exceptionless regularity would fare well in evading predators and obtaining food. This is another reason not to be concerned about the unavailability at the nonlinguistic level of the idea that causes are sufficient for their effects. It may well be the case that every apparent example of probabilistic (or indeterministic) causation at the macro level can be explained in terms of hidden variables, so that what looks like a probabilistic regularity is really a manifestation of a deeper underlying exceptionless regularity. If this were the case then the only reasons for adopting a probabilistic understanding of causation would be apparent examples of indeterministic causation at the microphysical level. But the emphasis is very different when it comes to nonlinguistic creatures' understanding of protocausation. As far as the practicalities of foraging and reproducing are concerned, the apparent probabilistic regularities are paramount.

Protocausal understanding tracks relationships, which can be either deterministic or probabilistic, between states of affairs. This is why an understanding of protocausation is available at the nonlinguistic level. It also explains why primitive versions of certain fundamental inference forms are available at the nonlinguistic level. Let us return to the three basic inference forms. We are looking for analogues at the nonlinguistic level of the basic inference forms of disjunctive syllogism, *modus ponens* and *modus tollens*. The basic logical operations involved here are negation and the conditional. If negation at the nonlinguistic level is understood in terms of the mastery of pairs of contrary predicates, as suggested in the earlier discussion of protonegation, and if we view the relevant conditionals as protocausal conditionals holding between states of affairs rather than between complete thoughts (e.g., between modes of presentation of those states of affairs), then we have all we need for nonlinguistic analogues of our three basic forms of inference. *Modus ponens* can be understood straightforwardly in terms of a causal conditional together with an understanding, which may take the form of a perception or a memory, that the antecedent holds. The consequent will straightforwardly be detached. We can view *modus tollens* in terms of the combination of a causal conditional with the protonegation of the consequent of that causal conditional resulting in the detachment of the protonegation of the antecedent. As I showed earlier, the disjunctive syllogism "A or B, not-A, therefore B" can be understood in terms of a causal conditional with not-A as its antecedent and B as its consequent.

By way of concluding this section, I shall relate this discussion of the forms of inference available at the nonlinguistic level to the earlier discussions of nonlinguistic rationality. The first point to make is that nothing that has been said about these types of inference is incompatible with the claim that what I termed the inference-based conception of practical reasoning is unavailable at the nonlinguistic level. The mere fact that some types of inference (or protoinference) can be deployed by nonlinguistic creatures does not mean that we can understand practical reasoning at the nonlinguistic level in terms of the inference-based conception. Let us look again at the passage from Davidson in which this conception of practical reasoning (and, concomitantly, of rationality) is sketched out.

> If someone acts with an intention then he must have attitudes and beliefs from which, had he been aware of them and had he the time, he could have reasoned that his act was desirable. . . . If we can characterise the reasoning that would serve we will, in effect, have described the logical relations between descriptions of beliefs and desires and the description of the action, when the former gives the reasons with which the latter was performed. We are to imagine, then, that the agent's beliefs and desires provide him with the premises of an argument. (Davidson 1978/1980a, 85–86)

The proposal is to understand an agent's practical reasoning in terms of the reasoning that might have led him, starting with his beliefs and desires, to fix on the relevant course of action. There are two principal reasons why the three basic forms of protoinference I have been considering will not support this form of reasoning. One of these reasons is a consequence of my earlier argument that intentional ascent requires semantic ascent, while the other has to do with the distinctive and restricted character of nonlinguistic protoinferences.

I shall start with the general reason. Davidson's conception of practical reasoning has the practical reasoner starting with a particular belief-desire pair (or, more realistically, a particular set of beliefs and pro-attitudes) and reasoning from those to an intention to act in a certain way. One might expect this type of reasoning to involve, at the very least, reflection on what outcomes would be the best way of satisfying those relevant desires or pro-attitudes and on the likelihood of different courses of action generating those outcomes. Yet reflection of this type seems a clear example of second-order reflection on one's own motivations and on the information one possesses about the world. In order to be able to engage in this form of practical reasoning, one needs to be able to take one's beliefs and desires as objects of thought—to think about the consequences that follow from one's desires in the light of one's beliefs. And, if the argument in 8.2 is sound, such intentional ascent requires semantic ascent and hence cannot be available at the nonlinguistic level.

Even putting this general worry to one side, there is a more specific reason blocking the application of the inference-based conception of practical reasoning at the nonlinguistic level. The first is that protoinferences at the nonlinguistic level are not made in virtue of their form. Creatures who engage in, for example, proto-*modus tollens* need not have any grasp of the form of an inferential transition as truth-preserving. In fact, they cannot have any such grasp, since that would involve second-order reflection on the evidential relations between propositions and hence semantic ascent (which explains why, as I showed in chapter 5, there is no evidence that nonlinguistic creatures have any grasp of logical concepts). Connected with this is the fact that any given creature will only be able to make a limited number of protoinferences. This is particularly clear in the case of protonegation, which can only be deployed by a creature that has at its disposal the appropriate pair of contrary concepts. A nonlinguistic thinker can only negate those thoughts with a predicative component for which it can generate a contrary. That is the limitation of protonegation—as opposed to propositional negation, which permits the negation of any thought that can be entertained.

In terms of the three levels of nonlinguistic rationality identified in chapter 5, the protoinferences I have been discussing offer a further perspective on behavior that is a candidate for level 2 rationality. The key feature of practical reasoning that is a candidate for level 2 rationality is that it involves instrumental beliefs— instrumental beliefs that might feature in thinking about how to manipulate tools or about how an action might lead to a particular outcome. These instrumental beliefs can be understood as causal conditionals connecting a particular type of action with a particular type of outcome, and the three different types of protoinference offer different ways that these instrumental beliefs can feed into action. Not all causal conditionals, of course, are instrumental beliefs. A causal conditional relates states of affairs, and there is no need for either of those states of affairs to involve an action on the part of the agent. Causal conditionals can track regularities holding between events in the physical world as well as regularities in the behavior of other agents, and so one would expect some form of protoinference to feature in behavior that is a candidate for level 1 rationality (although not in behavior to be judged by the norms of level 0 rationality). It may well be that proto–*modus ponens* is more widespread than either of the two protoinferences involving protonegation—simply because creatures might plausibly be expected to become capable of tracking regularities between states of affairs before they are capable of grasping pairs of contrary concepts. Certainly the empirical evidence strongly suggests that rudimentary forms of causal cognition are very widespread in the animal kingdom and operative early on in ontogeny (Sperber 1995).

8

Language and Thinking about Thoughts

At various points in this book I have examined different conceptions of the relation between linguistic and nonlinguistic thought, and correspondingly of the scope and limits of nonlinguistic thought. These different conceptions fall naturally into two broad groups. At one extreme are views that seek to drive as much of a wedge as possible between linguistic and nonlinguistic thought. In chapter 3, for example, I considered the minimalist conception of nonlinguistic thought, according to which nonlinguistic creatures are capable only of an etiolated and imagistic type of thinking, the vehicles of which are "spatial images superimposed on spatial perceptions." If the minimalist conception is correct then it will provide us with a very clear sense of the differences between linguistic thought and nonlinguistic thought. So too would a view that goes naturally with the minimalist conception—the view, namely, that considerations of sense and mode of presentation can get no grip in the absence of language. But much of this book has been devoted to arguing that, initial appearances to the contrary, there is indeed room at the nonlinguistic level for the ascription of thoughts that have determinate content and compositional structure—and, more strongly, that such thoughts are indispensable for the purpose of psychological explanation. So where does this leave us? Are there any genuine differences at all between linguistic thought and nonlinguistic thought?

The principal claim of this chapter is that there is an important class of thoughts that is in principle unavailable to nonlinguistic creatures. In the first section I briefly discuss some of the claims that have been made about how language can function as a cognitive tool. It emerges that many of these functions do not actually require a full-fledged language. If language is to have a distinctive, unique, and essential cognitive function, so that the difference between linguistic and nonlinguistic cognition is qualitative rather than merely quantitative, then we must look elsewhere. In section 8.2 I develop my own account of the contribution that language can make to cognition—and explain why it is a contribution that can only be made by language. The central claim is that all thinking that involves intentional ascent (roughly, all thinking that involves thinking about thoughts) requires the capacity for semantic ascent (roughly, the capacity to think about words). In the next chapter I will go on to explore the practical implications of this result.

8.1 Language as a Cognitive Tool

Andy Clark (1998) has usefully plotted out six fundamental respects in which language can function as a tool, enhancing, extending, and facilitating thought and cognition), as follows.[1]

1. *Memory augmentation.* The acquisition of a public language offers us powerful means of systematically storing data (not simply in written language but also in communicated oral traditions).
2. *Environmental simplification.* Applying linguistic labels is one way that the perceived environment can be broken down into persisting objects and properties.
3. *Coordination.* Language permits the mutual control of attention and resource allocation in coordinated activities.
4. *Transcending path-dependent learning.* The learning patterns of linguistic creatures are not constrained by the particular cognitive paths they have followed, since linguistic communication allows ordinary learning patterns to be circumvented and short-circuited.
5. *Control loops.* Language allows us to create control loops for our future behavior (by writing down plans that might be too complicated to keep in one's head, for example) as well as to register and respond to the instruction and regulation of others.
6. *Data manipulation and representation.* "Extended intellectual arguments and theses are almost always the product of brains acting in concert with multiple external resources. These resources enable us to pursue manipulations and juxtapositions of ideas and data which would quickly baffle the un-augmented brain" (Clark 1998, 173).

These are all, no doubt, important ways that language possession serves to extend and enhance thinking. But they do not, I think, mark types of thinking that are in principle available only to language-using creatures. As a first step in plotting out the scope of nonlinguistic thought, it will be useful to explore how several of the functions that Clark identifies can be carried out by nonlinguistic processes.

By "nonlinguistic process" I mean one or other of two things. On the one hand a process can be straightforwardly nonlinguistic in virtue of not relying on any symbols at all.[2] On the other a process can be nonlinguistic even though it is dependent on symbols, simply because it does not rely on the right sort of symbols. Of course, to describe a process as nonlinguistic in this second sense is hostage to a principled distinction between linguistic and nonlinguistic symbol systems, and I shall have some more to say about that shortly. First, though, consider how far one can get with the prosthetic functions of language at an entirely nonsymbolic level.

The mutual control of attention and resource allocation in coordinated social activities does not require the intervention of language. Coordination requires a degree of communication, but this communication can perfectly well be nonsymbolic (hence, uncontroversially, nonlinguistic). It is well known, for example, that human infants engage from a very early age in sustained periods of coordinated activity with their caregivers. The process has aptly been called one of *affect attunement* (Stern 1985). It is a process of exploring and communicating emotional states through changes in facial expression, vocalizations, and gesture.

> Affect attunement is the performance of behaviors that express the quality of feeling of a shared affect state without imitating the exact behavioral expression of the inner state. . . . The reason attunement behaviors are so important is that true imitation does not permit the partners to refer to the internal state. It maintains the focus of attention on the forms of the external behaviors. Attunement behaviors, on the other hand, recast the event and shift the focus of attention to what is behind the behavior, to the quality of feeling that is being shared. (Stern 1985, 142)

In affect attunement, emotional states are communicated by being shared. The infant's participation in this sort of communication is intentional (as, of course, is the caregiver's), and the process of affect attunement is a type of coordinated activity in which there is a mutual control of resource allocation. Nonetheless, the process is not one of symbolic communication, because facial expressions and vocalizations are not *symbols* for the emotional states that are being communicated. The link between a scowl and a feeling of disagreeableness, for example, is expressive rather than symbolic. The behavioral manifestations of emotions and feelings cannot be divorced from the emotions and feelings that are being manifested. That is to say, the link between them is not arbitrary and conventional, which is the essence of the symbolic.

A further example of coordination without symbols comes with the well-studied dances carried out by worker honeybees (von Frisch 1967).[3] Although the details of the dances vary among the seven known species of the genus *Apis,* the basic principles are similar. Worker bees returning to the nest site after successful foraging land on the horizontal top of the nest and perform what has come to be known as a waggle dance to inform their fellow workers of the location of the food source. In the waggle dance the bee flies in a figure-of-eight pattern, moving its abdomen back and forth laterally on the straight line in between the two circles. Although there is of course a degree of error, the waggle dances communicate information about the direction, distance, and desirability of the food source. Each of these three dimensions of variation is correlated with a dimension of variation in the dance. The angle of the dance relative to the position of the sun indicates the direction of the food source. The duration of a complete figure-of-eight circuit indicates the distance to the food source (or rather the flying time to the food source, because it increases when the bees would have to fly into a headwind). And the vigor of the dance indicates the desirability of the food to be found. Variation in all three environmental features is preserved in the relevant dimensions of the bee dance.

The bee dance is an even clearer example than affect attunement of coordination in resource allocation—and, as in the affect attunement case, it does not seem appropriate to describe the coordination as resting on symbolic communication. The bee dance is nonsymbolic because it does not involve arbitrary signals. To appreciate the point, and in particular the distinction between arbitrary and iconic signals, it is worth making a small digression into the theory of signals. There can be no transfer of information without rules for the encoding and decoding of signals (Green and Marler 1979). Viewed in broad and abstract terms, the rules for the encoding of a signal govern the transformations that lead from stimuli received at the sensory surfaces to signaling behavior. The simplest such rules yield deterministic links from input to output, as when the signaling behavior is what is sometimes called an 'instinctive behavior pattern' or an 'innate releasing mechanism.' Newly hatched herring gulls, for example, are particularly sensitive to the sensory input correlated with the length, movement, and coloration of the adult herring gull's bill. A transformation rule maps this onto the chick's characteristic signaling behavior, vigorous pecking at the adult's bill tip (Tinbergen 1973). In this case the decoding signal is equally straightforward. The adult herring gull responds by feeding the chick. More complex signaling behaviors might involve a series of rules governing a series of transformations. In affect attunement, for example, there will be rules governing the extraction of various qualitative and quantitative aspects of vocal exclamations and gestures by the partner in the exchange; rules mapping those aspects onto an amodal 'common currency'; and rules that then generate responsive gestures or vocalizations (Stern 1985).

In an iconic signal system there is, for each dimension of variation in the relevant environmental feature (the distance of the food source in the honeybee case, for example), a single transformation rule mapping variation in that parameter onto variation in the relevant dimension of the signal. The receiver of the signal will decode the signal by an inverse mapping.[4] Signs are arbitrary, as opposed to iconic, when no such general and continuous rules exist to map variations in environmental parameters onto variations in signals. Each member of the signal set is linked to a particular environmental feature by specific assignments that can only be characterized one by one. Within the framework set by the distinction between arbitrary and iconic signals, it seems relatively uncontroversial, first, that the bee dances are iconic rather than arbitrary signaling practices and, second, that no practice that does not involve arbitrary signals can plausibly be described as linguistic.

The bee dances, then, clearly illustrate how coordination in resource allocation and communal activity can be achieved at the nonlinguistic level. They also illustrate how control loops can be created without language and, moreover, how path-dependent learning can be transcended. The whole point of the bee dances is that the vast majority of worker bees do not need to seek the food for themselves. The worker bees that remain in the hive can profit from the explorations of a small number of bees to circumvent the standard search procedures.

Imitative learning is perhaps the most fundamental way of overcoming path-dependence through permitting the social transmission of knowledge. Imitation is extremely widespread in the animal kingdom and is present in human infants more or less from birth (Meltzoff and Moore 1977, 1983). The most straightforward form of imitative learning is simple mimicry, of the sort that can be seen in the social transmission of bird songs and in neonatal imitation of facial expressions. In many species, individual birds deprived (e.g., by neonatal deafening or by being raised in isolation) of the opportunity to imitate the songs of conspecifics develop either only very rudimentary version of the standard songs or radically abnormal songs (see, e.g., Marler 1970). At a more sophisticated level we can identify various types of mimetic learning, of different degrees of sophistication. It is known from studies of chimpanzee tool use, for example, that chimpanzees are skilled at learning about the dynamic properties of objects from observing them being manipulated by others (Boesch and Boesch 1992). There is some debate about whether tool-using chimpanzees are actually imitating patterns of behavior (Tomasello 1996), as opposed to picking up the dynamic affordances of objects and learning about features of the environment, but these clearly illustrate some form of the social transmission of knowledge.

The cognitive significance of mimetic learning within phylogeny has been recognized by Merlin Donald in his speculative reconstruction of the emergence of the modern mind (Donald 1991). Donald suggests that a long period of *mimetic culture* served as the bridge between the episodic form of cognition characteristic of the apes and earliest hominids and the language-based culture that emerged after the transition from the Middle Paleolithic to the Upper Paleolithic. He associates mimetic culture with a wide range of social cognitive phenomena that collectively served as an adaptive foundation for the evolutionary emergence of language. The enormous development in techniques of tool manufacture characteristic of the Middle Paleolithic period must have been linked with new means for the transmission of information across a community. From what we know of contemporary hunter-gatherer societies, the process of tool manufacture is very much a social process, and clearly dependent on successful communication among the participants (Reynolds 1993). If we follow the majority of archeologists in dating the emergence of linguistic communication after the Middle Paleolithic (Bickerton 1990, 1996, Liebermann 1984) then it is hard to see any alternative to group mimetic learning as the crucial cognitive mechanism underpinning complex tool manufacture. Mimesis can also plausibly be viewed as the foundation for the social expression of emotion—again a form of nonlinguistic communication that circumvents the path-dependence of language.

Returning to Clark's list of the instrumental cognitive functions served by language, I have already shown in some detail that at a very basic level the function of environmental simplification does not require any sort of communication, symbolic or otherwise. Human infants are born able to parse the perceived environment into object-like segments that are taken to obey certain basic higher-order physical principles. This is probably not enough, however, for the type of environmental simplification that Clark intends. His view, I suspect, is that the environmental simplification that language provides applies to a perceived environment that is already parsed into objects or object-like entities. Language does not enable us to perceive an environment composed of discrete and continuously existing objects in the way that many philosophers have argued.[5] What it allows us to do is to impose a simplified pattern that will allow us to make sense of the discrete and continuously existing objects that we encounter in perception and action.

Even when the function of environmental simplification is understood in this sense, however, it still seems clear that it can be achieved at the nonlinguistic level. It is at this point that it becomes pressing to say something about quite how "linguistic" and "nonlinguistic" are being understood here. There has been considerable discussion among philosophers, linguists, and psychologists as to what constitutes a language. Savage-Rumbaugh has argued, for example, that language emerges with the appearance of symbolic communication (Savage-Rumbaugh 1986). Most linguists, on the other hand, think that some form of grammar and syntactic structure is essential for a symbol system to count as a genuine language (Chomsky 1980). The majority of philosophers have followed the linguists in this respect (Bennett 1976), although David Lewis (1983) has proposed in a rather more inclusive spirit that languages are simply functions from expressions onto meanings. Confronted with this it is hard not to be pulled in two directions. On the one hand it is tempting to think that there is little point in trying to arbitrate in this debate. It is unclear what criteria we should use to judge any of these proposals. If we are trying to capture the essence of human language then it is clear where the answer lies—but our project is broader than that. The ordinary meaning of the word "language" is too vague to help us. After all, ordinary language allows us to talk freely of the language of architecture and the language of the body. But, on the other hand, it seems impossible to investigate the nature and scope of nonlinguistic thought without a demarcation line between the linguistic and the nonlinguistic.

I will adopt a middle way between these two extremes. A genuine language must allow for the formation of complex symbols from simple symbols. The essence of language is the combination of symbols with each other to express thoughts, taking thoughts to be complex entities that can be assessed for truth or falsity. The possibility of truth appears only with complex symbols. It emerges only when a state of affairs is asserted to be the case, and this requires, at a bare minimum, the combination of a naming symbol and a predicate symbol. A lexicon of simple symbols will not support communicative utterances that are assessable for truth or falsity (although they may, of course, be adequate to perform speech acts such as issuing injunctions). So complex symbolic systems allow the formation of complex symbols, symbols whose meaning is determined by the meaning of the symbols of which they are composed. That is to say, complex symbol systems display what is often known as *compositionality*, the possibility of recombining the members of a finite number of simple symbols to produce a range of complex symbols. This characteristic of complex symbol systems is frequently stressed in both philosophical and psychological discussions of language. It tends to be taken as a unitary phenomenon, but compositionality can be displayed in two fundamentally different ways, corresponding to two fundamentally different types of complex symbol systems.

In the first category, the category of sequentially complex symbol systems, complex symbols are formed in a purely additive or successive manner. Correlatively, understanding a sequentially complex symbol is a matter of successively understanding the simple symbols that make it up. A good example of such a sequentially complex symbol system comes with the communication systems spontaneously developed by very young children born deaf but whose parents do not use sign language to them. Such children tend without instruction to develop elementary signing systems employing combinations of two signs (Goldin-Meadow 1979). The two-sign combinations typically involve a pointing gesture combined with an action sign. An example might be pointing at a door combined with a turning gesture to signify that it should be opened. Pygmy chimpanzees, or bonobos (*Pan paniscus*), have acquired similar abilities (Greenfield and Savage-Rumbaugh 1990). It is clear that we are dealing here with the formation of complex symbols. In the given example, it is the formation of a complex symbol communicating an injunction—the injunction to open the door. But the mode of formation is extremely simple. The syntactic rules of the symbol system are such that the action sign (the turning gesture) can only be conjoined with a sign that picks out an object. There is no way of using the syntactical rules to build up further complex symbols.

In what might be termed a hierarchically complex symbol system, on the other hand, the logical and semantic relations between the components of a complex symbol cannot in every case be read off from the sequential ordering of simple symbols. The basic feature of a hierarchically complex symbolic system is that it possesses a hierarchically organized compositional semantics operating in such a way that understanding a complex symbol will not always be a matter of successively understanding the simple symbols that make it up. To get from a sequentially complex to a hierarchically complex symbol system we must lift the basic restriction that complex symbols can *only* be formed by combining a predicate symbol and the appropriate number of naming symbols. Hierarchically complex symbol systems possess a variety of mechanisms that allow the formation of complex symbols. Operators analogous to the definite and indefinite articles in English will allow the formation of complex names (i.e., definite and indefinite descriptions), while reiterable operators that apply to complete sentences will allow the formation of complex symbols compounded from sentences. The logical constants are a case in point, but so too are the operators indicating possibility and necessity and indeed tense. I will have more to say about these in the next chapter (particularly in sections 9.4–9.7).

Returning to the matter at hand, it seems plausible that the function of environmental simplification identified by Clark can be carried out by "labeling" environmental features with a simple symbol system. Environmental simplification does not require complex symbols (although of course it would be greatly enhanced by a complex symbol system) and hence does not require a language. A classic example of how this might work (and one that provides a further example of how the instrumental functions I have already considered can be effected at the nonlinguistic level) comes with the alarm calls of vervet monkeys (Cheney and Seyfarth 1990). Vervet monkeys have three alarm calls, each geared to a different category of predator—eagle, leopard, and snake. When vervets hear a particular alarm call they do not display an indiscriminate fear or avoidance response, but rather behave in ways appropriate to the predator to whose presence they have been alerted. When they hear the eagle alarm call, for example, they look up and scan the sky. Vervets also have two further calls, the "wrr" and "chutter" calls, which communicate the nearby presence of strange groups of vervets. According to Cheney and Seyfarth, vervet monkeys are more likely to issue alarm calls when there are close kin in the vicinity (1990, ch. 5). Something similar holds for the food signals issued by macaque monkeys, who seem to scan for members of their social group before issuing a food signal (Hauser and Marler 1993). Even if we assume that the vervet alarm calls are symbolic, they do not constitute a complex symbol system, since there is no scope for the formation of complex symbols. Yet it is clear that the alarm calls are serving a function of environmental simplification, and indeed permit the creation of control loops for regulating each individual's future behavior and the behavior of other members of the group.

Nor is it only in primates that we find such behaviors. A classic ethological example of environmental simplification and control loop creation comes with the ways that different species of birds hide caches of seeds at specific locations. Clark's nutcrackers are known to deploy multiple cues to identify the locations of nut caches. Experiments have shown that they are able to reidentify nut stores even when experimenters manipulate the most obvious landmarks (Balda and Turek 1984). In creating food stores, birds both simplify the environment in terms of markers that allow them to reidentify the caches and create control loops for future behavior in terms of a structure of intercache trajectories that will determine their movements when retrieving food.

As far as Clark's original list of six instrumental functions is concerned, therefore, it looks as if we can make sense of at least four of them operating at the nonlinguistic level. And the two that are left (memory augmentation and data manipulation) do not seem very likely candidates for marking a distinctive type of cognition only made available by the acquisition of language. There are all sorts of ways that nonlinguistic creatures can augment their limited memory capacities, some of which I have already considered in thinking about how path-dependent learning might be transcended at the nonlinguistic level. And data manipulation is a characteristic of all thought. The only differences between linguistic and nonlinguistic thought in either of these dimensions are likely to be differences of degree. It would seem, therefore, that if there indeed are any fundamental differences of type between linguistic and nonlinguistic cognition, they will lie elsewhere. In the next section I will turn to a fundamentally different type of argument for the distinctiveness of linguistic cognition.

8.2   Intentional Ascent and Semantic Ascent

In the same article in which he puts forward the six instrumental functions of language that I considered in section 7.1, Andy Clark offers the following conjecture about the role of language in underpinning the distinctiveness of human cognition.

> Perhaps it is public language that is responsible for a complex of rather distinctive features of human thought—viz., our ability to display *second-order cognitive dynamics*. By second-order cognitive dynamics I mean a cluster of powerful capacities involving self-evaluation, self-criticism and finely honed remedial responses. Examples would include: recognizing a flaw in our own plan or argument, and dedicating further cognitive efforts to fixing it; reflecting on the unreliability of our own initial judgements in certain types of situation and proceeding with special caution as a result; coming to see why we reached a particular conclusion by appreciating the logical transitions in our own thought; thinking about the conditions under which we think best and trying to bring them about. The list could be continued, but the pattern should be clear. In all these cases we are effectively thinking about our own cognitive profiles or about specific thoughts. (Clark 1996, 177)

He explains how language makes these types of thought available in the following terms.

> It is easy to see in broad outline how this might come about. For as soon as we formulate a thought in words (or on paper), it becomes an object both for ourselves and for others. As an object it is the kind of thing we can have thoughts about. In creating the object we need have no thoughts about thoughts—but once it is there, the opportunity immediately exists to attend to it as an object in its own right. The process of linguistic formulation thus creates the stable structure to which subsequent thinkings attach. (Clark 1996, 177)

It seems to me that the basic idea Clark is putting forward is essentially correct. My aim in this section of the chapter will be to formulate the basic idea more precisely and to provide an argument to back it up.

Clark's explanation of the role language plays in second-order cognitive dynamics is incomplete, at least for my purposes. For one thing, all he really offers is an account of how, given that we have language, we are able to engage in second-order cognitive dynamics—whereas what we need is an argument that second-order cognitive dynamics can only be undertaken by language-using creatures. This links up directly with a more fundamental worry. The natural way to derive an argument for the necessity of language from Clark's suggestions would be to claim that language is required for thinking about our own thoughts. But this claim is hardly uncontroversial. It would be instantly denied, for example, by language of thought theorists. It is an integral part of the language of thought hypothesis that reflexive thinking is available in the language of thought. Once again we find ourselves caught in the familiar grey area between public languages and the language of thought. We need to investigate not simply whether some form of language is required but what type of language that must be.

The basic premise from which we need to start here is that reflexive thoughts can only be possible if the target thoughts have vehicles that allow them to be the objects of further thoughts. The question, then, is what form these vehicles must take. Broadly speaking, the candidates fall into two broad categories. They might be either personal-level vehicles or subpersonal vehicles. Any argument to show that reflexive thinking requires the target thoughts to be vehicled in a public language will have to establish, first, that the vehicles must be at the personal level and, second, that the only available vehicles at the personal level are public language sentences.

The plausibility of the first step in the argument emerges when we reflect that reflexive thinking will paradigmatically involve a direct and conscious cognitive access to the target thoughts. As the first passage quoted from Clark at the beginning of this section makes clear, typical examples of reflexive thinking might include evaluating evidential and inferential relations between thoughts. Such reflexive thinking involves having the target thoughts in mind—entertaining them consciously and considering how they relate to each other logically and evidentially. Yet it seems clear that we do not have the appropriate sort of direct and conscious cognitive access to subpersonal states. Second-order cognitive dynamics is a matter of the conscious regulation and policing of one's own thoughts-and we do not consciously regulate and police sentences in the language of thought. It might well be the case that certain types of hypothesis testing and refinement do take place at the subpersonal level. Something like this happens, according to Fodor, when we learn a language. Nothing I say is incompatible with that proposal, since my claim is simply that such processes would not count as instances of second-order cognitive dynamics. Nonetheless, one might want to question the proposal on other grounds, such as the availability of alternative models of language acquisition, particularly those developed within the connectionist tradition (for a survey of recent work see McLeod et al. 1998).

It is hard to see how a defender of the language of thought hypothesis could maintain that we do have conscious access to sentences in the language of thought, given that the language of thought hypothesis is a hypothesis about subpersonal cognitive architecture, not about the medium of conscious thought. It is generally accepted that subpersonal states are inferentially insulated from the conscious processes of cognitive evaluation and self-criticism. This is precisely the distinction between the personal and subpersonal levels (see, for example, Stich 1978). A fortiori, therefore, it follows that the vehicles of the thoughts that are the objects of what Clark calls second-order cognitive dynamics cannot be sentences in a subpersonal language of thought.[6]

There are versions of the language of thought hypothesis, however, that are not put forward purely as hypotheses about subpersonal cognitive architecture and hence are not directly blocked by this line of argument. Some authors have suggested that there might be a modular internal language in which thoughts are encoded for conscious consideration. This general approach would sit well with (although neither entails nor is entailed by) higher-order thought theories of consciousness (Rosenthal 1991). It seems to me, however, that this proposal lacks phenomenological plausibility. All the *propositional* thoughts that we consciously introspect, whether thoughts that come unbidden into our minds or thoughts that we consciously instigate and consider in solving a problem, take the form of sentences in a public language. We do, of course, engage in various types of nonsentential thinking—what, in chapter 3, I termed thinking-how in contrast to thinking-that—and it is only mistaking nonpropositional thinking-how for propositional thinking-that that leads to the view that we can be aware of "pure" thoughts without any sentences featuring among the contents of introspection.[7] There are certain types of problem that we solve by manipulating mental images and exercising the visual imagination. And we are, of course, conscious of bodily sensations, emotional feelings, and other such qualitative states (although these are not properly described as types of thinking at all). But we are not, I think, ever conscious of *propositional* thoughts that do not have linguistic vehicles. When we are conscious of propositional thoughts we are conscious of imaged sentences.[8] What we introspect when we introspect our propositional thoughts in the manner required for the processes of second-order cognitive dynamics is inner speech.

This brings me to the second step of the argument. What needs to be shown is that public language sentences are the only possible personal-level vehicles for thoughts that are to be the objects of reflexive thinking. The conclusion so far is that sentences in the language of thought are not appropriate vehicles. The only way to proceed is by elimination—showing that there are no viable alternatives to public language sentences. How else might the representation relation work? There seem to be two possibilities. On the one hand representation might be secured symbolically through the complex symbols of a natural language (complex symbols being required since what are being represented are thoughts about states of affairs). A thought would be represented, therefore, through its linguistic expression and would appear as a potential object of thought qua linguistic entity. On the other hand, representation might be secured in an analogue manner, through some kind of pictorial model. On this conception of the vehicles of thought, which we find developed in different ways in mental models theory in the psychology of reasoning (originally proposed in Craik 1943 but most comprehensively developed in Johnson-Laird 1983) and in the conception of mental maps put forward by Braddon-Mitchell and Jackson (1996), the vehicle of a thought is a pictorial representation of the state of affairs being thought about.[9]

The idea of structural isomorphism is at the heart of both theories. Both mental models and maps are spatially isomorphic with what they represent. The relations (or at least some of them) holding between elements of the mental model/map can be mapped on to the relations holding between objects in the represented state of affairs. In this way representation is secured through the relations of exemplification and resemblance. The mental model/map represents a state of affairs by exemplifying the structure of that state of affairs—that is to say, by itself possessing a structure that resembles (at some suitable level of abstraction) the structure of the represented state of affairs. It does so, however, in a way that does not have an independently identifiable structure corresponding to the state of affairs exemplified. Braddon-Mitchell and Jackson put the point clearly.

There is no natural way of dividing a map at its truth-assessable representational joints. Each part of a map contributes to the representational content of the whole map, in the sense that had that part of the map been different, the representational content of the whole would have been different. Change the bit of the map of the United States between New York and Boston, and you change systematically what the map says. This is part of what makes it true that the map is structured. However, there is no preferred way of dividing the map into basic representational units. There are many jigsaw puzzles you might make out of the map, but no single one would have a claim to have pieces that were all and only the most basic units. (Braddon-Mitchell and Jackson 1996, 171)

We need, therefore, to distinguish weak and strong senses in which a representational vehicle might be structured. In the weak sense there is structure whenever a structural isomorphism can be identified between the vehicle and what it represents. In the strong sense, however, structure requires the existence of basic representational units combined according to independently identifiable combinatorial rules. Natural language sentences (or for that matter sentences in the language of thought) are clearly structured in the strong sense, whereas mental maps/models only possess structure in the weak sense.

In mental models and maps, the representation relation will be secured through some combination of isomorphic resemblance and exemplification holding primarily between the model/map as a whole and the represented state of affairs as a whole (and only derivatively at the level of the distinguishable elements of the map/model and state of affairs, respectively). There are important questions to ask about the nature, and even the possibility, of resemblance and exemplification-based representation—questions that go back to early criticisms of the British Empiricists (and that have arisen more recently in criticisms of the picture theory of the proposition offered by Ludwig Wittgenstein in the *Tractatus Logico-Philosophicus*). I shall prescind from these, however. There is a fundamental problem with either version of the analogue proposal as an account of how it is possible for thoughts to have vehicles that allow them to become the objects of further thoughts.

Second-order cognitive dynamics involves sensitivity to the inferential relations between thoughts, and we do not yet have an understanding of how images can be inferentially connected to each other. The problem once again derives from the intimate relation between inference and structure explored in earlier chapters. There is a sense in which mental models and maps are structured, since they contain elements that can feature in further mental models/maps. Nonetheless, they do not seem to be structured in the right sort of way to permit the reflexive type of second-order cognitive dynamics under discussion. It will be helpful to take maps and mental models separately.

A canonical example of second-order cognitive dynamics might be coming to see the evidential basis for a particular belief and then evaluating the inferential transition made on that basis. (This would be an example of what in section 9.1 I will term *reflective doxastic modification*.) An example might be the realization that one has made an overly rash inductive generalization, or a faulty deductive in-ference. It is perfectly easy to see how there could be some very basic forms of in-ferential transition between maps. Such transitions might be modeled on broadly associationist lines, and it is the possibility of such transitions that enables maps to serve as guides to action. What is not possible, however, is for such transitions to be understood and evaluated in terms of either deductive validity or probabilistic support. Those very features of maps (their analogue nature and structural isomor-phism with what they represent) that make them so useful for guiding action serve to make them inappropriate for the type of inferential evaluation characteristic of second-order cognitive dynamics. In order for such evaluation to take place, the maps must be interpreted in broadly propositional terms. We must interpret one map as expressing one proposition and the second as representing a further propo-sition, and then evaluate the inferential relations (be they deductive, inductive, or probabilistic) between those two propositions. Once again, our only understanding of how to do this rests on the two propositions being linguistically formulated.

Braddon-Mitchell and Jackson do not directly address this issue, but they do offer the following explanation of how maps can evolve over time in what is clearly intended to be an analogy with inferential transitions between linguistically vehicled representations.

> Maps are physical entities whose structure can govern the way they evolve over time. When cartographers update maps or put two maps together to make one that incorpo-rates all the information in a single map, these operations are governed in part by the structures of the maps they are working on. And in order to find a target, rockets use a kind of internal map that gets continually updated as new information comes in. In these rockets, later maps are causal products of earlier maps plus what comes in via the rocket's sensors. Hence map theorists can tell an essentially similar story to lan-guage of thought theorists about how thoughts evolve over time as a function of their propositional objects. (Braddon-Mitchell and Jackson 1996, 173)

There is a fundamental disanalogy here, however. The issue is not really about how thoughts evolve over time. In a very important sense individual thoughts quite simply do not evolve over time. It is systems of thought that evolve, and they do so as a function of the inferential relations between the thoughts that compose them. These inferential relations hold between distinct thoughts, and nothing that Braddon-Mitchell and Jackson say in this short passage gives us any way of under-standing how we should understand inferential relations between distinct thoughts at the level of mental maps. The process of combining maps has only very limited analogies with the process of inferring one thought from another. We do not have, for example, any idea what a conditional map might look like—and consequently little understanding of how conditional reasoning might take place at the level of mental maps. A fortiori, therefore, there seems no sense in which we can under-stand second-order cognitive dynamics as applying to the inferential transitions between mental maps.

The situation is somewhat more complicated with mental models theory. How can mental models not be suitable targets for the type of reflexive thinking characteristic of second-order cognitive dynamics, given that mental models are explicitly proposed as providing a unified account of deductive, probabilistic, and modal reasoning (Johnson-Laird 1999)? It is important to be clear, however, about the precise claims of mental models theory. Mental models theory is proposed as an alternative to the so-called mental logic theory (Rips 1994), according to which reasoning is an exclusively syntactic matter grounded in formal rules of inference.[10] The key idea of mental models theory is that arguments are evaluated by the construction of mental models of the relevant premises. An argument is judged to be deductively valid if the conclusion holds in all the constructed models of the premises, probabilistically valid if it holds in most of the models, and so forth. The claim made is that this model of reasoning provides a better explanation of the patterns discovered in the experimental study of how subjects reason than the idea that reasoning involves the manipulation of sentential representations according to formal rules. Some of these patterns involve systematic susceptibility to formal fallacies, which it is obviously difficult to explain on the mental logic approach. Others are simply patterns in the time taken to carry out certain inferences, which advocates of the mental models approach claim is directly correlated with the number of models that the reasoner needs to construct (Johnson-Laird and Byrne 1991).

Mental models are indeed supposed to be structurally isomorphic to the states of affairs described in the premises. But like mental maps, their structure is derivative. It is derived from the premises that they are modeling. The models are constructed from constituents and properties that feature in the premise being modeled. And those premises are of course linguistic entities. It would be a mistake to think that mental models theory construes inference in terms of transitions between mental models—any more than a model-theoretic approach to the sentence calculus construes inference in terms of transitions between truth tables. Mental models theory construes inference as a matter of transitions between sententially encoded propositions. What is distinctive about it is that it construes those transitions between sententially encoded propositions as taking place in virtue of relations between analogue representations of the states of affairs portrayed in those sententially encoded propositions (as opposed to formal relations holding between the syntactic structures of the relevant sentences). Mental models theory is not a genuine alternative to the sentential conception of reasoning, since the whole idea of a mental model only makes sense within the framework of the sentential conception. Mental models theory offers a particular way of developing the sentential conception, not of supplanting it. Mental models are not the vehicles of inference, but rather, as their name suggests, models of those inferences.

By a process of elimination, therefore, we have reached the conclusion that thoughts can only be the objects of the type of reflexive thinking in which thoughts are the objects of thought if they have natural language vehicles. This is not, of course, to say that we cannot deploy mental maps and mental models. It is clear that we do, and it is highly likely that nonlinguistic creatures do as well. Nor is it to say that mental models and mental maps cannot be the objects of thought. It seems clear that we can think about mental models and mental maps as well as think by means of them. The point is that we cannot use mental maps or mental models for thinking about thoughts in the manner demanded by second-order cognitive dynamics. Natural language sentences are the only proxies that will permit thoughts to function as the objects of thought in this manner. To put the matter in the form of a slogan, there can be no intentional ascent without semantic ascent. We think about thoughts through thinking about the sentences through which those thoughts might be expressed. The significance of this thesis depends, however, on the types of thinking that constitutively involve intentional, and hence semantic, ascent. We began this section with Clark's programmatic suggestion that only language-users can be capable of the types of cognitive self-criticism and self-monitoring that he terms second-order cognitive dynamics. In the next chapter I will work toward a more wide-ranging classification of the scope and limits of nonlinguistic thought.

9

The Limits of Thinking without Words

In the previous chapter I showed that a certain type of thinking is unavailable at the nonlinguistic level. Forms of thinking that involve thinking about thought (hence taking particular thoughts as the objects of thought) are only available to creatures participating in a public language. Thoughts can only be the objects of further thoughts if they have suitable vehicles, and the only suitable vehicles are public language sentences. Intentional ascent requires semantic ascent. In this chapter I consider the practical implications this has for the scope and limits of nonlinguistic thought. I am concerned in particular with the following two questions. What types of thinking are in principle unavailable to nonlinguistic creatures? What sort of primitive precursors might there be at the nonlinguistic level for types of thinking that involve intentional ascent in their full-fledged form?

It will turn out that intentional ascent is a broader category than immediately appears. There are two types of intentional ascent, which might be termed explicit and implicit intentional ascent respectively. The first type includes all those forms of thought that involve *metarepresentation*, or the ability to have thoughts that take further thoughts as their direct objects. I consider examples of metarepresentational thinking in the first three sections of this chapter. In section 9.1 I explain the distinctive type of belief revision available only to language-using creatures, contrasting it with the more primitive ways that nonlinguistic creatures can modify their beliefs and behavior in the light of changing evidence, whether supporting or countervailing. Section 9.2 discusses how the possibility of a certain type of higher-order desire involves intentional ascent (the taking of a cognitive attitude toward a particular desire) and hence depends on language. In section 9.3 I discuss the relation between language possession and what is often called theory of mind. I argue that the attribution of beliefs, certain types of desires (what I earlier called situation-desires), and propositional attitudes in general is only available to linguistic creatures—again because it involves thinking about thinking. A primitive type of psychological explanation, involving the attribution of goal-desires and perceptual states, is nonetheless possible at the nonlinguistic level.

Metarepresentational thinking, however, is not the only form of thinking that involves intentional ascent. Intentional ascent can also occur implicitly. Implicit intentional ascent does not involve taking thoughts as the objects of further thoughts. Rather, it involves embedding thoughts to create more complex thoughts whose contents are states of the world, rather than one's own mental states (as when one engages in second-order cognitive dynamics) or someone else's mental states (as when one is attributing beliefs and desires to others). In section 9.4 I explain in the abstract how and why embedding requires intentional ascent with particular reference to the truth-functional propositional operators and to the formation of quantified thoughts. I go on to suggest that tense and modal operators may best be viewed as analogous to adverbial modifiers, qualifying complete thoughts, with the result that tense-based thinking involves a form of intentional ascent. Section 9.5 explores the different ways of thinking about generality available at the linguistic and nonlinguistic levels and shows how a limited type of general thought is available at the nonlinguistic level. In section 9.6 I discuss the role that the acquisition of the relative pronoun might play in making possible the move from domain-specific cognition to domain-general cognition.

9.1   Belief Revision and Second-Order Cognitive Dynamics

The distinctiveness of linguistic cognition was introduced in the previous section through Clark's notion of second-order cognitive dynamics. Here again is how Clark characterizes this notion:

> By second-order cognitive dynamics I mean a cluster of powerful capacities involving self-evaluation, self-criticism and finely honed remedial responses. Examples would include: recognizing a flaw in our own plan or argument, and dedicating further cognitive efforts to fixing it; reflecting on the unreliability of our own initial judgements in certain types of situation and proceeding with special caution as a result; coming to see why we reached a particular conclusion by appreciating the logical transitions in our own thought; thinking about the conditions under which we think best and trying to bring them about. (1999, 177)

In this section I delineate more precisely the scope of the distinctive type of reflection that is made available by the presence of language. It turns out that this distinctive type of reflection has two broad components—the availability of a distinctively second-order variety of belief revision and the availability of second-order desires.

In order to appreciate what is really distinctive about linguistic cognition, two distinctions are needed. The first concerns the relation between behavior and its effects. Many types of behavior (indeed, plausibly, all types of behavior that are not tropistic, generated by innate releasing mechanisms, or classically conditioned) are driven by what might broadly be termed outcome-sensitivity. Animals and infants will modify all but the simplest behaviors according to their outcomes. This is the essence of trial-and-error learning, as well as being an indispensable adaptive trait. But these are two different types of outcome-sensitivity. We can term them practical outcome-sensitivity and doxastic outcome-sensitivity, respectively. A creature is practically outcome-sensitive when it modifies its behavior directly as a function of exposure to evidence of that behavior's success or failure. A creature is doxastically outcome-sensitive, on the other hand, when it modifies its behavior as a function of modifications in its beliefs, having modified its beliefs in response to evidence of the truth or falsity of those beliefs.

Practical outcome-sensitivity can be illustrated through the distinction between classical conditioning and instrumental conditioning. In classical conditioning, a neutral stimulus (e.g., the sound of a bell) is followed by an unconditioned stimulus (e.g., the presentation of food) that elicits a reaction (e.g., salivation). The outcome of classical conditioning is that the conditioned response (the salivation) comes to be given to the conditioned stimulus (the sound of the bell) in the absence of the unconditioned stimulus. In instrumental or operant conditioning, the presentation of the reinforcing stimulus is contingent on the animal making a particular behavioral response (such as pecking a lever). If the behavioral response does not occur, the reinforcing stimulus is withheld. Classically conditioned behavior is not outcome-sensitive in any interesting sense, since it is not the behavior that is reinforced. The conditioning is a function of the strength of the association between the conditioned response (e.g., the sound of the bell) and the unconditioned stimulus (e.g., the presentation of food). The process of conditioning is not determined by anything the animal actually does.

Instrumental conditioning, on the other hand, is clearly outcome-sensitive. It is the behavior itself that is reinforced. Nonetheless, most varieties of instrumental conditioning are not doxastically outcome-sensitive. The category of instrumentally conditioned behavior is not fully homogenous, and, although a case can be made for regarding certain types of instrumental conditioning as resting on instrumental beliefs (see, e.g., Dickinson and Balleine 1993, Heyes and Dickinson 1993, and the experiments by Rescorla and Skucy, and Hammond discussed hereafter), the vast majority of instrumentally conditioned behaviors are not best interpreted in terms of beliefs about the contingency between behavior and outcome.

Clear examples of doxastic outcome-sensitivity come with behaviors exemplifying what in chapter 6 I termed level 2 rationality. Level 2 rationality involves instrumental beliefs about the contingencies between courses of action and outcomes and no creature can properly be credited with such instrumental beliefs unless those beliefs are evidentially sensitive to the contingency in question. We considered a clear example of this sensitivity in the lever-pressing experiments. Rats trained to press a lever to obtain food will cease lever-pressing when the schedule is changed so that the food appears irrespective of whether the rat presses the lever or not. They are sensitive to the evidential connection between the action of lever pressing and the appearance of the food and modify their behavior accordingly (Rescorla and Skucy 1969, Hammond 1980). Creatures (such as Hershberger's chicks who persist in moving toward a food-source that retreats from them at twice the rate at which they approach it) clearly lack this sensitivity (see section 6.4 above). Similarly, a direct sensitivity to the outcomes of action is an integral part of tool construction and use. One cannot devise tools without being sensitive to their aptness or not for the job for which they are being devised. Supporting and/or countervailing evidence needs to be taken into account in modifying the tools.

As the example of level 2 rationality shows, doxastic outcome-sensitivity is not simply a matter of behavior modification resulting from changes in beliefs. If, for example, a creature stops stalking one kind of prey because it has noticed an easier quarry within closer reach then its behavior has been modified as a consequence of changes in its (perceptual) beliefs. Nonetheless, it has not displayed doxastic outcome-sensitivity because the beliefs in question are not beliefs about the outcome of the behavior and the means by which that outcome is to be achieved. Nor are the relevant changes in belief the result of changes in the balance of evidence for the original belief (as they would be if, for example, the creature noticed that what it had taken for one kind of prey was really another). Bearing this in mind, many forms of behavior exemplifying level 1 rationality are going to come out as practically but not doxastically outcome-sensitive. I showed in chapter 6 that a wedge needs to be driven between the normative and descriptive dimensions of our theories of practical decision-making as applied to behaviors falling within the general category of level 1 rationality. We as observers can model level 1 choice behavior in terms of some normative theory such as expected utility theory, which has a manifestly instrumental dimension (given that the calculation of expected utility rests on the relevant utilities and probabilities of the different possible outcomes consequent on any given behavioral option). But this does not mean that the practical decision-making resulting in the behavior itself involved any instrumental reasoning—nor, a fortiori, any degree of doxastic outcome-sensitivity. A clear example of this emerged in the red deer roaring contexts. The louder a red deer stag roars, the stronger it is—since the same thoracic muscles are employed in roaring and fighting. To the extent that a deer acts because it recognizes that it is roaring louder than its antagonist, it will be acting in a way that can be analyzed instrumentally as maximizing its expected utility. But it is not acting the way it does because it has engaged in any consequence-sensitive reasoning. Therefore, even if during the roaring contest the stag discovers that its antagonist can in fact roar louder than initially appeared and consequently withdraws from the roaring contest, this would still not count as doxastic outcome-sensitivity.

It is clear, therefore, that doxastic outcome-sensitivity, although relatively circumscribed within the nonlinguistic realm, is not the preserve of language-using creatures. To see what is epistemically distinctive about the realm of the linguistic, we need to make a further distinction between two different types of doxastic outcome-sensitivity. Doxastic outcome-sensitivity involves, as I have shown, behavioral modification as a consequence of doxastic modification—and not simply doxastic modification per se but rather the modification of beliefs about the instrumental connection between a particular course of action and an intended outcome.

There are two different ways that the relevant doxastic modification can take place. The examples I have been considering up to now are of what might be termed *direct doxastic modification*. That is to say, beliefs are modified in direct response to changes in the structure and nature of available evidence. When it becomes apparent to the rat, for example, that the food reward will appear irrespective of whether or not it presses the lever, this new piece of evidence has a direct effect on the rat's belief about the dependence of food on lever-pressing, and that original belief is accordingly modified. A similar process might occur during the process of tool construction—when the stone fractures one way rather than another, the experienced stone-knapper might revise his instrumental beliefs about the appropriate way to detach flakes to construct a hand-axe. What is characteristic of both these examples is that perceptually registered countervailing evidence impacts immediately on the belief in question. The instrumental belief controlling the behavior is instantly modified in response to the perceived discrepancy between actual outcome and envisaged outcome.

In direct doxastic outcome-sensitivity, therefore, there is no need for the rat or the tool-maker to reflect on the relations of evidential support holding between what they perceive and what they believe. Such reflective changes of belief are, in contrast, characteristic of the second type of doxastic modification (which we can term *reflective doxastic modification*). The distinction can be put in terms of the different norms governing each type of belief revision. Direct doxastic modification can be seen as a process of maintaining and/or restoring coherence within the belief system (and, of course, between the belief system and the deliverances of perception). What matters is that the belief system should be coherent and integrated enough for the creature in question to preserve a unified epistemic perspective on the world and to be able to act accordingly. There should be no tension (more realistically: as little tension as possible) between the evidence that is available to a creature and the beliefs that that evidence supports. When there is tension between evidence and beliefs, modifications are made to restore coherence.

Reflective doxastic modification, on the other hand, is governed by the norm of truth rather than the norm of coherence. Coherence is a desideratum but it is not the sole desideratum. What matters above all is that the evidence should be such as makes the beliefs that it supports likely to be true. Reflective doxastic modification concerns itself explicitly with the logical and probabilistic relations between evidence and beliefs (as well, of course, as between the individual beliefs within a belief system). At the reflective level a belief might be rejected or modified in the absence of countervailing evidence or tension with existing beliefs—it might, for example, be rejected simply because the believer recognizes that it is not warranted by the evidence. Although the notions of warrant and justification can be applied in an attenuated sense at the level of direct belief revision (most prominently in a broadly externalist sense according to which, roughly speaking, a set of beliefs is warranted to the extent that it is produced by reliable mechanisms and modified according to principles that tend to preserve truth and eliminate error), there is no sense in which the extent to which their beliefs are warranted or justified can be an issue for creatures operating solely at that level. That is to say, internalist notions of warrant and justification can get a grip only at the reflective level, because these notions can be applied only to thinkers capable of explicit reflection on the relations between thoughts and perceptions and between thoughts and other thoughts.[1]

The link between reflective doxastic modification and language should be clear, given the discussion in the previous chapter. It is only possible to evaluate and reflect on the extent to which one belief implies another (more precisely: the extent to which acceptance of one belief commits one to acceptance of another), or the extent to which a belief is supported by a particular type of evidence, if one is able explicitly to hold those beliefs in mind. And, as I discussed at some length earlier, thoughts can only be the objects of further thoughts in the way that this requires if they have linguistic vehicles. It is clear, moreover, that reflective belief revision will involve explicit consideration of the formal logical relations between thoughts—and we have no understanding of the logical relations between thoughts except when those thoughts have linguistic vehicles.

The discussion so far has concentrated on processes of belief revision. But once the mechanisms of reflective belief revision are in place, broader possibilities emerge for reflective self-monitoring and epistemic self-criticism. Reflective subjects can evaluate beliefs without changing them. They can distinguish between those beliefs that are candidates for revision and those that are not candidates for revision. They can plot out the evidential connections between the different components of their belief systems, working out what rests on what and which beliefs are bearing the greatest weight. Reflective subjects can also identify and learn from their past mistakes, settling on epistemic policies that are designed to avoid those mistakes. The notion of second-order cognitive dynamics that Clark originally introduced includes all these high-level forms of epistemic self-monitoring. They are all rooted, however, in the distinctive type of belief revision that I have termed reflective doxastic modification—itself a particular type of outcome-sensitivity. The process of emancipation from the doxastic here-and-now is a gradual one.

9.2   Higher-Order Desires

Nonlinguistic creatures are incapable of intentional ascent. I have shown the role that intentional ascent plays in certain types of belief revision and, more broadly, in epistemic self-monitoring. Are there comparable phenomena in the realm of desire? It is useful at this point to advert to Frankfurt's influential distinction (1971) between first-order and second-order desires. In the terminology I have been adopting, first-order desires can be either goal-desires or situation-desires. They are first-order because they are directed at objects and/or properties (in the case of goal-desires) or states of affairs (in the case of situation-desires). Second-order desires, in contrast, are situation-desires that take first-order desires as their objects. A second-order desire is a desire to the effect that one should have a particular first-order desire.[2]

When we consider the structure of second-order desires, it becomes clear why an important class of second-order desires should be language-dependent. The content (that is to say, the satisfaction-condition) of a second-order desire is that one should have a particular first-order desire. The content of the first-order desire is embedded within the content of the second-order desire. It is, so to speak, the target of the second-order desire. But then it looks very much as if second-order desires involve intentional ascent and therefore, by the argument of section 8.2, the capacity for semantic ascent. Still, some qualification is required. In particular we need to distinguish cases in which the target first-order desire is a goal-desire from cases in which it is a situation-desire. The satisfaction-condition for a second-order desire embedding a goal-desire is the state of affairs in which the desirer stands in an extensionally specifiable desiring relation to a particular object or property. This does not seem to involve intentional ascent in the strict sense of the word, since the content of the target desire is specified only at the level of reference. There is no embedded thought, which there clearly is when the target desire is a situation-desire. The satisfaction-condition of a situation-desire is the state of affairs in which the desirer stands in the desiring relation to the state of affairs in which she has a desire with a determinate structured content at the level of sense.[3]

Of course, the capacity to form second-order desires is not an isolated capacity. Just as reflective belief revision comes as part of a package of strategies and abilities for epistemic self-assessment and self-monitoring, so too should the capacity for second-order desires be viewed as part of a complex set of strategies and abilities for determining the sort of person one is going to be. The second-order desirer is capable not simply of assessing her first-order desires but also of evaluating her first-order desires one by one and indeed of comparing and weighting them. New possibilities of decision-making open up. The second-order desirer can reflect on desires and preferences in a way that will allow her to adopt something like the primitive version of decision theory that I considered at the beginning of chapter 7. One would expect, moreover, that this type of reflection would be linked with a particular type of self-awareness—the awareness of oneself as an agent with distinctive projects, goals, and aims. The agent who can reflect on her own desires will also be able to see how they fit together, which ones are more fundamental, and which are more basic to her character. The analogy with the epistemic case is very close. In each category the basic capacity for intentional ascent is linked with reflective abilities that have no analogue at the nonlinguistic level.

9.3   *Intentional Ascent and Understanding Other Minds*

It is natural to think that the conclusions of the previous two sections can be extended from the intrasubjective case to the intersubjective case. I have argued that intentional ascent, and therefore language, is required for reflection on one's own beliefs and desires. Might a parallel argument hold for reflection on the beliefs and desires of other subjects and agents? Is it possible for nonlinguistic creatures to participate in practices of attributing psychological states to their conspecifics, or indeed to any other creatures? I have shown that nonlinguistic creatures can have a surprisingly rich psychological life. But to what extent can they understand the psychological lives of others? Unsurprisingly, it turns out that everything depends on which psychological states are in question. In this section I argue that only a very limited range of psychological attributions is possible at the nonlinguistic level. In essence, all that is available at the nonlinguistic level is an understanding of the perceptual states of other creatures, an understanding of their desires, and, relatedly, an understanding of the goal-directed nature of intentional action.

In the light of the preceding discussion, it is not hard to see why a very broad class of psychological attributions should be unavailable to nonlinguistic creatures. To attribute, for example, a belief or a situation-desire to another creature is essentially to view that creature as standing in a particular relation to a thought—the relation of believing the thought to be true or the relation of desiring that the state of affairs characterized in the thought come to pass. Clearly, therefore, the attribution of a belief requires thinking about a thought. It is a canonical form of intentional ascent that requires being able to "hold a thought in mind." As such, it is immediately susceptible to the argument sketched out in section 8.2 to the effect that intentional ascent requires the possibility of semantic ascent and hence is only available to language-using creatures. A belief can only be attributed if the thought that is the content of the belief can be represented by the attributer, which requires that it have a vehicle—and, as I have shown, the only candidate vehicles are linguistic.

The argument applies to the attribution of all mental states that are traditionally known as propositional attitudes—that is, to the attribution of all those mental states that involve the subject's taking a particular attitude (the attitude of hoping, say, or fearing) to a thought. This is closely connected, of course, with two familiar facts about ascribing propositional attitudes. The first is that propositional attitude ascriptions create opaque contents—they are intensional. A creature may believe a particular state of affairs to be the case under one "mode of presentation" (under one way of characterizing it) but not under another. Opacity is one fundamental reason why we need to take the objects of propositional attitudes to be thoughts, rather than the states of affairs or situations that are the truth-conditions of those thoughts. The second familiar fact (and the reason for the opacity of propositional attitude ascriptions) is the possibility of error. One can believe things that are not true and one can desire things that do not exist (that, for example, will not come into existence unless the desire is satisfied). How can the object of belief be a situation or state of affairs if it is possible to believe things that are not in fact the case? What could the object of belief be other than a thought? For these two reasons, then, there can be no attribution of propositional attitudes without intentional ascent.

So any mental state that involves taking an attitude to a thought can only be attributed by language-using creatures (although of course it can perfectly well be *had* by nonlinguistic creatures). If there are any mental states that can be attributed by nonlinguistic creatures, therefore, they can only be mental states that do not involve taking an attitude to a thought—and that, in turn, means that they can neither be opaque nor admit the same type of possible error that we find in the canonical propositional attitudes. It is easy to identify one candidate on the basis of the distinction between goal-desires and situation-desires. The distinction is effectively between desire construed as a propositional attitude (in situation-desires, which are attributed via that-clauses picking out the thought that is the object of desire) and the more fundamental goal-desires that are directed not at thoughts but rather at objects or features. It will be recalled that goal-desires, unlike situation-desires, are extensional. There is no reason, therefore, why nonlinguistic creatures should not be able to attribute goal-desires to other agents. The argument from intentional ascent cannot get a grip, since goal-desires are relations between a subject and an object/feature, rather than between a subject and a proposition.

The ability to attribute goal-desires goes hand in hand with a basic understanding of intentional, that is to say goal-directed, behavior. Although there will be many different degrees of complexity in goal-directed behavior, depending on the richness of the desires and beliefs by which it is driven, a creature that is capable of attributing goal-desires will be able to make the basic distinction between purposeful behaviors on the one hand and random movements and instinctive reactions on the other. A purposive action is an action for which a motivating goal-desire can be identified.

Goal-desires cannot be the only mental states identified and attributed by nonlinguistic creatures. It is hard to see, for example, how a goal-desire can be attributed to a creature without some evidence of the information that the creature possesses about its environment. At the bare minimum this information will be perceptual. To know what goal-desire might be motivating a creature at a given moment we need to know, first, what end it is pursuing and, second, how it might reasonably expect that end to be realized by its current behavior. Both of these require knowing to which features of its environment the creature is perceptually sensitive. If, therefore, a nonlinguistic creature is to be able to attribute goal-desires to a fellow creature, it must be able to formulate hypotheses about what that creature is perceiving.

This presents us with a puzzle. Reports of perception are usually taken to bear significant structural commonalities with propositional attitude reports. Except for those philosophers adopting some version of the epistemic theory of perception (according to which perception can be reductively analyzed in terms of the acquisition of dispositions to belief), there is a consensus that the content of perception cannot straightforwardly be assimilated to the content of belief (Crane 1992, Dretske 1981, Peacocke 1983, 1992). Nonetheless, the acknowledged differences between the content of belief and the content of perception are not usually taken to stand in the way of reporting the content of perception with "that—" clauses specifying the perceiver's relation to a thought—the thought in question being the propositional content of the belief to which the perception might be expected to give rise.[4] But this, by the familiar argument from intentional ascent, seems to place the understanding of perception beyond the reach of nonlinguistic creatures—and therefore (by the argument of the previous paragraph) bars them from identifying and attributing goal-desires.[5]

The resolution of the puzzle comes with a distinction between two different types of perception and, correspondingly, between two different types of perceptual report. I will call the two types of report SS reports and ES reports, respectively.[6] SS reports have the following three characteristics. They

1. Take nonpropositional complements
2. Create transparent contexts
3. Are made true by direct perceptual relations between perceivers and particulars

ES reports differ from SS reports in all three dimensions. ES reports

1. Take propositional complements
2. Create opaque contexts
3. Are made true by perceptually based epistemic relations between perceivers and propositions

Many philosophers endorse the idea that SS reports and ES reports characterize different modes of perception. In Dretske's terms, SS reports describe what can be termed *simple seeing*, while ES reports characterize *epistemic seeing*.[7] The basic idea is that simple seeing and epistemic seeing are dissociable components in normal visual perception. Dretske, in the book that put this sort of distinction on the map, explicitly suggests that what we see in simple seeing (or what he calls nonepistemic seeing) "is a function solely of what there is to see and what, given our visual apparatus and the conditions in which we employ it, we are capable of visually differentiating" (1969, 76). That is to say, the distinction between simple seeing and epistemic seeing is phenomenologically salient. Dretske explicitly draws a parallel with the conception of the sensory given that was at the core of the sense-datum theory of perception. Whereas the sense-datum theorist believed, or is alleged to have believed, that we can strip away from the rich manifold of perceptual experience to reach a level at which what is really seen are colored expanses, the simple seeing theorist holds that what we really reach after such a process is correctly characterized by an SS report.

For present purposes we can remain neutral on the question of whether this dissociability thesis is correct at the level of perception itself. It may or may not be the case that we can strip away the epistemic dimension from the perceptions of creatures capable of epistemic seeing in a way that will allow us to characterize these perceptions entirely in nonepistemic terms. It is certainly true, however, that the dissociability thesis is perfectly correct at the level of perceptual reports. An episode of epistemic seeing can perfectly well be characterized, albeit incompletely, by an SS report. The SS report can be viewed as specifying the objects of perception—I am taking the objects of perception here to be whatever it is that stands at the other end of the causal chain leading to perceptual states. On this report, an SS report simply states that the perceiver stands in an appropriate perceptual relation to a certain object—the relation that will allow her to discriminate that object from the perceptual background. It has nothing to say about how that object is perceived (about its mode of presentation), which of course is why SS reports create transparent contexts.

The significance of this should be clear. The argument from intentional ascent shows that nonlinguistic creatures are not capable of the sort of understanding of vision that might be expressed through ES reports, since ES reports require specifying a perceiver's relation to a thought. But this is perfectly compatible with nonlinguistic creatures being capable of SS reports and, correlatively, of thinking about the direct perceptual relations between other creatures and objects in the world. Nor are SS reports, and the understanding that goes with them, quite as restricted as initially appears. Although many of those who have made the distinction between simple seeing and epistemic seeing have specified the former in terms of relations purely between a perceiver and an object, there is no reason why this has to be the case. The *relatum* of simple seeing can be a state of affairs where a state of affairs might minimally be construed as an object exemplifying a property or two or more objects exemplifying a particular relation.[8] It seems natural to suggest that a nonlinguistic creature can include in the complement of an SS report pretty much anything it can think about directly—that is, anything it can think about directly it can think about as the object of another's perceptual state.

The availability of SS reports to nonlinguistic creatures allows them to engage in a primitive form of psychological explanation. Psychological explanation, as traditionally construed, is not available to nonlinguistic creatures since it depends on the attribution of beliefs and situation-desires. Nonetheless, a combination of SS reports and the attribution of goal-desires will permit nonlinguistic creatures to make some progress on explaining and predicting the behavior of their conspecifics and potential predators. If one knows what a creature desires and has some sense of its perceptual sensitivity to the environmental layout (as well of course as an understanding of its motor capabilities) one can expect to be able to predict its behavior with some success.

To take stock, then, it appears that propositional attitude ascriptions are beyond the capacity of nonlinguistic creatures. The argument from intentional ascent shows us that language is required for all psychological attributions that specify a thinker's relation to a thought. The only psychological attributions that escape the argument from intentional ascent are attributions of goal-desires and the SS reports that characterize simple seeings (and the equivalent, of course, in other sensory modalities). Nonlinguistic creatures, therefore, are capable only of a highly circumscribed understanding of other minds that falls far short of what is often described as possession of a theory of mind.

It should be noted that this restrictive interpretation of the "mind-reading" abilities of nonlinguistic creatures is compatible with much recent research into the extent to which nonhuman primates can properly be described as possessing a "theory of mind." There are well-documented examples of primate behavior that some prominent students of animal behavior have thought can only be interpreted as examples of interpersonal deception (de Waal 1982, Premack and Woodruff 1978, and some of the essays in Byrne and Whiten 1988). But the consensus opinion among primatologists is that a more parsimonious interpretation of these behaviors is to be preferred (see, e.g., Gómez 1996, Hauser 2000, and Povinelli 1996).[9] Many of the examples of what has come to be termed *tactical deception* (Byrne 1995) can be understood as the manipulation not of another's propositional attitudes but simply of their visual perspective. Here is an example of a tactical deception in a troupe of baboons in Ethiopia that lends itself to such an interpretation:

> An adult female spent 20 min in gradually shifting in a seated position over a distance of about 2 m to a place behind a rock about 50 cm high where she began to groom the subadult male follower of the group—an interaction not tolerated by the adult male. As I was observing from a cliff slightly above [the animals] I could judge that the adult male leader could, from his resting position, see the tail, back and crown of the female's head, but not her front, arms and face: the subadult male sat in a bent position while being groomed, and was also invisible to the leader. The leader could thus see that she was present, but probably not that she groomed. (Report by Hans Kummer, quoted in Byrne 1995, 106)

The behavior of the female baboon, assuming that it is indeed to count as an instance of tactical deception, does not seem to require assuming an intention to manipulate the beliefs of the alpha male (e.g. an intention to bring it about that he believe that she is not grooming the subadult male). What she is doing is profiting from an understanding of the alpha male's visual "take" on the situation to escape detection. The female baboon needs only to appreciate the alpha male's line of sight and the fact that he would be prevented from seeing the subadult male by the intervening rock. This seems firmly at the level of simple seeing rather than epistemic seeing.

It is interesting to note that a recent survey article draws a basic distinction between two different levels of understanding vision that can be mapped without too much effort onto the distinction between simple seeing and epistemic seeing and that can be put to work to distinguish between different ways of understanding the experimental and ethological evidence for primate "mind-reading." Daniel Povinelli (1996) has distinguished three different types of knowledge about visual perception and its mechanisms. The first level is a simple sensitivity to the presence of eyes and eyelike stimuli. This sensitivity is exploited, for example, by the many species of moth and butterfly that are patterned to resemble eyes. Such sensitivity is clearly widespread throughout the animal kingdom and is too primitive to concern us. The second level seems closely correlated with an appreciation of nonepistemic seeing. Povinelli describes it as an understanding of perception as a cognitive connection between organisms and world. The third level seems much closer to an understanding of epistemic seeing. This is "the understanding that in addition to linking an individual's mental state of attention to the external world, visual perception also alters one's internal experiences, states of knowledge and belief" (Povinelli 1996, 313). Within this classification the standard understanding of primate social deception would place it squarely at the third level, while the proposal being developed in this section is that it can be understood at the second level.

Considerable laboratory research has recently been carried out on primate understanding of visual perspective and the direction of gaze. Some of this research has been negative. There is solid experimental evidence that chimpanzees are not very good at understanding the visual perspective of humans (Povinelli and Eddy 1996a, 1996b). In particular, when given the choice of begging for food from an experimenter who can see them from one who cannot, they are only capable of making very crude discriminations. They successfully distinguish between, for example, an experimenter facing them and one whose back is turned toward them, but they do not seem to understand the difference between an experimenter who is directly looking at them and one who cannot see them because he has a bucket over his head. Some experimenters have taken this to cast doubt on chimpanzee understanding of vision and visual perspective. Others have pointed out, however, that the paradigm is a highly unnatural one for primates, not simply because it involves humans rather than conspecifics but because the natural situation for chimpanzees is one of competition for scarce resources, rather than cooperation or collaboration (Hauser et al. 1993). Recent investigation of chimpanzees' understanding of the visual perspective of conspecifics in competitive situations shows that chimpanzees can monitor the visual perspective of a competitor and information to guide their own actions (Hare, Call, and Tomasello 2001, Hare et al. 2000). One group of experiments involved pairs of chimpanzees, one subordinate and one dominant, placed in separate rooms and separated by occluders (Hare, Call, and Tomasello 2001). Experiments hid food in full view of the subordinate chimpanzee who could expect that the dominant chimpanzee would be successful in competing for any food that both had seen hidden. The various conditions manipulated the dominant chimpanzee's visual access to the location of the food—in some he saw where the food was hidden, in others not, while in a third condition he was misinformed about the location of the food because it was moved after he had initially seen it being placed. In all conditions the subordinate was able to monitor the dominant's visual access to the location of the food. The subordinate chimpanzee was consistently able to make use of this information to its own advantage, refraining from directly competing with the dominant chimpanzee for food about whose location the dominant had accurate information and preferentially retrieving food items about which the dominant was either uninformed or misinformed.

A natural way of interpreting these experimental data, in conjunction with the ethological data that originally gave rise to them, is as manifesting a form of social understanding reliant on the use of information about vision and goal-directed action, rather than on the attribution of beliefs, desires, and other propositional attitudes. If the argument of this chapter is correct then this form of social understanding is all that is available at the nonlinguistic level and is sufficient to explain the various forms of social deception, social interaction, and social cognition that have been identified in nonlinguistic creatures. This proposal is line with that offered by primatologists such as Tomasello and Call (1997) and Whiten (1996), who complain that the existing discussions of primate social cognition are unnecessarily polarized between interpretations of primate social behavior in terms of full-fledged belief-desire psychology on the one hand and unthinking reinforcement on the other.

9.4   Embedding and Intentional Ascent

The role played by intentional ascent is very clear in the three types of thinking I have considered. Thoughts are part of what is being thought about in second-order cognitive dynamics, in second-order desires, and when one speculates about the mental states of others. When, for example, one attributes a belief to another creature, one is effectively attributing to that person a relation to a thought. Similarly, in evaluating a piece of reasoning in the manner characteristic of second-order cognitive dynamics, one is considering the logical or probabilistic relations holding between the thoughts of which it is made up. It does not make sense to suppose that either of these types of thinking could be engaged in without the capacity for intentional ascent—and hence, by the argument of the previous chapter, without the possibility of semantic ascent. It would be a mistake, however, to conclude that intentional ascent is involved only when thoughts are explicitly targeted on other thoughts—that is to say, when thoughts are part of the content of what is being thought. I bring out in this section how the capacity for intentional ascent is required for all thinking that involves compound thoughts with further thoughts embedded in them, irrespective of whether those embedded thoughts feature in the content of thinking.

We can start with a basic class of compound thoughts—namely, those involving the basic logical connectives, such as disjunction, conjunction, and the material conditional. Consider a disjunctive thought of the sort that might be expressed in the sentence "*A* or *B*." What is it to be capable of entertaining such a thought? It is to be capable of understanding that a certain relation holds between two thoughts—the relation of their not both being false (and, on some understandings of 'or,' their not both being true). Of course, the disjunctive thought itself is not a thought about the two thoughts expressed by *A* and *B*. It is a thought about the states of affairs that serve as the truth-conditions for the thoughts. Nonetheless, the disjunctive thought is not available to be thought by any creature not capable of thinking about how the truth-value of one thought might be related to the truth-value of another thought.[10] The same holds of the other truth-functional propositional operators. Understanding a truth-functional operator is understanding how it serves to form compound thoughts whose truth-value is a function of the truth-values of their parts. No creature that was not capable of thinking about thoughts could have any understanding of truth-functional compound thoughts.[11]

The example of the truth-functional propositional operators shows that a particular type of thinking can presuppose the capacity for intentional ascent, even though the thoughts instantiating that type of thinking are not themselves thoughts about thoughts. Compound thoughts formed through the truth-functional propositional operators involve intentional ascent *implicitly* rather than explicitly. Are there other types of complex thoughts of which the same can be said? Extrapolating from the truth-functional operators suggests that a similar argument will apply to complex thoughts formed by operators that can only be understood via the notion of truth—and this, of course, can hold for operators that are not truth-functional. Let me offer a conjecture with respect to modal operators (in the sense of 'modal' on which modal operators are those attributing possibility and necessity). It seems very plausible that our understanding of necessity cannot be divorced from the understanding of truth. Our primary understanding of the notion of necessity may well be in terms of a propositional (or, for that matter, a sentential) operator, and a proposition is necessary just if it is true in every possible situation (in every possible world). If this is the case then modal thoughts would presuppose intentional ascent, and with it semantic ascent, no less than compound thoughts formed by means of the truth-functional propositional connectives.

Modal thinking is in many respects similar to tensed thinking. The logical systems that have been developed to display the logical structure of tensed thought are analogous to those that have been developed to elucidate the logical structure of modal thought. They are all what might be termed adverbial extensions of nonmodal and nontensed logics.[12] That is to say, they can be derived from nonmodal and nontensed logics by the application of operators that function as adverbs.[13] The following passage is a classic statement of this approach as applied to tense logic.

> If an expression constructs a sentence out of one other sentence it is an adverb or an adverbial phrase, like 'not' or 'It is not the case that' or 'allegedly' or 'It is alleged that' or 'possibly' or 'It is possible that'. . . . I want to suggest that putting a verb into the past or future tense is exactly the same sort of thing as adding an adverb to the sentence. 'I *was* having my breakfast' is related to 'I am having my breakfast' in exactly the same way as 'I am *allegedly* having my breakfast' is related to it, and it is only a historical accident that we generally form the past tense by modifying the present tense, e.g. by changing 'am' to 'was,' rather than by tacking on an adverb. In a rationalized language with uniform constructions for similar functions we would form the past tense by prefixing to a given sentence the phrase 'It was the case that' or 'It has been the case that' and the future tense by prefixing 'It will be the case that.' (Prior 1968, 7, quoted in Evans 1985)

The central implication of the adverbial nature of the tense and modal operators is that, where "T" is an operator of the relevant class and "p" the name of a sentence, the meaning of "Tp" will be a function of the meaning of "p" and the meaning of the relevant operator.

Perhaps it is equally the case that our understanding of temporal order is inextricably linked with our understanding of truth, so that understanding tense is a matter of understanding that propositions can have different truth-values at different times. On this view, our basic understanding of temporal relations is not an understanding of temporal relations holding between events or states of affairs. It is, rather, an understanding of the temporal relation between the truth of different propositions. We understand the idea that event A took place earlier than event B by understanding that it was true that event A took place before it was true that event B took place. This is because thinking about the temporal relations between events requires thinking about events holding at particular times, and the understanding of an event holding at a time other than the present is parasitic on the understanding of a particular proposition being true at a particular time. Thinking about temporal relations (or so I am suggesting) requires being able to think about the possibility of propositions being true or false at different times. It may well be that the capacity to think about possibility, to think about time, and to think about the truth-values of propositions are all interdependent and interlinked. If this were so, then modal and tensed thinking would be just as unavailable to nonlinguistic creatures as thinking involving the truth-functional propositional connectives.

This suggestion about the language-dependence of tensed thinking enables us to make sense of a puzzling transition in the prehistory of the human race. The consensus among archeologists and students of human evolution is almost universal that the crucial stage in human cognitive evolution occurred about 40,000 to 35,000 years ago, with the transition from the Middle Paleolithic to the Upper Paleolithic. This transition involved a sudden explosion in tool technology and social/cultural organization, with the emergence for the first time of forms of life that are recognizably congruent with those of modern humans. With the transition to the Upper Paleolithic come the first decorative objects; the first really compelling evidence for totemistic/religious behavior, as revealed in burial practices and totemic representations; sophisticated hunting strategies that capitalize on seasonal migrations and fluctuations in animal numbers; and far more complex forms of tool production that seem to have drawn on detailed knowledge of natural history to tailor tools for particular hunting tasks, as opposed to the more general-purpose tools of the Lower and Early Paleolithic (for overviews see Donald 1991, ch. 8, Mellars 1996, and Mithen 1996a, ch. 9). From this point on, the rate of cognitive evolution accelerated exponentially. It is, of course, for this reason that many cognitive archeologists have identified this transition as involving the emergence of a recognizably human language.

One striking feature of the type of cognition emerging in the Upper Paleolithic is the way it exemplifies a novel conception of time. It is a type of thinking reflecting a conception of time that goes beyond a simple ability to discriminate events that are taking place in the present from those that have taken place in the past or that will take place in the future. There are ways of being oriented toward the past or the future that are available to relatively simple organisms—most simply, in the form of expectations about future events and memories of past events. But these need to be sharply distinguished from modes of thought that depend on thinkers being able to locate themselves within a temporal narrative.[14] What the fossil record tells us about the earlier hominids strongly suggests that they behaved in ways that involved distinguishing the past, the present, and the future. But there is nothing to suggest patterns of behavior available only to creatures capable of narrative thought. In contrast such patterns of behavior seem extremely widespread in the Upper Paleolithic.

A very clear illustration comes with the hunting strategies that emerged during this period. Archeologists studying the Upper Paleolithic have found a vastly increased sensitivity to seasonal changes in the density and movements of animals. Whereas in the Middle Paleolithic hominids tended to hunt single animals in a very opportunistic way (or indeed perhaps only to scavenge on their remains), the later hominids appear to have shown far more long-range planning in their foraging behavior. They prepared tools long before they needed them, designing them for specific prey and specific hunting techniques. Their excavated campsites seem to have been prepared for long occupations and were systematically moved to intercept prey or harvest food resources (Binford 1989, Mellars 1996, Mithen 1996a). There is also evidence that, at least after the earlier stages of the Upper Paleolithic, the targets shifted from isolated animals to large herds of animals like reindeer and red deer, which were ambushed on their migration paths at particular times of year (Mithen 1990).

If, as I have suggested, tensed thinking is only available to language-using creatures, then it is easy to see why the evolution of a recognizable human language should have been connected with the emergence of these types of cognition and behavior in the transition from the Middle to the Upper Paleolithic. These forms of hunting behavior presuppose a type of narrative thinking that is quite simply unavailable in the absence of language. And this is, in fact, consistent with influential views about when natural language emerged in the course of evolution (Mithen 1996).

I have so far in this section considered several ways that intentional ascent might be involved implicitly in types of thinking that are not explicitly targeted on further thoughts. I argued that the formation of compound thoughts by means of the truth-functional propositional connectives presupposes the capacity for intentional ascent and suggested, more tentatively, that similar capacities may be presupposed by the ability to entertain thoughts involving temporal or modal notions. In the remainder of this section I discuss a further way that the capacity for intentional ascent can be presupposed by different types of thinking. The types of thinking that I have been considering up to now have involved the formation of complex thoughts by what we can think of as adverbial operators on propositions, such as the truth-functional connectives and the modal and tense operators. I turn now to a different way of forming complex thoughts.

Consider the inference form of existential generalization. This is the pattern of inference instantiated by the transition from "Fa" to "$\exists x Fx$"—that is to say, from an atomic sentence to the effect that a named individual has a given property to the general proposition that at least one individual has that property. The logical operations involved in this transition are clear enough (Dummett 1973). The first is breaking down the atomic sentence into two components, a predicative component and a nominative component (or, in Fregean terms, a function and an argument). Once the internal structure of the atomic sentence is manifest, the next operation is to replace the nominative component with a variable. The final operation is to bind that variable with an existential quantifier. This sequence of logical operations gives us an important clue as to what is involved in a subject's being able to understand the existential quantifier in a manner that permits existential generalization. In order to understand how a given sentence can imply an existential generalization, a thinker needs to be able to view it as being composed in such a way that the nominative component can be replaced by an arbitrary name (hence by a variable). The sentence needs to be "broken down" in thought before the existential quantifier can be applied. But this breaking down in thought of an atomic sentence presupposes the capacity for intentional ascent. It involves holding the thought in mind and determining its structure in a way that creates a space for the variable that will be bound by the existential quantifier. The same point holds, *mutatis mutandis*, for thinking involving the universal quantifier (as I will discuss further in section 9.5).

It would seem, then, that there are two principal ways that the capacity for intentional ascent can be presupposed in the generation of complex thoughts. First, the formation of compound thoughts by means of the truth-functional propositional operators presupposes the capacity for intentional ascent because grasping a complex thought is a matter of grasping the way in which its truth-value is determined by the truth-value of its constituent thoughts, and truth is a notion that applies primarily to thoughts. Second, complex thoughts involving quantification presuppose the capacity for intentional ascent because mastery of the mechanisms of quantification requires the ability to determine the structure of a thought. I suggested also that the capacity to form complex thoughts involving modal and tense operators may well also be dependent on the capacity for intentional ascent, but this suggestion will play no further role in the argument.

If this line of argument is well founded, then it follows that logic requires language—a conclusion reached on very different grounds by Jonathan Bennett (1976). So what are the consequences for reasoning at the nonlinguistic level? I have already explored some relevant terrain in chapter 7, where I showed how nonlinguistic creatures could be capable of certain forms of protoinference that do not involve intentional ascent. Conditional reasoning, it was suggested, can be understood in causal terms, while protonegation can be understood in terms of mastery of contrary concepts (as opposed to the ability to apply a truth-functional operator to propositions). This still leaves open an important question, however. If thinking involving quantifiers presupposes the capacity for intentional ascent, hence is unavailable to nonlinguistic creatures, should we conclude that nonlinguistic creatures cannot be credited with any form of general thoughts? This question will be addressed in the next section.

The proposed analysis of quantificational thinking raises a further question. I have argued that the key feature in quantificational thinking is the ability to break down a thought in such a way as to open up a space for a variable. Given the highly plausible suggestion, already discussed in chapter 4, that the variable of quantification is the analogue of the relative pronoun in natural language, it is natural to wonder whether the ability to break down thoughts that comes with the capacity for intentional ascent might not have cognitive implications that I have not yet discussed. In section 9.6 I shall propose that this type of intentional ascent makes possible (and may well be required for) the integration of different types of domain-specific thinking.

9.5   Two Types of General Thought

In the previous section I argued that quantificational thinking requires language. This conclusion seems to entail that nonlinguistic creatures cannot have general thoughts. This section argues that this conclusion only follows on one way of understanding generality.

Philosophers have distinguished two ways of thinking about generality (Bennett 1977, Lewis 1969). The distinction goes back at least as far as the twelfth century—we find it in Abelard's distinction between generality *in sensu composito* and generality *in sensu diviso*. If I believe, *in sensu composito*, that every F is a G then the content of my belief is a general proposition to the effect that everything that is an F is also a G. There may, of course, be individual things that are F but that I do not believe to be G—since I may be unaware that they are in fact Fs, for example. Nonetheless, as far as I am concerned it is a general truth that nothing can be an F without also being a G. So, for example, I might believe *in sensu composito* that all tigers are dangerous even though, unaware that an albino tiger is still a tiger, I might find myself in front of a tiger and fail to recognize that it is dangerous. If, on the other hand, I believe *in sensu diviso* that every F is a G, the content of my belief is not a general proposition at all. Rather, what I have is a certain disposition to form singular beliefs. Whenever I encounter an F, or indeed whenever I think about one, I tend to come to the view that it is a G. It would be evidence against ascribing to me the belief *in sensu diviso* that every tiger is dangerous if I were to fail to identify the albino tiger as dangerous.

The distinction is sometimes termed the distinction between collective generality (*in sensu composito*) and distributive generality (*in sensu diviso*). It can most easily be viewed as a distinction of scope. Universal quantifiers will feature in the attribution of both types of general belief, but in the case of general beliefs *in sensu diviso,* the universal quantifier will fall outside the scope of the belief operator, while in the case of general beliefs *in sensu composito,* it will fall within the scope of the belief operator.

It is plausible to interpret the distinction between general beliefs *in sensu composito* and general beliefs *in sensu diviso* as entailing that only general beliefs *in sensu composito* take quantified propositions as their objects. This in turn implies that general beliefs *in sensu composito* are only available to creatures that have the capacity for intentional ascent (for reasons brought out in the previous section). An analogous point holds, of course, for existential beliefs (and is, in effect, the distinction between *de re* and *de dicto* existential beliefs). A nonlinguistic creature can have a belief to the effect that some F is a G in the etiolated sense that there is some F of which it believes that it is a G (with the existential quantifier falling outside the scope of the belief operator). Only a language-using creature, however, can have a belief that is correctly characterized with an existential quantifier falling within the scope of the belief operator.

Of course, the plausibility of this thesis about the language-dependence of a distinctive kind of thinking about generality stands or falls with the original distinction between two types of general belief. Some authors have put forward what appears to be an intermediate conception of general beliefs, suggesting that there is really only one type of belief about generality that fits into neither the distributive nor the collective mold. Braithwaite, for example, offers an account of belief according to which believing that *p* is a matter of behaving as if *p* were true. He extends this to general beliefs as follows:

> A third advantage of my doctrine [the first two advantages being (1) that it lends itself to an account of degrees of belief and (2) that it can serve as the basis for an account of justified inductive belief] is that it assists in one of the most subtle problems of logic, that of the analysis of general propositions. For action appropriate to belief in a general proposition does not present any special problems. 'I am disposed to act appropriately to every P being Q' means that, whenever I am disposed to act appropriately to a thing's being P, I am disposed to act appropriately to its being Q. (Braithwaite 1932–33, 39–40)

Although Bennett, for example, suggests that Braithwaite is offering an account of distributive generality (Bennett 1977, 104 n. 3), there is a crucial difference between Braithwaite's proposal and the distributive construal. Braithwaite does not suggest that the general belief that all *F*s are *G* requires behaving, with respect to everything that is *in fact* an *F*, as if it were a *G*. Rather, he requires simply that the believer should behave with respect to everything that *he takes to be* an *F* as if it were a *G*. Failing to respond appropriately to the dangerousness of an albino tiger would not, therefore, disqualify me from believing that all tigers are dangerous (hence the belief would not be correctly characterized with a universal quantifier outside the scope of the belief operator in the way that general beliefs *in sensu diviso* would be correctly characterized).

But it is far from clear that Braithwaite has really given us a satisfying account of general beliefs. One problem with his view is that it lacks the appropriate counterfactual implications. A believer might be disposed to behave with respect to everything that she in fact takes to be an *F* as if it were a *G* without being disposed to behave with respect to everything that she *might* take to be an *F* as if such things were *G*s. A genuinely universal belief to the effect that all *F*s are *G*s is completely incompatible with the possibility that something might be taken to be an *F* and yet not be believed to be a *G*—but Braithwaite's account seems to leave this possibility open. Of course, though, a simple modification will rescue the theory. All we need require is that the believer be disposed to behave with respect to everything that she is disposed to believe to be an *F* as if it were a *G*. But this brings us to the real problem. Braithwaite is suggesting not only that creatures can have fully general beliefs even though they do not have the resources to mark that generality in any way (either at the linguistic level or at the level of thought) but, more strongly, that there are no general beliefs for which markers of generality are required. And it is this second claim that must be challenged. It cannot be the case that there is no significant cognitive difference between a creature that has a generalized Braithwaitean disposition, on the one hand, and a creature for which such a disposition is grounded in an explicitly formulated general thought of the type expressible by a universally quantified sentence. The difference is easily capturable when we consider the logical form of the appropriate belief ascriptions. I have already shown that general beliefs *in sensu diviso* should be characterized in the following manner:

For all x, if x is an F then β believes (is disposed to act as if) x is a G

General beliefs in the Braithwaite style are specifiable in a broadly similar manner, with a slightly expanded antecedent.

For all x, if x is an F and is taken by β to be an F, then β believes (is disposed to act as if) x is a G

But this still falls short of general beliefs *in sensu composito* specifiable as follows:

(3) β believes that, for all x, if x is an F then x is a G.

Nothing could persuade me that there is no significant difference between (2) and (3).

It would seem, then, that there is a real and genuine distinction to be drawn between two types of thinking about generality. Although one of these ways of thinking about generality (that which involves contents containing quantified general beliefs) is restricted to creatures capable of intentional ascent (and hence of semantic ascent), the distinction offers a type of thinking about generality that is indeed available at the nonlinguistic level. As such, it provides a primitive analogue for quantificational thinking in the same manner that the forms of protoinference discussed in chapter 7 provide primitive analogues of the truth-functional propositional connectives.

9.6   *From Domain-Specificity to Domain-Generality*

The hypothesis of domain-specificity has become increasingly popular among theorists in cognitive archeology, evolutionary psychology, and developmental psychology. (Barkow, Cosmides, and Tooby 1992, Hirschfeld and Gelman 1994, Mithen 1996; but see Fodor 2000 for criticism of extreme versions of the hypothesis). This section suggests that the apparent domain-specificity of various types of nonlinguistic thinking may in fact reflect a structural limitation on the types of thinking available at the nonlinguistic level.

The basic tenet of the hypothesis of domain-specificity is that certain fundamental types of cognitive activity are carried out by modular systems that have evolved to deal with particular types of problem and particular types of situation. Popular candidates for domain-specific modules include the interpersonal competences involved in social interactions; the basic principles about objects and their interactions that are usually collectively labeled naive physics; and an intuitive grasp of folk biology and natural history. These modules operate on a highly selective and domain-specific set of inputs with a fixed and limited amount of background information. For present purposes, there is systematicity within each module, but not across modules. An example of this failure of systematicity can be found in the archeological record—namely, the failure of early hominids to integrate their practical abilities in tool construction with their detailed knowledge of natural history in order to produce hand-axes for specific purposes. In the Middle Paleolithic, for example, we find what seem to be highly developed tool-making skills existing side by side with a subtle and advanced knowledge of the natural environment, but it is not until the Upper Paleolithic that we see these two bodies of knowledge being integrated in the form of tools specially designed for dealing with different plants and animals, together with hunting strategies that are tailored to the habits of specific animals (Mithen 1996a).

The proposal I want to consider is that language is required for the integration of domain-specific modules.[15] The argument here hinges on the distinctive role of the relative pronoun in permitting the construction of relative clauses. This was briefly discussed in chapter 4 when I considered Quine's account of the psychogenesis of reification. I rejected Quine's argument that reification depends on the linguistic mechanisms of quantification and the relative pronoun (the natural language equivalent of the bound variable of quantification). But nonetheless I saw no reason to dispute Quine's general claim about the enormous cognitive significance of the linguistic device of the relative pronoun. The crucial feature of the relative pronoun in this respect is that it permits the formation of relative clauses. One way of thinking about relative clauses is as a way of distinguishing within a sentence between the object that is the logical subject of the sentence (what the sentence is about) from what the sentence says about that object (Quine 1974, sec. 24, 1995).[16] In English, for example, from a sentence like "The red deer comes to the water just before nightfall" we can extract the relative clause "that comes to the water just before nightfall," which can be used to characterize other animals, or be embedded in further sentences, and so forth. Once the relative clause has thus been constructed and detached from the original sentence, the information it provides is available in a form that can be employed in a variety of different contexts. Consider a simplified model of domain-specific cognition in which a thinker can think about two separate domains, each of which contains two objects and four properties. The properties from one domain can only be applied in thought to the objects in that domain, and no object or predicate features in more than one domain. Suppose that a is an object in the first domain and G a predicate in the second domain. How might such a creature come to be capable of the thought that Ga? Only be forming a conception of what it is for something to be a G that is no longer tied to the objects in the second domain. That is to say, only by forming a conception of what it is for an arbitrary object to be a G. And it is this that the introduction of the relative pronoun makes possible. The relative clause is the most basic way of extrapolating complex predicates from complete sentences in a form that will allow them to be applied to objects falling under other cognitive domains—and the defining feature of domain-general cognition is that objects from one domain can be thought about in terms formerly associated only with objects from another domain, as in totemic art when an artifact is attributed the properties of an animal, or as in advanced tool construction when the design of a tool is specifically tailored to properties of the intended prey.

Let us assume, therefore, that the integration of different types of domain-specific cognition must involve some cognitive mechanism that operates in a manner analogous to the relative pronoun to distinguish within thoughts between what the thought is about and what the thought affirms of that object. At this point the close relation between the relative pronoun and the variable of quantification becomes relevant once again. One might expect this cognitive mechanism to operate in a manner very similar to that involved in extracting an existential generalization from a given sentence—namely, by breaking the thought down in such a way that the predicative component is detached from the nominative component. In the case of quantified thought, the result of this "decomposition" of the thought is to allow the insertion of a variable bound by a quantifier into the place occupied by the name. In the case of the transition from domain-specific to domain-general thinking, however, the result of the "decomposition" is to make it possible to insert an arbitrary name into the place of the name. In both cases, however, the reliance on the capacity for intentional ascent is clear. What is required is the ability to hold a thought in mind in order to identify and manipulate its structure. And this, by the argument of chapter 8, is only possible when that thought has a linguistic vehicle.

In the first seven chapters of the book I defended at some length the thesis that it can be appropriate and correct to attribute to nonlinguistic creatures thoughts that have determinate contents, are compositionally structured, and reflect the mode of presentation under which the creature in question apprehends the immediate environment. Not only is the ascription of such thoughts often mandated by the requirements of psychological explanation, but the explanatory practices within which such thought-ascriptions take place can be embedded within viable conceptions of nonlinguistic reasoning and nonlinguistic rationality.

The principal claim of the two final chapters has been that there are significant limitations to the cognitive abilities of nonlinguistic creatures. Certain types of thinking are in principle only available to creatures that dispose of a language. The fundamental reason for the restriction developed in chapter 8 is that thoughts can only be the objects of further thoughts when they have linguistic vehicles. Intentional ascent (that is to say, thinking about thoughts) requires the possibility of semantic ascent. The argument from intentional ascent to semantic ascent places significant restrictions on the scope of thinking without words, Many types of thinking involve intentional ascent explicitly, because they are directly targeted on first-order thoughts. This is the case, for example, in the types of reflection associated with second-order cognitive dynamics (section 9.1) and most forms of higher-order desire (section 9.2). Explicit intentional ascent is also involved in all forms of psychological understanding that involve attributing thoughts to others (section 9.3). In section 9.4 I showed that intentional ascent can also be involved implicitly even in types of thinking that are not explicitly targeted on first-order thoughts—that is to say, in types of thinking whose contents do not involve further thoughts. These are types of thinking into which a creature cannot enter without the capacity for intentional ascent. The principal example discussed in section 9.4 was logical thinking involving the truth-functional propositional connectives and quantifiers (although it was also suggested that modal and tensed thought might fall into this category). In section 9.5 I identified a type of general belief that does not presuppose intentional ascent and hence is available to nonlinguistic creatures. The final section of the chapter explored the role of language in making possible the transition from domain-specific to domain-general cognition. It was argued that the mechanisms required for domain-general thinking are very similar to those that make possible quantificational thought.

The picture that has emerged of the scope of nonlinguistic thinking provides principled grounds for thinking that many cognitive abilities that have traditionally been taken to be uniquely human are indeed unique to language-using humans. Only language-using creatures can be logical thinkers, monitor their own processes of belief formation and argument, and reflect on the desires that they want to have. Only language-using creatures are capable of attributing thoughts to other creatures. Yet the gulf between linguistic and nonlinguistic thought should not be exaggerated. Many of these uniquely human cognitive abilities have analogues at the nonlinguistic level. Logical thinking may be the preserve of language-users, but forms of general belief and types of protoinference are available at the nonlinguistic level. Nonlinguistic creatures cannot monitor their own processes of belief formation, but they are nonetheless capable of sophisticated forms of belief revision. The attribution of thoughts is not possible at the nonlinguistic level, but there are still relatively complicated ways that nonlinguistic creatures can think about the perceptions and desires of other creatures and hence in which they can explain and predict behavior in, broadly speaking, psychological terms. The cognitive separation between creatures that have language and creatures that do not is very real. But it is a separation between two types of *thinking*—between two ways of representing the social and physical environment—rather than between thought and the absence of thought.

Afterword

The conception of nonlinguistic thought developed in this book has been formulated with a view primarily to the requirements of, and constraints imposed by, those disciplines studying the cognitive abilities of nonlinguistic creatures, namely, cognitive ethology, developmental psychology and cognitive archeology. I have stressed, not simply the nature and content of the thoughts that might be attributed to nonlinguistic creatures, but also the practices of explanation within which those attributions take place. Indeed, the accounts eventually reached of the nature and content of nonlinguistic thinking were formulated in the light of particular ways of understanding those practices of explanation. The plural here is important. Different types of explanation are appropriate for different types of behavior at the nonlinguistic level, and those types of explanation bring with them different and distinctive ways of understanding the thoughts that lie behind the behaviors in question.

The most obvious contrast is between, on the one hand, those explanations that presuppose some nonlinguistic analogue of belief-desire psychology and, on the other, explanations that appeal to non-propositional perceptual states. We do not have to make a general choice between understanding the thoughts of nonlinguistic creatures on the model of propositional attitudes and understanding them as essentially perceptual in form (in the manner proposed by the minimalist approach discussed in chapter 3). Each model is suitable for different types of behavior. Most examples of thinking behavior in nonlinguistic creatures should no doubt be accommodated in more or less the way that the minimalist proposes—as involving, in Dummett's phrase, the superposition of spatial images upon spatial perceptions. Behaviors for which the minimalist approach is appropriate are characterized by being circumscribed by the here-and-now. The information on which the animal or infant acts is available in the content of perception. No abstraction away from the environmental context is required. There is, in short, no form of reasoning involved. This does not mean, however, that there is no sense in which behavior of this type can be assessed for rationality. The notion of rationality is inextricably linked with the practice of psychological explanation. An explanation works by making an action comprehensible and, broadly speaking, an action is made comprehensible when it becomes clear why it was a rational thing for the agent in question to carry out, in the light of their motivations and the information at their disposal. But rationality does not require reasoning. There are different ways in which the notion of rationality can be deployed with respect to nonlinguistic creatures, and what I termed level-1 rationality is clearly applicable in the context of minimalist explanations. Minimalist explanations are appropriate for behaviors that can be understood as responses to perceptually available information, and the rationality of those responses can be understood according to a range of normative criteria even though the responses in question are not *reasoned* responses.

Yet, the minimalist approach has its limitations. There are behaviors that outstrip the bounds of the here-and-now in a way that the minimalist approach cannot accommodate. These behaviors have in common a type of consequence-sensitivity that involves instrumental reasoning about the outcomes of actions—reasoning that exploits the particular connections between actions and outcomes. It is with behaviors of this type that we come to the domain of propositional attitude psychology. We need to attribute beliefs and desire to make sense of these behaviors. This is so for two reasons. The first is that the types of mental state invoked in the minimalist mode of explanation do not support instrumental reasoning of the appropriate type. The second is that the form of explanation appropriate to consequence-sensitive behavior requires mental states with contents that have structure (that is to say, that are made up of constituents that can feature in further thoughts) and whose contents can be linguistically expressed in a relatively determinate manner and without remainder. These reasons are of course related. We have difficulty making sense of the idea of reasoning defined over states lacking determinate contents and intrinsic structure.

The proposal to apply propositional attitude psychology to nonlinguistic creatures brings its own peculiar difficulties. In particular there is the problem of explaining both how the beliefs and desires of nonlinguistic creatures can have determinate and linguistically expressible contents and how we can find out what those contents are. The version of success semantics proposed in this book tackles these questions simultaneously. The requirements of successful action fix the content of belief in such a way that what a creature believes can be worked out from how it behaves and what it wants to achieve. Of course, the way in which a creature behaves needs to be understood broadly, as involving not just how it actually did behave but how it would behave in different circumstances. And, in order to know what a creature believes about the world one needs to have an idea of the sorts of discriminations that it is capable of making between categories of objects, of the similarities to which it is sensitive and of the general expectations that it possesses about how bodies behave. This sort of understanding of how a creature carves up its environment is not easy to gain, but we have seen that there are ways in which it can be gained, drawing upon existing research paradigms for studying infants and animals.

The beliefs and desires attributed to nonlinguistic creatures feature in instrumental reasoning. Yet the forms of reasoning available at the nonlinguistic level are fundamentally different from those in terms of which reasoning at the linguistic level is usually understood. Animals and infants are not capable of applying formal rules of inference defined over propositions. Not only is the evidence usually taken to reveal mastery of formal principles of inference in nonlinguistic creatures highly inconclusive, but there are good grounds for thinking that there can be no logic without language. These grounds derive from the general line of argument, developed in chapter 8, to the effect that intentional ascent requires semantic ascent. Public language vehicles are required for thoughts to be the objects of further thoughts, and (as I argued in section 9.4) it is not possible to understand either the truth-functional logical connectives or the mechanisms of quantification without being capable of intentional ascent of this type. So, we cannot understand the way in which a nonlinguistic creature's beliefs and desires can lead to action by thinking about how it might reason deductively or inductively from those beliefs and desires to a particular intention to act. In chapter 7 I offered an alternative way of understanding reasoning at the nonlinguistic level, in terms of what I termed proto-inference. Proto-inferences are not made in virtue of their form. Rather, they trade on a creature's mastery of pairs of contrary concepts and on its understanding of causal connections between states of affairs. The mechanisms of proto-inference allow analogues at the nonlinguistic level of fundamental forms of reasoning, such as reasoning from an excluded alternative (the analogue of disjunctive syllogism) and what I termed proto-modus ponens and proto-modus tollens.

The question of nonlinguistic rationality reflects the more general issue of the differences between linguistic and nonlinguistic thought. The argument that intentional ascent requires semantic ascent imposes serious limits on the range of thoughts available at the nonlinguistic level. Most obviously, it means that animals and infants cannot be capable of attributing propositional attitudes in the interests of psychological explanation, since attributing a mental state effectively involves identifying a relation between an individual and a thought. Nor are nonlinguistic creatures capable of the type of second-order cognitive dynamics that involves explicitly reflecting on the inferential connections between thoughts and the likelihood of their truth, since this requires explicitly taking thoughts as the objects of thoughts. This does not entail, however, that no forms of psychological understanding or belief revision are available at the nonlinguistic level. As we saw in chapter 9 there are primitive forms of psychological understanding that do not involve attributing propositional attitudes. These forms of psychological understanding exploit perceptual connections between agents and states of affairs and an understanding of the goals of intentional action. Similarly, there are relatively sophisticated forms of belief revision that do not involve the type of metarepresentational thinking characteristic of second-order cognitive dynamics. This, of course, is precisely what one would expect. As I have stressed in earlier work (Bermúdez 1998), high-level cognitive abilities do not emerge *ex nihilo*. They arise from a basis of lower-level cognitive precursors that are both ontogenetically and phylogenetically primitive.

The overall picture that has emerged of nonlinguistic thought strikes a balance between the two conceptions of the relation between thought and language with which we began in chapter 2. I have stressed that thinking in general by no means requires the vehicle of a public language. Moreover, we can attribute to nonlinguistic creatures full-fledged thoughts that are the objects of propositional attitudes, in addition to the non-propositional and essentially perceptual types of thinking envisaged by the minimalist that we considered in chapter 3. As we saw in chapters 4 and 5 the full-fledged thoughts we can attribute to nonlinguistic creatures are composed of distinguishable components that can feature in further thoughts. These thoughts reflect the creature's ontological perspective on the world—the way in which it carves up the environment into bounded individuals and the object-properties to which it is sensitive. They have determinate contents that must be specified by means of a "that–"clause. And they reflect the aspectuality and intensionality of the modes of presentation under which objects and properties are thought about. Nonetheless, in opposition to the conception of the relation between language and thought favored by language of thought theorists, we cannot simply analyze the thinking of creatures who do not possess a public language by crediting them with an internal language of thought that has the expressive capacity of a public language. The argument that intentional ascent requires semantic ascent places significant limitations on the expressive power of nonlinguistic thought. And hence, even if it is thought that nonlinguistic thought must be realized in a language of thought, that language of thought must be significantly different to that hypothesized to account for the thinking of nonlinguistic creatures.

The fact of the matter, however, is that we have little idea of what the vehicle of nonlinguistic thought might be. At the level of the vehicle, nonlinguistic thoughts are rather similar to scientific unobservables (Sellars 1956/1997). We can see their effects but (as yet) only speculate as to the intrinsic nature of their vehicles. They provide us with a powerful and indispensable tool for understanding the behavior of nonlinguistic creatures, a tool that we can employ even though we do not clearly understand the physical basis for it. What I have tried to bring out in this book, however, is that we can ascribe thoughts with structured contents to nonlinguistic creatures and employ those thoughts to give intentional explanations of their behavior *without* knowing what the vehicles of those thoughts are. Knowing what the vehicle of nonlinguistic thoughts are is not necessary to give intentional explanations of the behavior of nonlinguistic creatures. And nor is it sufficient. Even if we were convinced by arguments such as those put forward by proponents of the language of thought hypothesis this would not help us at all in determining the contents of those thoughts and how they might be employed in psychological explanation. What we need, and what I have tried to show that we can attain, is a way of working backwards from behavior to genuinely explanatory structured representations. This will ultimately yield a conceptual foundation for the various disciplines that are committed to giving psychological explanations of the behavior of nonlinguistic creatures.

Notes

Chapter 1

1. Interestingly, however, it has been suggested that some processes of instrumental conditioning are not in fact completely nonpsychological. See for example Heyes and Dickinson 1993 and Dickinson and Balleine 1993.

2. The remainder of this section draws on section 4.2 of Bermúdez 1998.

3. In the following, unless there is explicit indication to the contrary, I will be using "linguistic thought" to abbreviate "the thoughts of language-using creatures." It should not be thought that linguistic thoughts are necessarily linguistically expressed by the thinker.

Chapter 2

1. Dissenting interpretations of Frege of varying stripes will be found in, for example, Baker and Hacker 1984, Makin 2000, Weiner 1990, and Sluga 1980.

2. The interpreter most often mentioned in this context is Michael Dummett, who has done more than anyone both to promote Frege as a serious philosopher and to promote the idea that Frege's fundamental contribution to philosophy is the idea that we can only analyze thought through analyzing language.

3. For illuminating discussion of Frege's notion of force see Dummett 1973, ch. 10.

4. This claim has been challenged by the tradition of possible worlds semantics. According to Stalnaker (1987), for example, the objects of propositional attitudes are sets of possible worlds and as such do not have any constituent structure. He writes, for example, that "belief-desire explanations do presuppose that propositions stand in logical relations such as entailment, and one can generalize about entailment relations by describing propositions in terms of the way they are or might be determined. But as the possible worlds analysis of propositions makes clear, the assumption that propositions stand in logical relations does not imply that they have linguistic structure or logical form" (60–61).
A proper consideration of Stalnaker's position would take us too far afield, but it is worth noting that he does make room for structure in the way a thought (or proposition) is determined. The basic idea is that thinkers have a way of thinking about Socrates and the property of mortality that can be combined to determine a particular set of possible worlds (namely, all and only the possible worlds in which Socrates is mortal). Similarly, thinkers have a way of thinking about the property of mortality and the existential quantifier that can be combined to determine another set of possible worlds (namely, all and only the possible worlds in which at least one thing is mortal). The inference is valid just if the first set of possible worlds is a subset of the second. There are definite advantages to this way of thinking about inference (some of which will be considered later on in this book). For the moment I need note simply that structure has not been banished. It has merely been relocated—from the thought itself to the way in which that thought is determined.

5. There are nonetheless difficulties with Frege's suggestion that the structure of a

thought is given by the structure of the sentence that expresses it. For further discussion see Bell 1987, Dummett 1991a, and Bermúdez 2001a.

6. In fact, one of the key arguments for the language of thought hypothesis is that we cannot explain the possibility of language learning without assuming that there is a language of thought (Fodor 1975). The argument is, in essence, that language learning is a process of hypothesis formation and testing and hence requires a language-like medium in which those hypotheses can be formulated and evaluated. Ex hypothesi this cannot the language being learned. Hence, Fodor concludes, it must be a language of thought at least as expressively powerful as the language being learned.

7. Defenders of the language of thought hypothesis do have an alternative line of response. They can claim that the process of language learning is essentially a process of hypothesis formation and testing that requires postulating a language of thought. This is Fodor's view. It is unlikely to be widely accepted, however. There is little evidence that language learning is anything like what Fodor describes.

8. The remainder of this section develops arguments originally presented in Bermúdez 1995c.

9. A possible model for this type of explanation (although not one developed from the perspective of the language of thought theory) comes with the speculations about the relation between mirror neurons and empathetic understanding of conspecifics to be found in Gallese and Goldman 1998.

10. This problem arises for any theory of the semantics of sentences in the language of thought. Nothing in the argument to follow hinges on the earlier decision to consider causal covariance theories rather than, say, teleological theories.

11. This interdependence of syntax and semantics clearly poses the question of how languages are acquired in human development. Even if, as Chomsky and others have suggested, there is an innate basic syntactic competence, the problem still arises for the acquisition of semantics. It is widely accepted that prosodic cues (e.g., the fact that changes in frequency and lengthening indicate major clausal and phrasal boundaries) and a general, probably innate knowledge of the general characteristics of clauses and phrases play a significant part in language acquisition (Stromswold 2000). But it is hard to see how these could suffice without the operation of some sort of 'semantic bootstrapping,' where semantic bootstrapping is precisely the process of using the interdependence of semantics and syntax to work toward a semantic understanding (Pinker 1994). There are very real questions about the extent of the semantic knowledge required, although all parties are agreed that arguments from the poverty of the stimulus are less compelling for the acquisition of semantics than for the acquisition of syntax.

12. Compare Braddon-Mitchell and Fitzpatrick 1990, 14.

13. There is a nice example of how this might be done in Churchland and Sejnowski 1992, ch. 4, 183-188. They show (using a neural network model of how the shape of a figure can be computed from the patterns of shading on its surface) how individual neurons that seem to be responsive to particular stimuli (hence that look very much as if they are grandmother neurons) can be interpreted as forming parts of vectors processing information that does not in any straightforward way map onto the individual features to which the individual neurons are responsive.

Chapter 3

1. There are also analogies with the distinction made by cognitive psychologists between declarative memory (remembering-that) and procedural memory (remembering-how). See, e.g., Squire, Knowlton, and Musen 1993.

2. It is important to distinguish this proposal from a superficially similar claim. Theorists concerned with the subpersonal underpinnings of thinking-how have debated whether imagistic representations exist at the subpersonal level. Although certain well-known experimental results (Shephard 1982) seem to suggest that the subpersonal vehicles of certain personal-level types of reasoning are imagistic in form, other theorists have argued that the results are indeed compatible with versions of the language of thought theory (see Block 1991 and Tye 1991 for discussion from a philosophical point of view). But this debate is orthogonal to that with which I am currently concerned. Thinking-how is proposed as a personal-level phenomenon—and it is quite possible that the subpersonal vehicles of thinking-how might be propositionally encoded sentences in a language of thought. For present purposes I am taking "subpersonal" to be synonymous with "at the level of the organism" and hence not confined to persons as standardly understood. For further discussion of the relevance of the person/subpersonal distinction to psychology see Bermúdez 2000b and the other essays collected in Bermúdez and Elton 2000.

3. I am very grateful to David Chalmers for suggesting this way of presenting and engaging with the minimalist approach.

4. This is why the various types of indexical thought have traditionally posed problems for the propositional approach to thought. For further discussion see Kaplan 1989 and Perry 1977 and 1979.

5. Once again, of course, indexicals pose significant difficulties (Perry 1977, 1979). These are not, however, difficulties that have led theorists to propose indexical thought as an example of nonpropositional thought in the sense I am discussing.

6. It is also open to a theorist, at least in principle, to maintain linguistic expressibility and structure while denying the independence of content from context and the availability of the content/force distinction. But it is difficult to see what might motivate such a position.

7. For a short introduction to the terms of the debate see Bermúdez forthcoming-c. As I explained in the preface, the position I am developing in this book is intended to be neutral on the general question of conceptual versus nonconceptual content.

8. For discussion of what it is to take a perception "at face value" see Peacocke 1999 and Bermúdez 2002.

9. Cussins does not himself use these terms, but this way of putting the point is, I think, in the spirit of his account.

10. The theory of affordances has most frequently been applied to vision, but the thesis extends to the other sensory modalities (see Turvey 1996 for an ecological approach to haptic perception).

11. For a discussion of the extent to which the abilities of marsh tits and chickadees to hide and retrieve food is really due to place-memory rather than the deployment of simple heuristics and rules of thumb, see the articles by Sherry cited in the text and Shettleworth and Krebs 1986.

12. These differences are slightly diminished if the minimalist chooses to specify the contents of nonlinguistic desires in terms of situation-desires, rather than goal-desires, since a situation-desire is much closer to a propositional attitude than a goal-desire. Nonetheless, even with situation-desires there is still no need to move beyond perception in psychological explanation.

13. For a more detailed discussion of immediate perception and the issues that it raises in the epistemology of perception see Bermúdez 2000a.

14. See, for example, Armstrong 1961. There is an instructive discussion of the inferential approach to mediate perception in the first chapter of Jackson 1977.

15. The use of dishabituation experiments in infant and animal cognition will be discussed in more detail in chapter 4.

16. Nonetheless, some learned behaviors, such as the tool-use in cotton-top tamarins (Hauser 1997) discussed in the previous section, can be accommodated in terms of the direct perception of instrumental properties.

17. This distinction will be discussed further in chapter 6 in the context of rationality at the nonlinguistic level.

18. This is adapted from Baker 1995, 122. Baker is more cautious than I am. She holds EAC to be a sufficient but not a necessary condition of a genuine explanation. My second clause is also slightly different from hers. She has: (2) given that an F-type event did occur, the occurrence of a G-type event was inevitable. The difference is not important, however, as my clause 2 can be seen as a way of making plainer what inevitability might mean in this context.

19. Of course, EAC is roughly formulated, and there is an extensive literature devoted to making it more precise and less susceptible to counterexamples, but it is quite adequate for present purposes. A version of EAC is sometimes adopted as the main plank of counterfactual analyses of causation (e.g., Lewis 1973). Nothing I say here depends on the acceptability or otherwise of such counterfactual analyses.

20. I will discuss desires here purely for the sake of convenience—because we already have in play an understanding of how to go about establishing the content of a desire. It should be clear that the following argument could be applied equally effectively to beliefs.

21. See particularly the discussion of level 1 rationality in sections 6.3 and 7.1.

Chapter 4

1. In any case, worries about circularity could easily be dispelled through the mechanism of ramsification (Lewis 1972). Ramsification makes a virtue out of the interdependence of belief and desire attributions.

2. In fact, the content of both beliefs and situation-desires is given by the state of affairs *as apprehended in a particular way*. I shall return to this later; it is not important for the moment.

3. Readers of Peacocke 1999 will recognize this as an instance of what he calls the Integration Challenge. For further discussion see Bermúdez 2001d.

4. Various control experiments rule out the obvious explanations of the monkey behavior, such as their having a bias toward the bottom box (as a function, perhaps, of food always being on the ground). The details can be found in Hauser 2001.

Chapter 5

1. This is an idealization, of course. In practice, thoughts are not *that* fine-grained (nor do we need them to be for the purposes of psychological explanation and prediction). A subset of the descriptions will be adequate. The essential point is that some have to be excluded in order to narrow the field down until we have the type of localized indeterminacy that we are happy to accept in our ordinary social interactions.

2. There is a clear example of the subtraction fallacy in a well-known argument that has been used to argue for a range of theses in metaphysics, from four-dimensional conceptions of physical objects to the relativity of identity. The argument hinges on the claim that, since there is an object in existence at a time t at which, for example, I cut off my hand, there must have been an object in existence before time t corresponding to my physical body minus my hand. This claim is, of course, completely unwarranted. See Heller 1997, ch. 1, for a deployment of the claim in defense of four-dimensionalism about objects.

3. Clearly, these sentences cannot strictly speaking be atomic sentences, since food is

not a particular and hence not something that will be picked out by a singular term. I will put these difficulties to one side, however, as they do not affect the principal issue here, which is how we should view the predicative component of the sentences in the target-set.

4. This should not taken to imply the existence of an absolute space determining absolute spatial position—merely that there is some privileged coordinate system that fixes spatial location at the level of reference.

5. For further discussion see Campbell 1993, Evans 1982, and (with particular reference to nonlinguistic creatures) Bermúdez 1998, ch. 8.

6. It is natural to ask whether these four proposed ways of understanding how the location of the food is apprehended by the rat exhaust the range of possibilities. As will be explored further below, rats are very capable of deploying nongeometrical cues in situations where the geometrical structure of their environment is systematically perturbed, but there is considerable evidence that rats tend to use geometrical information when that information is available (Gallistel 1990, ch. 6, O'Keefe and Nadel 1978). Moreover, the experimental paradigms under discussion are designed to rule out the possibility that the rats are using nongeometrical cues. If, as this suggests, the only candidate modes of presentation of the location of the food are geometrical, then there are reasonable grounds for thinking that there are no further possibilities other than the four canvassed here. I am assuming, following Gallistel 1990, that the frames of reference deployed by rats (and within the animal kingdom generally) are metric systems.

7. As discussed in chapter 4, however, success semantics is most plausible when it is developed without the global explanatory pretensions of philosophical functionalism. I am offering success semantics solely as a theory of nonlinguistic thought. There are, I think, no prospects for using it to explain all types of propositional thinking.

Chapter 6

1. This conception of psychological explanation is held widely but not unanimously. According to the theory of intentional icons developed by Ruth Millikan, intentional states such as beliefs and desires should be understood in functional terms—in terms primarily of why they have come about and what jobs they are designed to do. A corollary of her approach to mental states is to downplay the rational connections holding between beliefs, desires, and other propositional attitudes. Psychological explanation, as Millikan construes it (in, for example, Millikan 1984, 1986) is a form of functional explanation, much closer to explanation in biology than to psychological explanation as traditionally conceived. Millikan's general approach has been sympathetically applied to the domain of cognitive ethology in chapter 6 of Allen and Bekoff 1997. There is much to be said for the view that psychology is a branch of biology, and it is also true that much explanation within psychology and ethology is functional rather than causal/predictive, but the cases that concern me in this book do not fit Millikan's framework, which works best for simple, subpersonal mechanisms.

2. This would effectively amount to a conception of everyday reasoning taking semantic, rather than syntactic, validity as fundamental.

3. In fact, as I show in chapters 8 and 9, there is an even more fundamental reason why nonlinguistic creatures cannot carry out the relevant reasoning. The type of practical syllogism envisaged by Davidson involves taking one's own beliefs and desires as premises. However, taking one's own thoughts as objects of thought in this way is only possible if they have linguistic vehicles—intentional ascent requires semantic ascent, as I argue in section 8.2. This is a further reason why the limited forms of protoinference available at the nonlinguistic level (see chapter 7) are irrelevant to the inference-based conception of practical reasoning.

4. It is known that vervet monkeys are sensitive to whether other individuals in the group are reliable sources of information about predators (Cheney and Seyfarth 1990).

5. As I will show in the next chapter, there is room at the nonlinguistic level for what I term protoinference, but it is a long way from that required for the inference-based conception of rationality.

6. Of course, this is to a certain extent a stipulation as to how words are to be used, but there is some justification for it in our ordinary ways of speaking. If I act completely randomly to resolve a deadlock in a situation where I really cannot see any advantage in acting one way rather than another, it would seem natural to describe this as my selecting a course of action without actually deciding on it.

7. There should be no implication that, for example, ethical deontologists are not advocating a method of decision-making. My comments should be understood as limited to "decision-making" as it might plausibly be identified in a nonlinguistic context. It seems clear, however, that making decisions on deontological grounds is not possible for creatures that are not capable of making decisions on consequence-sensitive grounds. Moreover, as I shall show in chapters 8 and 9, the type of reflection accompanying deontological decision-making is not available to nonlinguistic creatures.

8. It is worth pointing out, though, that the normative criteria of level 2 rationality incorporate elements of both internal and external rationality, in the sense introduced in section 6.1. The requirement that the relevant instrumental belief be accurate is clearly an external requirement. It is quite possible that an action will fail to qualify as rational in this external sense, even though it clearly satisfies the second, internal criterion. Arguably this would be enough for it to qualify as rational in our everyday sense—and, as I suggested, internal rationality is what is important for psychological explanation. In any case it is also possible to apply the normative criteria appropriate for level 0 and level 1 rationality to level 2 behaviors. We can assess the types of instrumental reasoning involved in, say, tool construction from the viewpoint of expected utility theory.

9. This at least is the interpretation favored by Heyes and Dickinson (1993). Their interpretation, which is formulated in the context of a more overarching attack on ethological attributions of propositional attitudes in nonlaboratory conditions, has been challenged (Allen and Bekoff 1995). One point Allen and Bekoff make is that the chick's behavior might be underwritten by a more general instrumental belief to the effect that approaching objects permits access to them, and there are good reasons why this belief might be robust in the face of the chick's experiences with the mirror—it is not always rational to revise deep-seated beliefs in the face of countervailing evidence. This point is well taken, and that may well be the correct interpretation of the chick's behavior. But the more general point stands, which is that instrumental beliefs involve a general sensitivity to contingencies, and where no such sensitivity can plausibly be identified, the attribution of an instrumental belief must be revoked. What Allen and Bekoff do, in effect, is offer a way that the behavior of the chicks can be interpreted as suitably contingency-sensitive. For further discussion see Heyes and Dickinson's (1995) reply to Allen and Bekoff.

Chapter 7

1. Fodor's model cannot be quite right as it stands. It is not (usually) the case that each behavioral option will have only one outcome, and what the creature will have to compute, for each behavioral option, are the likelihoods of the principal different outcomes that could occur. Intuitively, a creature will need to consider not simply the most desirable outcome that might be consequent on acting in a given way but also the less desirable and indeed

positively undesirable outcomes that might also occur. Each of these outcomes will have a different utility. The decision-maker will then need to weight the likelihoods of each different outcome by its desirability. The sum of these calculations will yield an expected utility for that behavioral option. The final stage will be simply to select the behavioral option with the greatest expected utility.

2. I shall say more about the particular type of inferences that might be deployed in level 2 rationality in section 7.2.

3. In the next section I will look in more detail at the form these instrumental beliefs might take—and at the inferences within which they might feature.

4. I am taking 'or' in its inclusive sense, according to which a disjunction remains true if both its disjuncts are true. The exclusive sense of 'or' can be defined by adding to the inclusive sense the further requirement that the two disjuncts not both be true. This requirement can itself be given a conditional reading. "Not-(P and Q)" is equivalent to "If P, then not-Q."

5. For an extended discussion of this view of negation see Frege 1918–19a.

6. For extended discussion of these and related matters see Sommers 1982 and Grice 1989. Bochvar 1981 provides a formal development of the idea that there are two fundamentally different types of negation.

7. And of course this also brings in modal notions, which, as I will show in the final chapter, may well not be available at the nonlinguistic level.

8. This is what Geach has called the *Latin prose theory of relative pronouns*, on which, for example, the sentence "Any man who owns a car drives it" is assimilated to "Any man, *if he* owns a car, drives it." See Geach 1967/68.

9. The most radical proposal in this area is that singular causal claims of the form "Event *c* caused event *e*" can be analyzed in terms of counterfactual conditional claims of the type "Had event *c* not occurred, event *e* would not have occurred." A counterfactual theory of causation is proposed in Lewis 1973.

10. These predictions are most frequently viewed as involving (non-truth-functional) subjunctive conditionals (about what would or would not happen), rather than truth-functional indicative conditionals. There is a useful discussion of causation and conditionals in the first chapter of Mellor 1995.

Chapter 8

1. As I will show hereafter, these six respects do not exhaust Clark's conception of the contribution that language can make to cognition.

2. I take it as uncontroversial that no system of communication can count as linguistic unless it involves symbols. The characteristic of symbols is that they are arbitrary as opposed to iconic signals (see further in the main text hereafter).

3. The bee dances have also received attention from philosophers. See Bennett 1964.

4. The definition of iconic signals just posed is significantly different from that suggested by Charles Sanders Peirce, who is usually credited with having first formulated the distinction between iconic and arbitrary signals (or rather, in his terms, between iconic and symbolic signs). Peirce defines an icon as a "Sign that represents its Object in resembling it" (1991, 270). He does not impose any requirement that continuous variation in the object be matched by continuous variation in the signal, and consequently takes as iconic signs that would not count as iconic on the criteria just outlined. For example, he holds that linguistic predicates are iconic as well as logical and mathematical proofs. Peirce's theory of signs is discussed in chapters 4 and 6 of Hookway 1985.

5. Consider, for example, the following two passages from Michael Dummett's book on

Frege. "Our apprehension of reality as decomposable into discrete objects is the product of our application to an originally unarticulated reality of the conceptual apparatus embodied in our language" (Dummett 1973, 505). And: "Our ability to discriminate, within reality, objects of any particular kind results from our having learned to use expressions, names or general terms, with which are associated a criterion of identity which yields segments of reality of just that shape: we can, in principle, conceive of a language containing names and general terms with which significantly different criteria of identity were associated, and the speakers of such a language would view the world as falling apart into discrete objects in a different way from ourselves. . . For Frege, the world does not come to us articulated in any way; it is we who, by the use of our language (or by grasping the thoughts expressed in that language), impose a structure on it" (1973, 503–504).

6. Nothing I say is intended to be incompatible with the substantive claims made by the theorists in the language of thought tradition. In particular, it may well be the case (as Fodor suggests) that the understanding of public language sentences involves in some sense translating them into the language of thought. My point is simply that reflexive thinking (in the sense in which I am understanding it, namely, as involving, e.g., the evaluation of epistemic links between propositions) is directed at the public language sentences rather than at the sentences in the language of thought that give their meaning.

7. The point was well put by Wittgenstein, who has plausible things to say about what is going on when it seems to one that one is introspecting a thought that is not sententially vehicled: "What happens when we make an effort—say in writing a letter—to find the right expression for our thoughts?—This phrase compares the process to one of translating or describing: the thoughts are already there (perhaps were there in advance) and we merely look for their expression. This picture is more or less appropriate in different cases.—But can't all sorts of things happen here?—I surrender to a mood and the expression *comes*. Or a picture occurs to me and I try to describe it. Or an English expression occurs to me and I try to hit on the corresponding German one. Or I make a gesture and ask myself: What words correspond to this gesture? And so on." (Wittgenstein 1953, sec. 335). For further discussion of Wittgenstein's complex views on the relation between language and thought see Budd 1989, chs. 5 and 6.

8. Peter Carruthers, who proposes that all domain-general cognition consists in the formation and manipulation of linguistic representations at the level of what Chomsky terms logical form, nonetheless thinks that we cannot be conscious of these "stripped down" linguistic representations (Carruthers 1996, forthcoming). We are only conscious of sentences with the full complement of natural language phonological and structural features from which the level of logical form is an abstraction.

9. I will count mental models theory as a conception of pictorial models even though the two notions cannot be straightforwardly mapped onto each other. It is true that mental models, as proposed by Johnson-Laird, are intended to be semiperceptual states that resemble the situations they represent. Nonetheless, there is a crucial ambiguity in mental models theory. On the one hand the manipulation of mental models is supposed to take place in working memory, the contents of which are generally thought to be open to conscious access and report. On the other hand it seems clear that introspection will have little role to play in deciding the issue between mental logic and mental models as far as the psychology of reasoning is concerned. To the extent that mental models theory is a theory of the subpersonal mechanisms of thought, it will be correspondingly of less use as a theoretical account of how thoughts might be vehicled in a way that would allow them to be the objects of further reflexive thinking.

10. The difference between the mental logic and mental models theories is frequently compared to that between proof-theoretic and model-theoretic approaches in logic.

Chapter 9

1. The distinction between direct and reflective doxastic modification is linked to the distinction drawn by Gilbert Harman between foundationalist and coherentist modes of belief revision (see Harman 1986). Harman's book contains much useful discussion of the different principles operating in the two different modes of belief revision. He does not take a view, however, on the relation between the coherentist/foundationalist distinction and the divide between the linguistic and the nonlinguistic.

2. Frankfurt makes a further distinction between second-order desires and second-order volitions, where a second-order volition is a desire not simply to have a particular first-order desire but also for that first-order desire to be one's will. I will use the term "second-order desire" to include second-order volitions.

3. As I noted in chapter 3, this type of second-order desire can be accommodated within the general paradigm of success semantics. I suggested there that those second-order desires that are targeted on specific first-order desires can be understood as states that cease when the relevant first-order desires come into being.

4. This is perfectly compatible with rejection of the epistemic theory of perception. The proposal is not that the propositional report says all that there is to say about the content of perception. One might think that perceptual states carry information in an analogue rather than digital manner, for example, while nonetheless thinking that the information carried can be propositionally reported. Nor, of course, does the suggestion that the propositional content of perception corresponds to the content of the perceptual belief to which it might be expected to give rise imply that perceptions are nothing more than dispositions to acquire belief. The canonical statement of the epistemic theory is Armstrong 1961.

5. It is worth noting that, strictly speaking, perceptual reports can only have one of the two characteristic features of propositional attitude reports. Clearly, the "that—" clauses reporting the contents of perception are intensional, but since perception is factive (that is, one can only perceive what is in fact the case), perceptual reports cannot be false. All this means, of course, is that we sometimes have to refer to "seemings-to-perceive" rather than to perceivings *tout court*.

6. The basic distinction here is made in various places, including Dretske 1969 and the final chapter of Jackson 1975. In the characterisation of SS reports and ES reports I am drawing on a more recent paper by Kevin Mulligan (1998).

7. As is frequently the case in the philosophy of perception, the modality of vision is really what is under discussion.

8. Mulligan (1998) suggests that the characterization of simple seeing should employ the machinery of tropes rather than properties.

9. Michael Tomasello (2000) has explicitly argued that (to put it in my terms) the capacity for intentional ascent is unique to humans and hence that the mind-reading interpretation of nonhuman apes cannot be correct. He does not, however, offer an argument for why intentional ascent should not be available to nonhumans. The argument from intentional ascent to semantic ascent would no doubt be congenial to him.

10. As discussed in chapter 7, analogues of disjunction are available at the nonlinguistic level—but these analogues do not employ anything like operators on propositions.

11. Of course, there are philosophers who think that the primary bearers of truth and falsity are sentences rather than thoughts. This would provide an even quicker way of arguing from truth-functional connectives to the need for semantic ascent.

12. I am taking 'extension' in a nontechnical sense here. But of course both modal and tense logics are extensions of classical logic in the technical sense that they incorporate the

vocabulary of classical logic and have the same theorems and inferences involving *only* that vocabulary.

13. The general approach has been challenged. See, for example, Evans 1985. But these challenges have not been accompanied by any alternative construals of tense logics.

14. My proposal bears certain resemblances to Donald's (1991) description of the Upper Paleolithic in terms of mythic culture. See also the discussion of different ways of understanding time in Campbell 1994.

15. A similar proposal is made in Carruthers forthcoming, although on very different grounds.

16. Geach has pointed out (1962, secs. 71–73) that this way of thinking about relative clauses does not extend easily to certain tricky cases. I am inclined to respond to this as Quine does (1974, 91) by distinguishing between the most plausible account of modern English and the most plausible account of the evolution of language.

References

Aiello, L. C.1996. Hominine preadaptations for language. In Mellars and Gibson 1996.

Allen, C., and M. Bekoff. 1995. Cognitive ethology and the intentionality of animal behaviour, *Mind and Language* 10, 313–328.

Allen, C., and M. Bekoff. 1997. *Species of Mind*. Cambridge, MA: MIT Press.

Armstrong, D. M. 1961. *Perception and the Physical World*. London: Routledge and Kegan Paul.

Armstrong, D. M. 1962. *Bodily Sensations*. London: Routledge and Kegan Paul.

Armstrong, D. M. 1997. *A World of States of Affairs*. Cambridge: Cambridge University Press.

Baier, A. 1979. Mind and change of mind. *Midwest Studies in Philosophy* 4, 157–176.

Baillargeon, R. 1987. Object permanence in 3.5- and 4.5-month-old infants. *Developmental Psychology* 23, 655–64.

Baillargeon, R. 1995. Physical reasoning in infancy. In Gazzaniga 1995.

Baker, G. P., and P. M. S. Hacker. 1984. *Frege: Logical Excavations*. Oxford: Oxford University Press.

Baker, L. R. 1995. *Explaining Attitudes: A Practical Approach to the Mind*. Cambridge: Cambridge University Press.

Balda, R. P., and R. J. Turek. 1984. Memory in birds. In Roitblat, Bever, and Terrace 1984.

Barkow, J. H., L. Cosmides, and J. Tooby. 1992. *The Adapted Mind: Evolutionary Psychology and the Generation of Culture*. Oxford: Oxford University Press.

Barwise, J., and J. Perry.1983. *Situations and Attitudes*. Cambridge, MA: MIT Press.

Bechtel, W., and J. Abrahamsen. 1991. *Connectionism and the Mind*. Oxford: Blackwell.

Bekoff, M., C. Allen, and G. M. Burghardt. 2002. *The Cognitive Animal*. Cambridge, MA: MIT Press.

Bell, D. 1987. Thoughts. *Notre Dame Journal of Formal Logic* 28, 36–50.

Bennett, J. 1964. *Rationality*. Indianapolis. Hackett.

Bennett, J. 1976. *Linguistic Behaviour*. Cambridge: Cambridge University Press.

Bermúdez, J. L. 1994. Peacocke's argument against the autonomy of nonconceptual content. *Mind and Language* 9, 203–218.

Bermúdez, J. L. 1995a. Aspects of the self (John Campbell's *Past, Space and Self*), *Inquiry* 38, 1–15.

Bermúdez, J. L. 1995b. Nonconceptual content: From perceptual experience to subpersonal computational states. *Mind and Language* 10, 333–369.

Bermúdez, J. L. 1995c. Syntax, semantics and levels of explanation. *Philosophical Quarterly* 45, 361–367.

Bermúdez, J. L. 1997. Practical understanding versus reflective understanding, *Philosophy and Phenomenological Research* 67, 635–641.

Bermúdez, J. L. 1998. *The Paradox of Self-Consciousness*. Cambridge, MA: MIT Press.

Bermúdez, J. L. 1999. Naturalism and conceptual norms. *Philosophical Quarterly* 49, 77–85.

Bermúdez, J. L. 2000a. Naturalized sense data. *Philosophy and Phenomenological Research* 61, 353–374.

Bermúdez, J. L. 2000b. Personal and subpersonal: A difference without a distinction. *Philosophical Explorations* 2, 63–82.

Bermúdez, J. L. 2001a. Frege on thoughts and their structure, *Philosophiegeschichte und logische Analyse* 4, 87–105.

Bermúdez, J. L. 2001b. Normativity and rationality in delusional psychiatric disorders. *Mind and Language* 16, 457–493.

Bermúdez, J. L. 2001c. Nonconceptual self-consciousness and cognitive science. *Synthese* 129, 129–149.

Bermúdez, J. L. 2001d. Review of C. Peacocke, *Being Known. Philosophical Psychology* 14, 250–256.

Bermúdez, J. L. 2002a. Sources of self-consciousness. *Proceedings of the Aristotelian Society* 102, 87–107.

Bermúdez, J. L. 2002b. Nonconceptual content. In *The Macmillan Encyclopedia of Cognitive Science.*

Bermúdez, J. L. Forthcoming-a. The domain of folk psychology. In O'Hear forthcoming.

Bermúdez, J. L. Forthcoming-b. Evans and the sense of "I". In Grush forthcoming.

Bermúdez, J. L. Forthcoming-c. *The Philosophy of Psychology: A Contemporary Introduction.* London: Routledge.

Bermúdez, J. L., and M. E. Elton (Eds.). 2000. *Personal and Subpersonal: Essays on Psychological Explanation* [Special issue]. *Philosophical Explorations* 3, 63–82.

Bermúdez, J. L., and A. Millar (Eds.). 2002. *Reason and Nature: Essays in the Theory of Rationality.* Oxford: Oxford University Press.

Bickerton, D. 1990. *Language and Species.* Chicago: Chicago University Press.

Bickerton, D. 1996. *Language and Human Behaviour.* London: UCL Press.

Binford, L. R. 1989. Isolating the transition to the cultural adaptations: An organizational approach. In Trinkhaus 1989.

Black, A. H., and Prokasy, W. F. (Eds.) 1972. *Classical Conditioning II: Current Research and Theory.* New York: Appleton Century Crofts.

Block, N. 1991. *Imagery.* Cambridge, MA: MIT Press.

Bochvar, D. A. 1981. On a three-valued logical calculus and its application to the analysis of the paradoxes of the classical extended functional calculus. *History and Philosophy of Logic* 2, 87–112.

Boden, M. (Ed.). 1990. *The Philosophy of Artificial Intelligence.* Oxford: Oxford University Press.

Boesch, C., and H. Boesch. 1992. Transmission aspects of tool use in wild chimpanzees. In Ingold and Gibson 1992.

Bower, T. G. R. 1966. The visual world of infants. *Scientific American* 215, 80–92.

Bower, T. G. R. 1982. *Development in Infancy.* San Francisco: Freeman.

Bradbury, J. W., and S. L. Vehrencamp. 1998. *Principles of Animal Communication.* Sunderland, MA: Sinnauer.

Braddon-Mitchell, D., and J. Fitzpatrick. 1990. Explanation and the language of thought. *Synthese* 83, 3–29.

Braddon-Mitchell, D., and F. Jackson. 1996. *Philosophy of Mind and Cognition.* Oxford: Blackwell.

Braithwaite, R. B. 1932–33. The nature of believing. *Proceedings of the Aristotelian Society* 33, 129–146.

Bremner, J. G. 1988. *Infancy*. Oxford: Blackwell.

Broome, J. 1991. Utility. *Economics and Philosophy* 7, 1–12.

Brown, C. R., M. B. Brown, and M. L. Shaffer. 1991. Food-sharing signals among socially roraging cliff swallows. *Animal Behavior* 42, 551–564.

Brunswik, E. 1943. Organismic achievement and environmental probability. *Psychological Review* 50, 255–272.

Budd, M. 1989. *Wittgenstein's Philosophy of Psychology*. London: Routledge.

Byrne, R. W. 1995. *The Thinking Ape*. Oxford: Oxford University Press.

Byrne, R. W., and A. Whiten (Eds.). 1988. *Machiavellian Intelligence: Social Expertise and the Evolution of Intellect in Monkeys, Apes and Humans*. Oxford: Blackwell.

Call, J., and P. Rochat. 1996. Liquid conservation in orangutans (*Pongo Pygmaeus*) and humans (*Homo sapiens*): Individual differences and perceptual strategies. *Journal of Comparative Psychology* 110, 219–232.

Call, J., and P. Rochat. 1997. Perceptual strategies in the estimation of physical quantities by orangutans (*Pongo Pygmaeus*). *Journal of Comparative Psychology* 111, 315–329.

Campbell, J. 1993. The role of physical objects in spatial thinking. In N. Eilan, R. McCarthy, and B. Brewer (Eds.), *Spatial Representation*. Oxford: Oxford University Press.

Campbell, J. 1994. *Past, Space and Self*. Cambridge, MA: MIT Press.

Carey, S., and R. Gelman (Eds.). 1991. *The Epigenesis of Mind: Essays on Biology and Cognition*. Hillsdale, NJ: Erlbaum.

Caron, A. J., R. F. Caron, and V. R. Carlson. 1979. Infant perception of the invariant shape of objects varying in slant. *Child Development* 50, 716–721.

Carruthers, P. 1996. *Language, Thought and Consciousness*. Cambridge: Cambridge University Press.

Carruthers, P. 2000. *Phenomenal Character*. Cambridge: Cambridge University Press.

Carruthers, P., and J. Boucher (Eds.). 1998. *Language and Thought: Interdisciplinary Themes*. Cambridge: Cambridge University Press.

Carruthers, P., and P. K. Smith. 1996. *Theories of Theories of Mind*. Cambridge: Cambridge University Press.

Cerella, J. 1979. Visual classes and natural categories in the pigeon. *Journal of Experimental Psychology: Human Perception and Performance* 5, 68–77.

Cheney, D. L., and R. M. Seyfarth. 1990. *How Monkeys See the World*. Chicago: University of Chicago Press.

Cheng, K. 1986. A purely geometrical module in the rat's spatial representation. *Cognition* 23, 149–178.

Child, W. 1994. *Causality, Interpretation and the Mind*. Oxford: Oxford University Press.

Chomsky, N. 1958. Review of B. F. Skinner's *Verbal Behavior*. *Language* 35, 26–58.

Chomsky, N. 1980. *Rules and Representations*. Oxford: Blackwell.

Churchland, P. M, 1989. *The Neurocomputational Perspective: The Nature of Mind and the Structure of Science*. Cambridge, MA: MIT Press.

Churchland, P. S. 1986. *Neurophilosophy: Towards a Unified Science of the Mind-Brain*. Cambridge, MA: MIT Press.

Churchland, P. S., and T. Sejnowski. 1992. *The Computational Mind*. Cambridge, MA: MIT Press.

Clark, A. 1996. Dealing in futures: Folk psychology and the role of representations in cognitive science. In McCauley 1996.

Clark, A. 1998. Magic words: How language augments human cognition. In Carruthers and Boucher 1998.

Clark, A., and A. Karmiloff-Smith. 1993. The cognizer's innards: A psychological and philosophical perspective on the development of thought. *Mind and Language* 8, 487–519.

Clayton, N. S., and A. Dickinson. 1999. Memory for the contents of caches by Scrub Jays. *Journal of Experimental Psychology: Animal Behavior Processes* 25, 82–91.

Clutton-Brock, T. H., and S. D. Albon. 1979. The roaring of red deer and the evolution of honest advertisement. *Behaviour* 69, 145–170.

Cohen, L. J. 1992. *An Essay on Belief and Acceptance*. Oxford: Oxford University Press.

Corballis, M., and E. G. L. Lea. 1999. *The Descent of Mind: Psychological Perspectives on Hominid Evolution*. Oxford: Oxford University Press.

Cosmides, L., and J. Tooby. 1994. Origins of domain-specificity: The evolution of functional organization. In Hirschfeld and Gelman 1994.

Cowie, R. 1977. Optimal foraging in great tits (*Parus Major*). *Nature* 268, 137–139.

Craik, K. 1967. *The Nature of Explanation*. Cambridge: Cambridge University Press.

Crane, T. (Ed.). 1990. The language of thought: No syntax without semantics. *Mind and Language* 5, 187–212.

Crane, T. 1992. *The Contents of Experience*. Cambridge: Cambridge University Press.

Cussins, A. 1990. The connectionist construction of concepts. In Boden 1990.

Cussins, A. 1992. Content, embodiment and objectivity: The theory of cognitive trails. *Mind* 101, 651–688.

Dancy, J. 1988. *Perceptual Knowledge*. Oxford: Oxford University Press.

Davidson, D. 1963. Actions, reasons and causes. *Journal of Philosophy 60*, 685–700. Reprinted in Davidson 1980a.

Davidson, D. 1967a. Causal relations. *Journal of Philosophy 64*, 691–703. Reprinted in Davidson 1980a.

Davidson, D. 1967b. Truth and meaning. *Synthese 17*, 304–323. Reprinted in Davidson 1980b.

Davidson, D. 1969. The individuation of events. In N. Rescher (Ed.). *Essays in Honor of Carl G. Hempel*. Dordrecht: Reidel. Reprinted in Davidson 1980a.

Davidson, D. 1970. Mental events. In L. Foster and J. W. Swanson, *Experience and Theory*. Amherst: University of Massachusetts Press. Reprinted in Davidson 1980a.

Davidson, D. 1975. Thought and talk. In S. Guttenplan (Ed.), *Mind and Language*. Oxford: Oxford University Press. Reprinted in Davidson 1980b.

Davidson, D. 1978. Intending. In Y. Yovel (Ed.), *Philosophy of History and Action*. Dordrecht: Reidel. Reprinted in Davidson 1980a.

Davidson, D. 1980a. *Essays on Actions and Events*. Oxford: Oxford University Press.

Davidson, D. 1980b. *Essays on Truth and Interpretation*. Oxford: Oxford University Press.

Davis, S. (Ed.). 1992. *Connectionism: Theory and Practice*. New York: Oxford University Press.

Dawkins, M. S. 1986. *Unravelling Animal Behaviour*. Harlow, UK: Longman.

Dennett, D. 1979. *The Intentional Stance*. Cambridge, MA: MIT Press.

Dennett, D. 1981. How to change your mind. In *Brainstorms*. Brighton, UK: Harvester Press.

Dennett, D. 1996. *Kinds of Minds*. New York: Basic Books.

De Sousa, R. 1971. How to give a piece of your mind: Or, the logic of belief and assent. *Review of Metaphysics* 25, 52–79.

Devitt, M. 1990. A narrow representational theory of the mind. In Lycan 1990.

Dickinson, A. 1980. *Contemporary Animal Learning Theory*. Cambridge: Cambridge University Press.

Dickinson, A., and B. Balleine. 1993. Actions and responses: The dual psychology of behaviour. In N. Eilan, B. Brewer, and R. McCarthy (Eds.), *Spatial Representation*. Oxford: Blackwell.

Dickinson, A., and D. Shanks. 1995. Instrumental action and causal representation. In Sperber, Premach, and Premach 1995.

Donald, M. 1991. *Origins of the Modern Mind*. Cambridge, MA: Harvard University Press.

Dretske, F. 1969. *Seeing and Knowing*. London: Routledge.

Dretske, F. 1981. *Knowledge and the Flow of Information*. Cambridge, MA: MIT Press.

Dretske, F. 1988. *Reasons in a World of Causes*. Cambridge, MA: MIT Press.

Dummett, M. 1973. *Frege: Philosophy of Language*. London: Duckworth.

Dummett, M. 1989. Language and communication. In A. George (Ed.), *Reflections on Chomsky*. Oxford: Blackwell.

Dummett, M. 1991a. More on thoughts. In *Frege and Other Philosophers*. Oxford: Oxford University Press.

Dummett, M. 1991b. Thought and perception: The views of two philosophical innovators. In *Frege and Other Philosophers*. Oxford: Oxford University Press.

Dummett, M. 1993. *The Origins of Analytical Philosophy*. London: Duckworth.

Evans, G. 1975. Identity and predication. *Journal of Philosophy* 72, 343–363.

Evans, G. 1981. Understanding demonstratives. In Parret 1981.

Evans, G. 1982. *The Varieties of Reference*. Oxford: Oxford University Press.

Evans, G. 1985. Is tense logic based on a mistake? In *Collected Papers*. Oxford: Oxford University Press.

Evans, W. E. 1973. The echolocation by marine delphids and one species of freshwater dolphin. *Journal of the Acoustic Society of America* 54, 191–204.

Field, J. 1976. Relation of young infants' reaching behaviour to stimulus distance and solidity. *Developmental Psychology* 12, 444–448.

Fisette, D. 1998. *Consciousness and Intentionality: Models and Modalities of Attribution*. Derdrecht: Kluwer.

Fodor, J. 1975. *The Language of Thought*. Cambridge, MA: Harvard University Press.

Fodor, J. 1983. *The Modularity of Mind*. Cambridge, MA: MIT Press.

Fodor, J. 1986. Why paramecia don't have mental representations. *Midwest Studies in Philosophy* 10, 3–23.

Fodor, J. 1987. *Psychosemantics*. Cambridge, MA: MIT Press.

Fodor, J. 2000. *The Mind Doesn't Work That Way*. Cambridge, MA: MIT Press.

Fodor, J., and B. P. McLaughlin. 1995. Connectionism and the problem of systematicity: Why Smolensky's solution doesn't work. In Macdonald and Macdonald 1995.

Fodor, J., and Z. Pylyshyn. 1988. Connectionism and cognitive architecture: A critical analysis. *Cognition* 28, 3–71.

Frankfurt, H. 1971. Freedom of the will and the concept of a person. *Philosophical Review* 68, 5–20.

Frankish, K. 1996. Natural language and virtual belief. In P. Carruthers and P. K. Smith (Eds.), *Theories of Theories of Mind*. Cambridge: Cambridge University Press.

Frege, G. 1918–19b. Negation. Translated by P. Geach and R. H. Stoothoff in B. McGuiness (Ed.), *Collected Papers on Mathematics, Logic, and Philosophy*. Oxford: Blackwell. (1984).

Frege, G. 1918–19a. Thoughts. Translated by P. Geach and R. H. Stoothoff in B. McGuiness (Ed.), *Collected Papers on Mathematics, Logic, and Philosophy*. Oxford: Blackwell. (1984).

Frisch, K. von. 1967. *The Dance Language and Orientation of Bees*. Cambridge, MA: Harvard University Press.

Gallese, V., and A. Goldman. 1998. Mirror neurons and the simulation theory of mind-reading. *Trends in Cognitive Science* 3, 493–501.

Gallistel, C. R. 1990. *The Organization of Learning*. Cambridge, MA: MIT Press.

Gallistel, C. R. 2000. The replacement of general purpose learning models with adaptively specialised learning modules. In Gazzaniga 2000.

Gallistel, C. R., A. L. Brown, S. Carey, R. Gelman, and F. C. Keil. 1991. Lessons from animal learning for the study of cognitive development. In Carey and Gelman 1991.

Gazzaniga, M. S. (Ed.). 1995. *The Cognitive Neurosciences*. Cambridge, MA: MIT Press.

Gazzaniga, M. S. (Ed.). 2000. *The New Cognitive Neurosciences*. Cambridge, MA: MIT Press.

Geach, P. T. 1962. *Reference and Generality*. Ithaca: Cornell University Press.

Geach, P. T. 1967/68. Identity. *Review of Metaphysics* 21, 3–12.

Gibson, J. J. 1979. *The Ecological Approach to Visual Perception*. Boston: Houghton Mifflin.

Gibson, K. R., and T. Ingold. 1993. *Tools, Language and Cognition in Human Evolution*. Cambridge: Cambridge University Press.

Goldin-Meadow, S. 1979. Structure in a manual communication system developed without a language model: Language without a helping hand. In H. A. Whitaker (Ed.), *Studies in Neurolinguistics,* Vol. 4. New York: Academic Press.

Gómez, J. L. 1996. Non-human primate theories of (non-human primate) Minds: Some issues concerning the origins of mind-reading. In P. Carruthers and P. K. Smith (Eds.), *Theories of Theories of Mind*. Cambridge: Cambridge University Press.

Gopnik, A., and A. Meltzoff. 1997. *Thoughts, Theories and Things*. Cambridge, MA: MIT Press.

Gould, J. L., and C. J. Gould. 1994. *The Animal Mind*. New York: Scientific American Library.

Gould, J. L., and C. J. Gould. 1998. Reasoning in animals. *Scientific American* 9, 52–59.

Gould, S. J., and R. Lewontin. 1979. The spandrels of San Marco and the panglossian paradigm: A critique of the adaptationist programme, *Proceedings of Royal Society of London* B 205, 581–598.

Green, S., and P. M. Marler, 1979. The analysis of animal communication. In P. M. Marler and J. C. Vanderbergh (Eds.), *Handbook of Behavioral Neurobiology: Vol 3. Social Behavior and Communication*. New York: Plenum Press.

Greene, E. 1987. Individuals in an osprey colony discriminate between high and low quality information. *Nature,* 329, 239–241.

Greenfield, P. M. 1991. Language, tools and brain: The ontogeny and phylogeny of hierarchically organised sequential behavior. *Behavioral and Brain Sciences* 14, 531–551.

Greenfield, P. M., and E. S. Savage-Rumbaugh. 1990. Grammatical combination in *pan paniscus*: Processes of learning and invention in the evolution and development of language. In S. Taylor-Parker and K. R. Gibson (Eds.), *Language and Intelligence in Monkeys and Apes*. Cambridge: Cambridge University Press.

Grice, H. P. 1989. *Studies in the Ways of Words*. Cambridge, MA: Harvard University Press.

Griffith, C. R. 1943. *Principles of Systematic Psychology*. Urbana: University of Illinois Press.

Griffin, D. 2001. *Animal Minds: From Cognition to Consciousness*. Chicago: University of Chicago Press.

Grush, R. Forthcoming. *Essays on Gareth Evans*. New York: Oxford University Press.

Guttenplan, S. (Ed.). 1975. *Mind and Language*. Oxford: Oxford University Press.

Hale, B., and C. Wright. 1997. *A Companion to the Philosophy of Language*. Oxford: Blackwell.

Hammond, L. J. 1980. The effect of contingencies upon appetitive conditioning of tree-operant behavior. *Journal of the Experimental Analysis of Behavior* 34, 297–304.

Hare, B., J. Call, B. Agnetta, and M. Tomasello. 2000. Chimpanzees know what conspecifics do and do not see. *Animal Behaviour* 59, 771–785.

Hare, B., J. Call, M. Tomassello. 2001. Do chimpanzees know what conspecifics know? *Animal Behaviour* 61, 139–151.

Harman, G. 1972. Logical form. *Foundations of Language* 9, 38–65.

Harman, G. 1986. *Change in View*. Cambridge, MA: MIT Press.

Hauser, M. D. 1997. Artifactual kinds and functional design features: What a primate understands without language. *Cognition* 64, 285–308.

Hauser, M. D. 1998. Expectations about object motion and destination: Experiments with a nonhuman primate. *Developmental Science* 1, 31–38.

Hauser, M. D. 2000. *Wild Mind: What Animals Really Think*. London: Penguin Books.

Hauser, M. D. 2001. Searching for food in the wild: A nonhuman primate's expectations about invisible displacement. *Developmental Science* 4, 84–93.

Hauser, M. D., and P. Marler. 1993. Food calls in rhesus macaques (*Macaca Mulata*). I & II. *Behavioral Ecology* 4, 194–205, 206–212.

Hauser, M. D., T. Williams, J. D. Kralik, and D. Moscovitz. 2001. What guides a search for food that has disappeared: Experiments on cotton-top tamarins. *Journal of Comparative Psychology*.

Heinrich, B. 2000. Testing insight in ravens. In C. Heyes and L. Huber (Eds.), *The Evolution of Cognition*. Cambridge, MA: MIT Press.

Heller, M. 1997. *The Ontology of Physical Objects*. Cambridge: Cambridge University Press.

Herman, L. M. 1980. Cognitive characteristics of dolphins. In L. M. Herman (Ed.), *Cetacean Behavior: Mechanisms and Functions*. New York: Wiley.

Herman, L. M. 1986. Cognition and language competencies of bottlenosed dolphins. In Schusterman, Thomas, and Woods 1986.

Herrnstein, R. J., and D. H. Loveland. 1964. Complex visual concepts in the pigeon. *Science* 146, 549–551.

Herrnstein, R. J., D. H. Loveland, and C. Cable. 1976. Natural concepts in pigeons. *Journal of Experimental Psychology: Animal Behaviour Processes* 2, 285–302.

Hershberger, W. A. 1986. An approach through the looking-glass. *Animal Learning and Behavior* 14, 443–451.

Heyes, C., and A. Dickinson. 1993. The intentionality of animal action. In Davies 1993.

Heyes, C., and A. Dickinson. 1995. Folk psychology won't go away: Response to Allen and Bekoff, *Mind and Language* 10, 329–332.

Heyes, C., and B. G. Galef. 1996. *Social Learning in Animals: The Roots of Culture*. New York: Academic Press.

Heyes, C., and L. Huber. 2000. *The Evolution of Cognition*. Cambridge, MA: MIT Press.

Hintikka, J. 1983. *The Game of Language*. Dordrecht: Reidel.

Hirschfeld, L. A., and S. A. Gelman. 1994. *Mapping the Mind: Domain-Specificity in Cognition and Culture*. Cambridge: Cambridge University Press.

Hood, B., and P. Willats. 1986. Reaching in the dark to an object's remembered position: Evidence for object permanence in 5-month-old infants. *British Journal of Developmental Psychology* 4, 57–65.

Hookway, C. 1985. *Peirce*. London: Routledge.

Horgan, T., and J. Tienson. 1992. Structured representations in connectionist systems. In Davis 1992.

Horgan, T., and J. Tienson. 1996. *Connectionism and the Philosophy of Psychology*. Cambridge, MA: MIT Press.

Hornsby, J. 1997. *Simple Mindedness*. Cambridge, MA: MIT Press.

Ingold, T., and K. R. Gibson. 1992. *Tools, Language and Intelligence: Evolutionary Implications*. Oxford: Oxford University Press.

Jackson, F. 1977. *Perception*. Cambridge: Cambridge University Press.

Jacob, P. 1997. *What Minds Can Do: Intentionality in a Non-intentional World*. Cambridge: Cambridge University Press.

Jeffrey, R. 1990. *The Logic of Decision*. Rev. 2nd ed. Chicago: University of Chicago Press.

Johnson-Laird, P. 1983. *Mental Models*. Cambridge: Cambridge University Press.

Johnson-Laird, P. 1999. Mental models. In Wilson and Keil 1999.

Johnson-Laird, P., and R. M. J. Byrne. 1991. *Deduction*. Hillsdale, NJ: Erlbaum.

Kacelnik, A. 1984. Central place foraging in starlings (*Sturnus vulgaris*). *Journal of Animal Ecology* 53, 283–299.

Kaplan, D. 1989. Demonstrations. In J. Almong et al. (Eds.), *Themes from Kaplan*. Oxford: Oxford University Press.

Karmiloff-Smith, A. 1993. *Beyond Modularity*. Cambridge, MA: MIT Press.

Kastak, C. R., R. J. Schusterman, and D. Kastak. 2001. Equivalence classification by California sea lions using class-specific reinforcers, *Journal of the Experimental Analysis of Behaviour* 76, 131–158.

Kim, J. 1984. Supervenient and epiphenomenal causation. In Kim 1993.

Kim, J. 1993. *Supervenience and Mind*. Cambridge: Cambridge University Press.

Köhler, W. 1925. *The Mentality of Apes*. New York: Harcourt Brace.

Krebs, J. R., and N. B. Davies. 1991. *Behavioural Ecology: An Evolutionary Approach*. Oxford: Blackwell Scientific.

Krebs, J. R., and A. Kacelnik. 1991. Decision-making. In Krebs and Davies 1991.

Lea, S. E. G. 1984. *Instinct, Environment and Behaviour*. London: Methuen.

Leslie, A. M. 1982. The perception of causality in infants. *Perception* 11, 173–186.

Leslie, A. M. 1984. Infant perception of a manual pick-up event. *British Journal of Developmental Psychology* 2, 19–32.

Lewis, D. 1969. *Convention*. Cambridge, MA: Harvard University Press.

Lewis, D. 1972. Psychophysical and theoretical identifications. *Australasian Journal of Philosophy* 50, 249–258.

Lewis, D. 1973. Causation. *Journal of Philosophy* 70, 556–567.

Lewis, D. 1983. Language and languages. In *Philosophical Papers,* Vol. 1. Cambridge: Cambridge University Press.

Lieberman, P. 1984. *The Biology and Evolution of Language*. Cambridge, MA: Harvard University Press.

Lowe, E. J. 1993. Rationality, deduction and mental models. In Manktelow and Over 1993.

Luce, R. D., and H. Raiffa. 1957. *Games and Decisions: Introduction and Critical Survey*. New York: Wiley.

Lycan, W. G. (Ed.). 1990. *Mind and Cognition*. Oxford: Blackwell.

McCauley, R. N. 1996. *The Churchlands and Their Critics*. Oxford: Blackwell.

Macdonald, C. 1995. Introduction: Classicism versus connectionism. In Macdonald and Macdonald 1995.

Macdonald, C., and G. Macdonald. 1995. *Connectionism: Debates in Psychological Explanation*. Oxford: Blackwell.

McDowell, J. 1994. *Mind and World*. Cambridge, MA: MIT Press.

McKenzie, B. E., and R. H. Day. 1972. Object distance as a determination of visual fixation in early infancy. *Science* 178, 1108–1110.

McKenzie, B. E., H. E. Tootell, and R. H. Day. 1980. Development of visual size constancy during the first year of human infancy. *Developmental Psychology* 16, 163–174.

Mackie, J. L. 1965. Causes and conditions, *American Philosophical Quarterly* 2, 245–264.

Mackintosh, N. 1983. *Conditioning and Associative Learning*. Oxford: Oxford University Press.

McLeod, P., K. Plunkett, and E. T. Rolls. 1998. *Introduction to Connectionist Modelling of Cognitive Processes*. Oxford: Oxford University Press.

Makin, G. 2000. *The Metaphysicians of Meaning: Frege and Russell on Sense and Denotation*. London: Routledge.

Malcolm, N. 1977. Thoughtless brutes. In *Thought and Knowledge*. Ithaca, NY: Cornell University Press.

Maloney, J. J. 1989. *The Mundane Matter of the Mental Language*. Cambridge: Cambridge University Press.

Manktelow, K. I., and D. E. Over (Eds.). 1993. *Rationality: Psychological and Philosophical Perspectives*. London: Routledge.

Marler, P. 1970. A comparative approach to vocal learning: Song development in white-crowned sparrows. *Journal of Comparative and Physiological Psychology* 71 (Supplement), 1–25.

Marler, P. 1991. The instinct to learn. In Hirschfeld and Gelman 1994.

Maynard Smith, J. 1982. *Evolution and the Theory of Games*. Cambridge: Cambridge University Press.

Mellars, P. 1996. Symbolism, language and the Neanderthal mind. In Mellars and Gibson 1996.

Mellars, P., and K. Gibson. 1996. *Modelling Early Human Minds*. Cambridge: McDonald Institute Monographs.

Mellor, D. H. 1991. *Matters of Metaphysics*. Cambridge: Cambridge University Press.

Mellor, D. H. 1995. *The Facts of Causation*. London: Routledge.

Meltzoff, A. N., and M. K. Moore. 1977. Imitation of facial and manual gestures by human neomnates. *Science* 198, 75–78.

Miles, H. L. 1990. Cognitive foundations for reference in a signing orangutan. In Taylor-Parker and Gibson 1990.

Millikan, R. 1984. *Language, Thought and Other Biological Categories*. Cambridge, MA: MIT Press.

Millikan, R. 1986. Thought without laws. *Philosophical Review* 95, 47–80.

Mitchell, R., and N. Thompson. 1986. *Deception*. Buffalo, NY: SUNY Press.

Mithen, S. 1990. *Thoughtful Foragers: A Study of Prehistoric Decision-Making*. Cambridge: Cambridge University Press.

Mithen, S. 1996. *The Prehistory of the Mind*. London: Thames and Hudson.

Møller, A. P. 1988. False alarm calls as a means of resource usurpation in the great tit *Parus Major*. *Ethology* 79, 25–30.

Montague, R. 1974. *Formal Philosophy*. New Haven: Yale University Press.

Moore, M. K., R. Borton, and B. L. Darby. 1978. Visual tracking in young infants: Evidence for object identity or object permanence? *Journal of Experimental Child Psychology* 25, 183–198.

Morgan, C. L. 1894. *An Introduction to Comparative Psychology*. London: Walter Scott.

Morgan, C. L. 1903. *An Introduction to Comparative Psychology*. New rev. ed. London: Walter Scott.

Morton, A. 2002. *The Importance of Being Understood: Folk Psychology as Ethics*. London: Routledge.

Mulligan, K. 1998. Perception, particulars and predicates. In Fisette 1998.

Munakata, Y., L. R. Santos, E. S. Spelke, M. D. Hauser, and R. C. O'Reilly. 2001. Visual representation in the wild: How rhesus monkeys parse objects. *Journal of Cognitive Neuroscience* 13, 44–58.

Munn, C. A. 1986. The deceptive use of alarm calls by sentinel species in mixed-species flocks of neotropical birds. In Mitchell and Thompson 1986.

Nagel, T. 1979. What is it like to be a bat? In *Mortal Questions*. Cambridge: Cambridge University Press.

O'Hear, A. (Ed.). Forthcoming. *Minds and Persons*. Cambridge: Cambridge University Press.

O'Keefe, J., and L. Nadel (Eds.). 1978. *The Hippocampus as a Cognitive Map*. Oxford: Oxford University Press.

Panaccio, C. 1992. *Les mots, les concepts et les choses*. Paris: Vrin.

Parret, H. 1981. *Meaning and Understanding*. Berlin: De Gruyter.

Peacocke, C. 1979. The problem of the essential indexical. *Nous* 13, 3–21.

Peacocke, C. 1983. *Sense and Content*. Oxford: Oxford University Press.

Peacocke, C. 1986. Analogue content. *Proceedings of the Aristotelian Society* Suppl. Vol. 60, 1–17.

Peacocke, C. 1992. *A Study of Concepts*. Cambridge, MA: MIT Press.

Peacocke, C. 1999. *Being Known*. Oxford: Oxford University Press.

Peirce, C. S. 1991. *Peirce on Signs: Writings on Semiotics*. Chapel Hill: University of Carolina Press.

Perry, J. 1977. Frege on demonstratives. *Philosophical Review* 86, 474 – 497.

Pettit, P. 1993. *The Common Mind: An Essay on Psychology, Society and Politics*. Oxford: Oxford University Press.

Piaget, J. 1952. *The Origins of Intelligence in the Child*. New York: Basic Books.

Piaget, J. 1954. *The Construction of Reality in the Child*. New York: Basic Books.

Pinker, S. 1994. *The Language Instinct*. London: Penguin Books.

Poole, J., and D. G. Lander. 1971. The pigeon's concept of pigeon. *Psychonomic Science* 25, 157–158.

Povinelli, D. J. 1996. Chimpanzee theory of mind. In Carruthers and Smith 1996.

Povinelli, D. J., and T. J. Eddy. 1996a. Chimpanzees: Joint visual attention. *Psychological Science* 7, 129–135.

Povinelli, D. J., and T. J. Eddy. 1996b. Factors influencing young chimpanzees' recognition of attention. *Journal of Comparative Psychology* 110, 336–345.

Premack, D., and A. J. Premack. 1983. *The Mind of an Ape*. Hillsdale, NJ: Erlbaum.

Premack, D., and G. Woodruff. 1978. Does the chimpanzee have a theory of mind? *Behavioural and Brain Sciences* 1, 515–526.

Prior, A. N. 1968. *Papers on Time and Tense*. Oxford: Clarendon Press.

Quine, W. V. O. 1960. *Word and Object*. Cambridge, MA: MIT Press.

Quine, W. V. O. 1974. *The Roots of Reference*. Cambridge, MA: Harvard University Press.

Quine, W. V. O. 1995. *From Stimulus to Science*. Cambridge, MA: Harvard University Press.

Ramsey, F. P. 1927[1978]. Facts and propositions. In *Foundations: Essays in Philosophy, Logic, Mathematics and Economics*. London: Routledge.

Ramsey, W. 1992. Connectionism and the philosophy of mental representation. In Davis 1992.

Rescorla, R. A., and J. C. Skucy. 1969. Effect of response-independent reinforcers during extinction. *Journal of Comparative and Physiological Psychology* 67, 381–389.

Rescorla, R. A., and A. R. Wagner. 1972. A theory of Pavlovian conditioning: variations in the effectiveness of reinforcement and non-reinforcement. In Black and Prokasy 1972.

Rey, G. 1997. *Contemporary Philosophy of Mind*. Oxford: Blackwell.

Reynolds, P. C. 1993. The complementation theory of language and tool use. In Gibson and Ingold 1993.

Rips, L. 1994. *The Psychology of Proof*. Cambridge, MA: MIT Press.

Ristau, C. A. 1991. Aspects of the cognitive ethology of an injury-feigning bird, the piping plover. In Ristau 1991.

Ristau, C. A. 1991. *Cognitive Ethology: The Minds of Other Animals*. Hillsdale, NJ: Erlbaum.

Rizley, R. C., and R. A. Rescorla. 1972. Associations in second-order conditioning and sensory preconditioning, *Journal of Comparative and Physiological Psychology* 81, 1–11.

Rizzolati, G., L. Fogassi, and V. Gallese. 2000. Cortical mechanisms subserving object grasping and action recognition: A new view on the cortical motor functions. In Gazzaniga 2000.

Roitblat, H. L., T. G. Bever, and H. S. Terrace. 1984. *Animal Cognition*. Hillsdale, NJ: Erlbaum.

Rosenthal, D. M. 1986. Two concepts of consciousness. *Philosophical Studies* 49, 329–359.

Rosenthal, D. M. 1993. Thinking that one thinks. In M. Davies and G. W. Humphreys (Eds.), *Consciousness*. Oxford: Blackwell.

Rumelhart, D. E., and J. L. McClelland. 1986. On learning the past tenses of English verbs. In Rumelhart, McClelland, and the PDP Research Group 1986b.

Rumelhart, D. E., J. L. McClelland, and the PDP Research Group. 1986a. *Parallel Distributed Processing: Explorations in the Microstructure of Cognition: Vol. 1. Foundations*. Cambridge, MA: MIT Press.

Rumelhart, D. E., J. L. McClelland, and the PDP Research Group. 1986b. *Parallel Distributed Processing: Explorations in the Microstructure of Cognition: Vol. 2. Psychological and Biological Models*. Cambridge, MA: MIT Press.

Ryle, G. 1949. *The Concept of Mind*. New York: Barnes and Noble.

Sainsbury, R. M. 2002. *Departing from Frege*. London: Routledge.

Samuelson, P. 1938. A note on the pure theory of consumers' behaviour, *Economica* 5, 61–71.

Savage-Rumbaugh, E. S. 1986. *Ape Language: From Conditioned Response to Symbol*. New York: Columbia University Press.

Savage-Rumbaugh, E. S., S. Shanker, and T. Taylor. 1998. *Apes, Language and the Human Mind*. Oxford: Oxford University Press.

Schusterman, R. J., J. A. Thomas, and F. G. Woods (Eds.). 1986. *Dolphin Cognition and Behaviour: A Comparative Approach*. Hillsdale, NJ: Erlbaum.

Schusterman, R. J., C. R. Kastak, and D. Kastak. 2002. The cognitive sea lion: Meaning and memory in the lab and in nature. In Bekoff, Allen, and Burghardt 2002.

Sellars, W. 1956/1997. *Empiricism and the Philosophy of Mind*. Cambridge, MA: Harvard University Press.

Shephard, R. 1982. *Mental Images and Their Tranformations*. Cambridge, MA: MIT Press.

Sherry, D. F. 1982. Food storage, memory and marsh tits. *Animal Behaviour* 30, 631–633.

Sherry, D. F. 1984. Food storage by black-capped chickadees: Memory for the location and content of caches. *Animal Behaviour* 32, 451–464.

Shettleworth, S. J., and J. R. Krebs. 1986. Stored and encountered seeds: A comparison of two spatial memory tasks. *Journal of Experimental Psychology: Animal Behaviour Processes* 12, 248–256.

Skinner, B. F. 1957. *Verbal Behaviour*. New York: Appleton-Century-Crofts.

Skryms, B. 1996. *Evolution of the Social Contract*. Cambridge: Cambridge University Press.

Slater, A. M., and V. Morrison. 1985. Shape constancy and slant perception at birth. *Perception* 14, 337–344.

Sluga, H. 1980. *Gottlob Frege*. London: Routledge Kegan Paul.

Smolensky, P. 1988. On the proper treatment of connectionism. *Behavioral and Brain Sciences* 11, 1–74. Reprinted in Macdonald and Macdonald 1995.

Smolensky, P. 1991. Connectionism, constituency and the language of thought. In Loewer and Rey 1991.

Smolensky, P. 1995. Constituent structure and explanation in an integrated connectionist/ symbolic cognitive architecture. In Macdonald and Macdonald 1995.

Sommers, F. 1982. *The Logic of Natural Language*. Oxford: Clarendon Press.

Spelke, E. S. 1990. Principles of object perception. *Cognitive Science* 14, 29–56.

Spelke, E. S., C. Hofsten, and R. Kestenbaum. 1989. Object perception and object-directed reaching in infancy: Interaction of spatial and kinetic information for object boundaries. *Developmental Psychology* 25, 185–196.

Spelke, E. S., and G. A. Van de Valle. 1993. Perceiving and reasoning about objects: Insights from infants. In N. Eilan, R. McCarthy, and B. Brewer (Eds.), *Spatial Representation*. Oxford: Blackwell.

Sperber, D., D. Premach, and A. J. Premack (Eds.). 1995. *Causal Cognition*. New York: Oxford University Press.

Squire, L. R., B. Knowlton, and G. Musen. 1993. The structure and organisation of memory. *Annual Review of Psychology* 44, 453–496.

Stalnaker, R. 1987. *Inquiry*. Cambridge, MA: MIT Press.

Stein, E. 1996. *Without Good Reason: The Rationality Debate in Cognitive Science*. Oxford: Clarendon Press.

Stephens, D. W., and J. R. Krebs. 1986. *Foraging Theory*. Princeton, NJ: Princeton University Press.

Sterelny, K. 1990. *A Representational Theory of Mind*. Oxford: Blackwell.

Stern, D. 1985. *The Interpersonal World of the Infant*. New York: Academic Press.

Stich, S. 1978. Beliefs and subdoxastic states. *Philosophy of Science* 45, 499–518.

Strawson, P. F. 1959. *Individuals*. London: Methuen.

Stromswold, K. 2000. The cognitive neuroscience of language acquisition. In Gazzaniga 2000.

Taylor, C. 1964. *The Explanation of Behaviour*. London: Routledge Kegan Paul.

Taylor-Parker S., and K. R. Gibson. 1990. *Language and Intelligence in Monkeys and Apes*. Cambridge: Cambridge University Press.

Terrace, H. S., L. A. Pettito, F. J. Sanders, and T. G. Bever. 1979. Can an ape create a sentence? *Science* 206, 891–900.

Tinbergen, N. 1951. *The Study of Instinct*. Oxford: Oxford University Press.

Tinbergen, N. 1973. *The Animal in Its World*. Cambridge, MA: Harvard University Press.

Tolman, E. C., and C. H. Honzik. 1930a. "Insight" in rats. *University of California Publications in Psychology* 4, 215–232.

Tolman, E. C., and C. H. Honzik. 1930b. Introduction and removal of reward, and maze learning in rats. *University of California Publications in Psychology* 4, 257–275.

Tolman, E. C., B. F. Ritchie, and D. Kalish. 1946. Studies in spatial learning II: Place learning versus response learning. *Journal of Experimental Psychology* 36, 221–229.

Tolman, E. C., B. F. Ritchie, and D. Kalish. 1947. Studies in spatial learning V: Response learning versus place learning via the non-correction method. *Journal of Experimental Psychology* 37, 285–292.

Tomasello, M. 1996. Do apes ape? In Heyes and Galef 1996.

Tomasello, M. 2000. Two hypotheses about primate cognition. In Heyes and Huber 2000.

Travis, C. 1994. On constraints of generality. *Proceedings of the Aristotelian Society* 94, 165–188.

Treisman, A. 1996. The binding problem. *Current Opinion in Neurobiology* 6, 171–178.

Treisman, A., and H. Schmidt. 1982. Illusory conjunctions in the perception of objects. *Cognitive Psychology* 14, 107–141.

Trinkhaus, E. (Ed.). 1989. *The Emergence of Modern Humans: Biological Adaptations in the Later Pleistocene.* Cambridge: Cambridge University Press.

Turvey, M. T. 1996. Dynamic touch. *American Psychologist* 51, 1134–1152.

Tye, M. 1991. *The Imagery Debate.* Cambridge, MA: MIT Press.

Tye, M. 1992. Visual content and visual qualia. In T. Crane (Ed.), *The Contents of Perception.* Cambridge: Cambridge University Press.

Tye, M. 1995. *Ten Problems of Consciousness.* Cambridge, MA: MIT Press.

Van Gelder, T. 1990. Compositionality: A connectionist variation on a classical theme. *Cognitive Science* 14, 355–384.

Vaughan, W., Jr. 1988. Formation of Equivalence Sets in Pigeons. *Journal of Experimental Psychology: Animal Behaviour Processes* 14, 36–42.

Von Hofsten, C. 1982. Foundations for perceptual development. *Advances in Infancy Research* 2, 241–261.

de Waal, F. 1982. *Chimpanzee Politics: Power and Sex among Apes.* London: Jonathan Cape.

Walker, S. 1983. *Animal Thought.* London: Routledge and Kegan Paul.

Weiner, J. 1990. *Frege in Perspective.* Ithaca, NY: Cornell University Press.

Whyte, J. T. 1990. Success semantics. *Analysis* 50, 149–157.

Whyte, J. T. 1991. The normal rewards of success. *Analysis,* 51, 65–73.

Wiggins, D. 1997. Sortal concepts: A reply to Xu. *Mind and Language* 12, 413–421.

Wilson, R. A., and F. C. Keil. 1999. *The MIT Encyclopedia of Cognitive Science.* Cambridge, MA: MIT Press.

Wimmer, H., and J. Perner. 1983. Beliefs about beliefs: Representation and constraining function of wrong beliefs in young children's understanding of deception. *Cognition* 13, 103–128.

Wittgenstein, L. 1953. *Philosophical Investigations.* Translated by G. E. M. Anscombe. Oxford: Blackwell.

Wright, C. 1997. The indeterminacy of translation. In Hale and Wright 1997.

Wynn, T. 1993. Layers of thinking in tool behavior. In Gibson and Ingold 1993.

Zeki, S. 1993. *A Vision of the Brain.* Oxford: Oxford University Press.

Index